REACHING
CLOUD
VELOCITY

This book is provided for informational purposes only. It represents Amazon Web Services, Inc. or its affiliates' ("AWS") current product offerings and practices as of the date of issue of this book, which are subject to change without notice. Customers are responsible for making their own independent assessment of the information in this book and any use of AWS's products or services, each of which is provided "as is" without warranty of any kind, whether express or implied. This book does not create any warranties, representations, contractual commitments, conditions or assurances from AWS, its affiliates, suppliers or licensors. The responsibilities and liabilities of AWS to its customers are controlled by AWS agreements, and this book is not part of, nor does it modify, any agreement between AWS and its customers.

www.reachingcloudvelocity.com

REACHING

CLOUD

VELOCITY

A Leader's Guide to
Success in the AWS Cloud

Jonathan Allen & Thomas Blood
With forewords by Werner Vogels,
Mark Schwartz, & Adrian Cockcroft

FOREWORD

by Dr. Werner Vogels, CTO, Amazon.com, Inc.

Innovation has always been part of the Amazon DNA, but about 20 years ago, we went through a radical transformation with the goal of making our iterative process—"invent, launch, reinvent, relaunch, start over, rinse, repeat, again and again"—even faster. The changes we made affected both how we built applications and how we organized our company.

Back then, we had only a small fraction of the number of customers that Amazon serves today. Still, we knew that if we wanted to expand the products and services we offered, we had to change the way we approached application architecture.

The giant, monolithic "bookstore" application and giant database that we used to power Amazon.com limited our speed and agility. Whenever we wanted to add a new feature or product for our customers, we had to edit and rewrite vast amounts of code on an application that we'd designed specifically for our first product—the bookstore. This was a long, unwieldy process requiring complicated coordination, and it limited our ability to innovate fast and at scale. And then if we wanted to enter a new country, we had to replicate all of our infrastructure and keep all of our code base in sync across multiple countries.

With that in mind, we created a blueprint for change with our "Distributed Computing Manifesto." This was an internal document describing a new architecture. With this manifesto, we began restructuring our application into smaller pieces called "services" that enabled us to scale Amazon dramatically.

But changing our application architecture was only half the story. Back in 1998, every Amazon development team worked on the same application, and every release of that application had to be coordinated across every team.

To support this new approach to architecture, we broke down our functional hierarchies and restructured our organization into small, autonomous teams—small enough that we could feed each team with only two pizzas. We focused each of these "two-pizza teams" on a specific product, service, or feature set, giving them more authority over a specific portion of the app. This turned our developers into product owners who could quickly make decisions that affected their individual products.

Breaking down our organization and application structures was a bold idea, but it worked. We were able to innovate for our customers at a much faster rate, and we've gone from deploying dozens of feature deployments each year to millions, as Amazon has grown. Perhaps more dramatically, our success in building highly scalable infrastructure ultimately led to the development of new core competencies and resulted in the founding of AWS in 2006.

And we continue to work in two-pizza teams today.

We're not alone in the quest to innovate quickly. To remain competitive, companies must increase their agility so that they can continually uncover new opportunities and create better products. This is why more and more customers are embarking on a similar journey.

Today, millions of customers in 190 countries around the world have made the AWS Cloud an important part of the way they do business—paying only for the cloud resources they need, when they need them and they have greatly benefitted from the performance, availability, security, reliability, scalability, and low cost it provides.

I have had the privilege of travelling the world and speaking to thousands of customers. Leaders of those customers always want to hear how other customers are benefiting from the cloud and how they made the change. One such leader, who successfully moved their business to AWS when he was the CIO of Dow Jones, was Stephen Orban. Stephen loved sharing what he had learned so much that he joined AWS in 2014 as our first AWS enterprise strategist. He has travelled the globe as I have, speaking with customers, sharing his lessons learned as a leader who moved to cloud.

Since then, the enterprise strategy team has grown. Customers are still looking to learn the lessons from other customers. And although there is no compression algorithm for experience, guidance that offers an empathetic narrative to the leader who wants an experiential and prescriptive approach to the AWS Cloud can be a powerful accelerant.

The authors, Jonathan and Thomas joined Stephen's team in 2016, bringing their own prior cloud transformation experience as executives. Subsequently they have worked with hundreds of AWS customers, which has given them a unique perspective on what it takes to fully unlock the benefits of cloud for your business.

Reaching Cloud Velocity is a guide to AWS Cloud adoption for decision makers and leaders, and points a way to using cloud as part of your digital transformation. In its pages, you will learn how cloud can improve your business operations; how to develop a cloud strategy; how to structure and build your cloud leadership team; the nuts and bolts of people, process, architecture, and migrations; cloud databases; machine learning; security and governance; and much more. There is no other book I know of that so completely details everything executives and other decision makers need to know to make the journey to cloud.

Take for example one of the most powerful methods to unlock agility, that of using serverless. This is used by thousands of customers, from iRobot to National Australia Bank. To quote from Jonathan and Thomas' compute, containers, and serverless chapter:

> *Today's Agile software development teams are rightly a heterogenous mix of skill types, including Software Development Engineer, Security Engineer, Software Quality Engineer, and Data Scientist. The tools they have to use to deliver solutions, even with microservices, can be diverse. It's not just the application code that you have to consider, it's the surrounding elements. Identity management, telemetry tracking, logs, security groups, databases, management information systems—the list goes on. Engineers and developers spending their time maintaining those tools is time they could have spent pulling forward user problems to solve them by applying logic, data, or a better UX experience. Removing the work (and continuing to abstract even higher and more efficiently) is where serverless comes in. And it has, and continues to have, a profound impact on development.*

The book is full of practical advice that you can use on your journey to the cloud. We are fortunate to have Jonathan and Thomas share their experiences and those of their AWS colleagues, and most important, the experiences of the hundreds of enterprise customers they have worked with as part of the AWS team.

I hope that as you read this book, you gain a better understanding of how to successfully make the journey to AWS Cloud, and the many advantages that will accrue to your organization when you do. Every day at Amazon is Day One, and every one of us at AWS stands ready to support you in your journey. The book you now hold in your hands is the first step.

WERNER

FOREWORD

by Adrian Cockcroft, VP Cloud Architecture Strategy, AWS

The pace of innovation has changed radically. It's no longer possible to stay competitive on an annual cycle of product or service updates, as the underlying technology capabilities change every day, and today's winners have figured out how to continuously adopt and drive new technology. Netflix is globally recognized as one of *the* most successful and innovative companies, and part of that success comes from a focus on working with AWS to maximize their cloud velocity. I've spent the last decade talking to a wide variety of organizations from around the world and trying to distill and share the lessons that can be learned from Netflix. The partnership between AWS and Netflix is an excellent example of long-term benefit on both sides. Netflix likes to be a very early adopter of new technologies as that provides great leverage to guide the technology to match their needs, with minimal upfront investment. As a result, there are many AWS services and features where Netflix was one of the first customers and that are an exact fit to Netflix's requirements. We've also seen many other customers use a deep partnership with AWS and gain cloud velocity to lead their markets, including Goldman Sachs, Intuit, Cerna, Verizon, and Volkswagen.

The competition question comes up often. Netflix also competes with Amazon Prime Video, and there are two separate points to consider. The first is that by using AWS—the most scalable, feature rich, and reliable cloud provider—Netflix is running on the same platform, which neutralizes any technology advantage that Amazon Prime Video could have. The second is that Netflix set out from the early days to be a strategically important and highly visible customer of AWS, and with a decade of success, also ended up as one of the largest customers. It turns out that the customer obsession that AWS talks about a lot is not limited to the biggest and most strategic customers, and I see examples every day of AWS catering to its entire customer base. Amazon Prime, Netflix, Hulu, Disney, Fox, Warner, HBO, and most of the other streaming video platforms around the world run on AWS.

The other big lesson from Netflix was copied from Amazon in the first place. Amazon calls it "two-pizza teams", and Netflix has many small autonomous teams with clear ownership and responsibility, with freedom to move quickly. In 2006, Werner Vogels published an ACM Paper which included the idea that developers should "run what they wrote." Netflix made this part of the cloud transition, and each team stopped building components of a monolith deployed by a central operations team, and turned those components into microservices with self-service automated continuous deployment into production. This approach to DevOps "teaches the developers to operate" on an automated cloud platform, encourages the shortest time-to-value possible, and is the best approach to getting out of the way of innovation. The most universal metric for innovation is actually time-to-value, (think of it as innovation latency) as it doesn't matter how big the organization is. If you can have an idea, and see it running later that day, you are lowering the barriers to innovation for everyone. Innovation velocity should scale up with size, but many organizations slow down so much as they get bigger that they don't see the velocity gains. One of the amazing things about a distributed organization is that velocity can increase faster than the growth rate, as each new generation of innovative services builds on top of the previous capabilities.

Finally, I'm very happy to see a section of this book dedicated to the strategic planning technique known as Wardley Mapping, using some examples I came up with to help map the evolution of technologies from custom, to products, to services, to utilities. These maps are a very useful approach to facilitate discussion and consider make vs. buy decisions, as data center-based applications migrate to cloud.

This book contains a lot of great examples and advice, written by authors who've been there and done that, on how to innovate quickly and leverage cloud.

ADRIAN

FOREWORD

by Mark Schwartz, Director Enterprise Strategy, AWS

The cloud is changing not just IT, but how business itself is conducted. More than that, it is deeply changing the world in which we live. Consider the work of the International Center for Missing and Exploited Children (ICMEC), which now uses AWS's facial recognition technology to scan social media to locate missing children and pass leads to law enforcement. Or the International Rice Research Institute (IRRI), which provisioned 37,000 cores of computing power in the cloud to sequence the genomes of 3,000 varieties of rice from 89 countries to find the most drought-resistant and productive strains of this grain, which is a staple in the diets of over half the world's population. When a company moves workloads from its own data center to the cloud, carbon emissions are reduced 88 percent—the cloud is drastically reducing the negative impacts of humanity on our environment.

In the business world, enterprises can innovate, get products quickly to market, earn the fruits of their creativity, and then innovate again when competitors catch up. McDonalds, for example, was able to develop and launch its food delivery mobile application in just four months, and then scale it globally. 3M assembled 600 of its employees, conducted a three-day hackathon to experiment with new cloud technologies like machine learning and IoT, tried out 70 or so new ideas, then chose the ones that seemed most promising for future investment.

This new, fast pace of development brings with it improvements in stability, quality, resilience, compliance, and security—perhaps just the opposite of what you would expect. With the cloud, an enterprise can use speed as a way to manage risk, respond quickly to attacks and failures, and automate repeated functions to make them more reliable and predictable. GE Oil and Gas reduced its P0 and P1 production issues (Priority 0 and Priority 1) by 98 percent when it moved to the cloud. This correlation between speed and stability was confirmed by studies reported in the book *Accelerate* and the annual State of DevOps reports.[1]

Even better: the cloud enables new software delivery techniques like DevOps and new architectures like microservices, which can further increase speed, quality, and resilience of systems. The combination of the cloud, new architectures, and new delivery processes are driving the competitive dynamics of the digital age, giving companies new ways to grow revenues, reduce costs, and reduce risks.

And it's easy. Anyone can go home from work, take out their credit card, and spin up some new virtual machines in the cloud. Their credit card might not even be charged, since AWS has a generous free tier. Compare that to yesterday's need to buy hardware, set it up, and operate and maintain it.

So, then—what's the problem?

Our Enterprise Strategy team at AWS meets with more than a thousand large-enterprise customers every year—enterprises filled with bright, creative people; enterprises that lead their industries because of their ability to execute and their innovative ideas that created and drove their market categories forward. And what we have learned is that, for them, although cloud technology may be straightforward, gaining all of the benefits the cloud offers is hard. To take advantage of all of those wonders of modern technology described in the paragraphs above, enterprises need to shift their cultures, develop new ways of evaluating IT investments, re-think their processes, devise new operating models, and evolve new skills. Those things are hard.

Indeed, in our meetings with enterprise executives across all industries and geographies, we find that a similar set of obstacles and challenges recur. Yes, every enterprise is different—the challenges manifest themselves in unique ways and the solutions will have different elements. Nevertheless, at their root, the impediments are those faced by any large organization looking to make a large transformation.

They are the challenges of an organization that has been successful in the past and thus has devised ways of working that have brought about that success. Their employees have the skills that they have needed in the past and their corporate culture reinforces the norms that have worked for them. But they realize that what has made them successful in the past will no longer make them successful in the new digital age of rapid change, uncertainty, and complexity. They need to unlearn much of what they have learned and develop a nimbleness that will allow them to face the uncertain future.

And that is hard.

So, they turn to our enterprise strategy team for prescriptive guidance. What have we seen that works? How did we lead our own companies' transformations before we joined AWS? What worked and what didn't work in those enterprises? How did we deal with cultural change, employee skill gaps, and changing security models?

Jonathan Allen and Thomas Blood wrote this book to answer those questions for a wider audience. They bring their experience, skills, and ability to formulate effective strategies and tactics and articulate them. They lay out, topic by topic, chapter by chapter, how an enterprise can and must adapt to the cloud-enabled world. The approaches they describe are well-tested and aimed at the key questions that enterprise leaders face as they transform their organizations. Just as they are in person, Jonathan and Thomas are witty, empathetic, and creative in their presentation of the critical techniques an enterprise can use to thrive in the digital cloud-enabled future.

Consider this excerpt from their chapter on culture:

Management, then, is not about enforcing control in a hierarchy of functional responsibilities. It is about gaining the power that the team-oriented approach offers by amplifying the teams' ideas, creating clarity around goals, removing impediments, and devising and allocating resources to support the teams' activities. You will have to engage the middle manager's ingenuity in accomplishing new goals where impact can be tied to business success and which collectively with other goals supports the new ways of working. An important task for leaders today is to creatively find ways to redefine the goals and incentives of their middle managers to align with transformation.

In just a paragraph, Jonathan and Thomas give us the key to overcoming the problem of the supposedly "frozen middle," the layer of management that appears to be resisting change. Later in the book, they introduce the notion of "seductive adoption"—the technique of making new ideas so compelling that they drive their own adoption. These are the techniques we see working for enterprises as they do the hard work of transforming to face the digital age.

As an example of a more nuts-and-bolts challenge that many of our customers face, they devote a chapter to the tactics of migrating from a mainframe into the cloud—safely, yet with determination and impact. Essential reading for the many organizations stymied by this challenge.

As these examples indicate, this book is the guide that IT leaders have been waiting for—the opinionated, no-fooling-around handbook for those who are serious about setting their companies up for future success...I mean, of course, taking advantage of the cloud. Read it and enjoy.

MARK

CONTENTS

PREFACE

"It is not the most intellectual of the species that survives; it is not the strongest that survives; but the species that survives is the one that is able best to adapt and adjust to the changing environment in which it finds itself."

– CHARLES DARWIN

Finding the right title for this book took nearly as long writing the book itself. How do you find a title for a leadership guide to AWS Cloud that expresses the sheer breadth of the subject, is succinct, prescriptive, memorable, and meets with one of the reader's greatest needs—that of finding a faster speed in business? *Reaching Cloud Velocity*, when we finally thought of it, fit the bill perfectly (that and the website address was actually available!).

The opportunity of working with hundreds of AWS customers over the last three years, and combining that with our own leadership experience as executives, has allowed us a privileged perspective on enterprise change in the cloud. The inflection point we are going through in the world of technology is a once-in-a-lifetime event and we are humbled to be part of it. It is so exciting to help customers suddenly see improvements across their business. When costs become understandable. Security is simplified. Flexibility improves. And for the first time, they are truly able to focus on customer outcomes for their own business. This is immensely rewarding.

Executives love to learn from fellow executives what works, and more important, what doesn't. The desire to Think Big and share these combined learnings with as many enterprise leaders as we can was the catalyst behind the book's creation. Along the way, it has been truly fascinating to engage with an unbelievable number of Amazonians, who have all unselfishly offered their own experience in such a customer-obsessed way to help with its creation. We thank them all.

One of the mechanisms intrinsic to Amazon is its effective use of tenets (or principles, if you like). You will hear more about them throughout the book, in virtually every chapter. We think it's very important for you the reader to understand the tenets that we established to write this book together. So, here they are:

1. **Prescriptive guidance.** Leaders are looking for cloud guidance they can copy and paste—and importantly—amend to fit the context of their business.

2. **Share what works.** Share the very best practices from our own experience and hundreds of customers that we have worked with.

3. **Share what doesn't work.** If we have seen something fail, time and time again, we will say so.

4. **Referenceable.** You don't have to read the entire book to get to the goodness and find value. Use the table of contents at the front, then fast forward to the bits you need to solve a particular problem.

5. **Enterprise leader focused.** This book is primarily written for enterprise leaders and managers to read and act to accelerate their cloud adoption.

6. **Concise writing.** This is not *War and Peace*. If a one-line answer works, we will use it.

7. **Human centric.** Focus on the people.

8. **Not a textbook.** No more than 320 pages. (darn it... we tried)

9. **The only constant is change.** Everything changes all the time, including best practices for cloud. We fully acknowledge that the best practices in this book will be superseded by new best practices.

10. **We are Amazonians, we are peculiar.** Amazon embraces diversity and thrives on uniqueness, our peculiar passion percolates prodigiously throughout.

Enjoy!

JONATHAN & THOMAS

PART 1
AWS CLOUD

1.1 INTRODUCTION

"There is no compression algorithm for experience."

– ANDY JASSY, CEO, AMAZON WEB SERVICES

Our experience has taught us (usually the hard way) that technology is actually the easiest part of transformation, because engineers love to build things and know how to solve technical problems. We have found that where most enterprises struggle is with the cultural, procedural, and business transformations necessary to maximize the results of adopting cloud. This often includes remembering how to do IT well after decades of outsourcing, and how to apply Agile and DevOps in the enterprise. It also includes the impact on other stakeholders, such as HR, Finance, Legal, and so on.

We are often amazed at how large companies that have brilliant, talented employees, and have brought staggering innovations to the market, can struggle to articulate their vision or measurable goals. They worry about the disruption that abounds and how companies are seemingly able to bring powerfully innovative new products to market in 90 days with just a handful of people.

They have forgotten the early years, when they were lean and hungry—when they had a clear goal to conquer the world. Now many companies, including well-known enterprises, are fiddling around the edges—making small, but unimaginative changes to their products—and somehow, they have enough marginal success for the investors to remain calm.

Such companies are ripe for disruption. Don't be one of them!

When we meet with customers, we like to start with what Amazon calls the "Voice of the Customer." Where are you going? What are your goals for this year, for next year, and for the foreseeable future? Some executives have a brilliant and cogent answer to those questions. Some do not. And it starts with vision. Once you can clearly articulate the *raison d'etre*—the reason you exist, your mission if you will—then you can rally your employees and get them excited and motivated for the next big thing. And more likely than not, that next big thing will require new ways of doing business and will probably benefit from going to the cloud. It will likely also require fairly significant changes to your people, process, technology, and ultimately, your corporate culture.

Good leaders know that your vision drives everything. The question is this: How will you make the vision a reality?

The vision is most likely based in meeting a need of your customers, and each department or functional unit will have to figure out how to align their purpose to the overarching vision. The product team will have to figure out what new feature or service will best meet the customer need. Marketing will have to figure out how to communicate with that customer about the new product, feature, or service. HR will have to understand what positions need to be filled to create and support the business and its vision. And IT has to figure out how best to support all of the functions in their efforts to realize the vision.

Being an IT leader in today's world is one of the most challenging jobs on the planet. Imagine having a 100-million-dollar system go live at 4:00 in the morning, with a thousand tasks to do, a very high likelihood of something going very wrong, and the literal success of your company in your hands. It's the IT leader's job to maintain existing systems in a cost-effective way while simultaneously creating new capabilities, minimizing risk, protecting corporate assets, and securing customer data. All too often, however, IT becomes the department of "not-so-fast," while being perceived as a cost center and necessary evil by other departments. Of course, the reality today is that IT is essential to the success of nearly every business on the planet. In a world where time to market, business agility, and innovation are on every executive's mind, IT must enable the business to go faster, be more agile, and innovate—all while meeting their traditional role of cost control and risk management.

This is where cloud comes in—and especially AWS.

Businesses come to AWS for many reasons. Often, it is to try and understand how Amazon is seemingly able to effortlessly innovate into so many adjacent businesses. Sometimes it's because the executive team has created a slide with words to the effect of "Cloud Strategy," "All-In," "Cloud First," or something similar, and IT feels compelled to explore what cloud has to offer. Sometimes there is a compelling event, such as the three-day, on-premise database outage Netflix suffered more than a decade ago, or the imminent expiration of the lease of a data center, or the possibility of selling off a part of the business, or the need to drive down operational costs more aggressively. Markets are desperate for cost savings and the accompanying desire to increase time to value (TTV) and the ability to ship features faster, while being secure and resilient. Whatever the initial impetus, once companies decide to explore AWS, they quickly realize that the benefits are far greater than they initially expected.

Early Amazon teams spent far too long building infrastructure rather than bringing amazing new ideas to life. They had to remove what

Werner Vogels, the Amazon CTO, called "undifferentiated heavy lifting," and instead create reusable building blocks. This was the catalyst that led to the creation and launch of the very first AWS service, which has grown to 175+ services that are just a click or an API call away. To emphasize this point, we often ask leaders if they would ever consider building their own email service. Invariably, when we ask that question, they look at us incredulously. But that is what many companies have in essence been doing all along—they have built and maintained systems that are essential to business operations, but don't actually drive business value. They certainly don't differentiate their business from the competition. Or as our AWS Enterprise Strategy colleague, Miriam McLemore (ex-corporate CIO of Coca-Cola), once said, "You may love your data center, but it doesn't love you!"

So, why then do businesses persist in maintaining systems that they could just consume as a service? "Why?" is a great question to ask when you encounter anything that is routine or bureaucratic. If something does not directly differentiate you from your competition and drive business value creation, see if there is an AWS building block that can take care of it for you. There probably is. Then use that building block instead of wasting your time and effort recreating something that is a utility.

Obviously, this is easy to say, but can be quite challenging when you have decades of legacy technology and processes. But, rest assured, every question you could possibly ask has almost certainly been asked before. The goal of this book is to condense some of the very best leadership guidance we can offer into actionable steps.

Now, let's get started!

1.2 AWS CLOUD

"Invention comes in many forms and at many scales. The most radical and often transformative of inventions are often those that empower others to unleash their creativity—to purse their dreams."

– JEFF P. BEZOS, FOUNDER AND CEO, AMAZON.COM, INC.

When Charles Phillips, the CEO of Infor, stood on stage at the AWS San Francisco Summit in 2014, he made an assertion that really resonated with us:

"Friends don't let friends build data centers."

2014 was also an inflection year of our own journeys to cloud, as it was then that we started building on AWS. We remember later that year hearing this same quote repeated at AWS re:Invent (the annual global AWS conference) in Las Vegas and reflecting deeply on the intent behind it. Why *do* we build data centers? Is building data centers actually the business we are in?

No—it's not.

In the tech industry, we have always been passionate debaters about the pros and cons of one solution over another. Whether we drink the

Kool-Aid of one tech over another, it's always interesting to see which ideas survive the white-hot crucible of business.

AWS Cloud is one case that has indeed survived the crucible of debate and has gone on to dramatically impact businesses of every size and every sector, including Netflix, National Australia Bank, Airbnb, Experian, Ancestry—the list goes on and on. How does cloud so significantly and positively impact these customers?

From our own experience and travels, we find that there are a vast number of ways cloud can positively impact a business. As Mark Schwartz writes about in his book, *A Seat at the Table*, build versus buy is finally an achievable reality. Says Schwartz, "Software development has changed...there are supporting APIs, platforms, frameworks, and tools that take care of much of the grunt work of development..." AWS calls this grunt work "undifferentiated heavy lifting." And removing swathes of this undifferentiated heavy lifting from customers ultimately lies at the crux of the cloud reality, which is changing the world. This in turn is tremendously liberating—upending decades of pent-up frustration of IT departments and their business colleagues, as well as powering the reality of Agile development and operations.

Before we go deeper into how to do this and the best practices, it's well worth taking a few pages to explore the global infrastructure of AWS as a foundation and to help level set.

What is cloud computing?

The term *cloud computing* refers to the on-demand delivery of IT resources via the internet with pay-as-you-go pricing. Instead of buying, owning, and maintaining their own data centers and servers, organizations can acquire technology such as compute power, storage, databases, and other services on an as-needed basis. It is similar to how consumers flip a switch to turn on the lights in their home and the power company sends electricity, along with a monthly bill for each kilowatt used. With cloud computing, AWS will manage and maintain the technology infrastructure in a secure environment, and businesses can access these resources via the internet to develop and run their applications. Capacity can grow or shrink instantly, and businesses only pay for what they use.

AWS Global Infrastructure components

Regions – AWS has the concept of a Region, which is a physical location around the world where it clusters data centers. AWS calls each group of logical data centers an Availability Zone. Each AWS Region consists of multiple, isolated, and physically separate AZ's within a geographic area. Unlike other cloud providers, who often define a region as a single data center, the multiple AZ design of every AWS Region offers advantages for customers. Each AZ has independent power, cooling, and physical security and is connected via redundant, ultra-low-latency networks. AWS customers focused on high availability can design their applications to run in multiple AZ's to achieve even greater fault-tolerance. AWS infrastructure Regions meet the highest levels of security, compliance, and data protection.

AWS now spans 69 Availability Zones within 22 geographic regions around the world, and has announced plans for sixteen more Availability Zones and five more AWS Regions in Indonesia, Italy, Japan, South Africa, and Spain.

Availability Zones – An Availability Zone (AZ) is one or more discrete data centers with redundant power, networking, and connectivity in an AWS Region. AZ's give customers the ability to operate production applications and databases that are more highly available, fault tolerant, and scalable than would be possible from a single data center. All AZ's in an AWS Region are interconnected with high-bandwidth, low-latency networking, over fully redundant, dedicated metro fiber providing high-throughput, low-latency networking between AZ's. All

Regions
Coming Soon

traffic between AZ's is encrypted. The network performance is suffi-cient to accomplish synchronous replication between AZ's. AZ's make partitioning applications for high availability easy. If an application is partitioned across AZ's, companies are better isolated and protected from issues such as power outages, lightning strikes, tornadoes, earthquakes, and more. AZ's are physically separated by a meaningful distance, many kilometers, from any other AZ, although all are within 100 km (60 miles) of each other.

AWS Wavelength – Enables developers to build applications that deliver single-digit millisecond latencies to mobile devices and end-users. AWS developers can deploy their applications to Wave-length Zones, AWS infrastructure deployments that embed AWS com-pute and storage services within the telecommunications providers' datacenters at the edge of the 5G networks, and seamlessly access the breadth of AWS services in the region. This enables developers to deliver applications that require single-digit millisecond latencies such as game and live video streaming, machine learning inference at the edge, and augmented and virtual reality (AR/VR). This brings AWS services to the edge of the 5G network, minimizing the latency to connect to an application from a mobile device. Application traffic can reach application servers running in Wavelength Zones without leaving the mobile provider's network. This reduces the extra network hops to the Internet that can result in latencies of more than 100 milliseconds, preventing customers from taking full advantage of the bandwidth and latency advancements of 5G.

AWS Outposts – AWS Outposts bring native AWS services, infrastruc-ture, and operating models to virtually any data center, co-location space, or on-premises facility. You can use the same AWS APIs, tools, and infrastructure across on-premises and the AWS cloud to deliver a consistent hybrid experience. AWS Outposts is designed for connected environments and can be used to support workloads that need to remain on-premises due to low latency or local data processing needs.

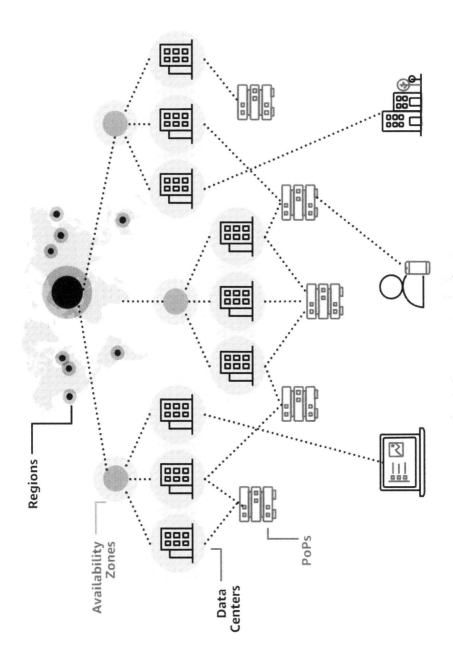

Regions

Availability Zones

Data Centers

PoPs

Services – AWS offers a very broad set of more than 175 global standardized building blocks that you can use to run your business and operate globally. Offering a broad set of global cloud-based products including compute, storage, database, analytics, networking, machine learning and AI, mobile, developer tools, IoT, security, enterprise applications, and much more. The general policy of AWS is to deliver AWS services, features and instance types to all AWS Regions within 12 months of general availability, based on a variety of factors such as customer demand, latency, data sovereignty and other factors. Customers can share their interest for local region delivery, request service roadmap information, or gain insight on service interdependency (under NDA) by contacting your AWS sales representative. Due to the nature of the service, some AWS services are delivered globally rather than regionally, such as Amazon Route 53, Amazon Chime, Amazon WorkDocs, Amazon WorkMail, Amazon WorkSpaces, Amazon WorkLink.

High Availability – Unlike other technology infrastructure providers, each AWS Region has multiple AZ's. Customers who care about the availability and performance of their applications want to deploy these applications across multiple AZ's in the same region for fault tolerance and low latency. AZ's are connected to each other with fast, private fiber-optic networking, enabling you to easily architect applications that automatically fail-over between AZ's without interruption.

The AWS control plane (including APIs) and AWS Management Console are distributed across AWS Regions and utilize a multi-AZ architecture within each region to deliver resilience and ensure continuous availability. This ensures that customers avoid having a critical service dependency on a single data center. AWS can conduct maintenance activities without making any critical service temporarily unavailable to any customer.

Network – AWS offers highly reliable, low latency, and high throughput network connectivity. This is achieved with a full redundant 100

Gbps network that circles the globe via trans-oceanic cables that run tens of thousands of kilometres and up to ten kilometres under the sea. Major links in the network are one or servers parallel 100 Gbps link. AWS is continually expanding this fibre network. For example, a trans-Pacific cable that spans 14,000 kilometres, linking Australia, New Zealand, Hawaii, and Oregon, is currently being built, expanding the network even further.

All data flowing across the AWS global network that interconnects the datacenters and Regions is automatically encrypted at physical level before it leaves the secured facilities. Additional encryption layers exist as well; for example, all Virtual Private Cloud (VPC) cross-region peering traffic, and customer or service-to-service Transport Layer Security (TLS) connections.

The network is designed to be highly redundant, have no single points of failure and are designed to survive many concurrent link failures.

Points of Presence – AWS has the largest global infrastructure footprint of any cloud provider in order to deliver customer's content through a worldwide network of Point of Presence (PoP) locations, which consists of Edge Locations and Regional Edge Cache servers. Amazon CloudFront is a fast delivery network (CDN) service that securely delivers data, videos, applications, and APIs to customers globally with low latency, high transfer speeds, all within a developer-friendly environment. AWS Global Accelerator is a service that acts as a fixed entry point to your applications running in a single or multiple AWS Regions and improves the availability and performance of your TCP and UDP traffics.

AWS has over 210 Points of Presence (199 Edge Locations and 11 Regional Edge Caches). With the cloud, this means you can easily deploy your application in multiple physical locations around the world—providing a lower latency while delivering applications closer to your customers.

Five reasons companies are moving so quickly to the AWS Cloud

The first reason is agility. AWS lets customers quickly spin up resources as they need them, deploying hundreds or even thousands of servers in minutes. This means customers can very quickly develop and roll out new applications, and it means teams can experiment and innovate more quickly and frequently. If an experiment fails, you can always de-provision those resources without risk.

The second reason is cost savings. If you look at how people end up moving to the cloud, the conversation starter almost always ends up being cost. AWS allows customers to trade capital expense for variable expense and only pay for IT as they consume it. And the variable expense is much lower than what customers can do for themselves because of AWS's large economies of scale. For example, Dow Jones has estimated that migrating its data centers to AWS will contribute to a global savings of $100 million in infrastructure costs.

The third reason is elasticity. As customers, we used to over provision to ensure we had enough capacity to handle our business operations at the peak level of activity. Now, using AWS, we could provision the amount of resources that we actually needed, knowing we could instantly scale up or down along with the needs of our business.

The fourth reason is that the cloud allows you to innovate faster because you can focus your highly valuable human resources on developing applications that differentiate your business and transform your customers' experiences. You no longer need to spend time and money building and maintaining things that are already available as a service and don't add value.

The fifth reason is that AWS enables you to deploy globally in minutes. This ability allows you to take an idea that works in one location, test it in another, and quickly deliver to customers worldwide.

In 2016, James Hamilton spoke at re:Invent about the depth and breadth of the decisioning and thoughtfulness that goes into the infrastructure, it's a fascinating glimpse into the long-term thinking that is typical of Amazon. Just search youtube for AWS re:Invent 2016: Amazon Global Network Overview with James Hamilton to go deeper.

1.3 ORIENTATION

"Absorb what is useful, discard what is useless, and add what is specifically your own."

– BRUCE LEE

You know precisely where you are. You are juggling 85 balls at the moment. You are reading or listening to this book in a carved-out precious moment of reflection.

We know this because we have been there.

Being the leader, you are attempting to run everything in harmony. You're working flat out to give yourself just a little more wriggle room to really focus on those things that matter—like growing the company through innovation or making sure you can get to the gym today.

But of those 85 balls you are juggling, some balls are heavier than others.

We have all been on the receiving end of *that* phone call—you know, the one at 3:00 a.m. to notify you that a critical company system just had a major problem. "We are escalating it to you as the leader." Forewarned is forearmed after all. Except now your sleep is broken, your adrenaline has just spiked your heart rate, and there is only a forlorn hope of getting back to proper rest, ready for battle tomorrow.

For those of us who have read The Phoenix Project, the adventures of Brent created an uncomfortable familiarity as the hero battles to deliver a Big Complex Project with impossible timelines, moving targets, and decreasing morale while simultaneously trying to improve efficiency and handle customer challenges. And this was all while trying to grow revenues in an ever-more-hostile internal and external environment with the added sweetener of a morphing and threatening security landscape. We read this book when it was first published in 2013, and we found it uncomfortably hilarious as we related with our own professional and personal experiences.

Continually orienting ourselves, checking our situational awareness of where we are, and ensuring the next step we take is the most-powerful action is what every leader does continuously. You will find actions steps in nearly every chapter, which provide suggestions for the next most powerful action you can take. And, as we know, change is very hard and exhausting, and change fatigue can become a real thing. We want our efforts to deliver results, we obsess about the perceived risk of fundamental change, but in our hearts, we know continuous change is required. We want to make a profound difference across cost efficiency, time to market, security, and employee morale—all with the goal of growing our business and delighting our customers.

There is no right or wrong approach for structuring technology decision making across an organization, but there are tradeoffs between centralization (efficiency, standardization) and autonomy (time to market, innovation). Increasingly, most of the executives we talk with favor the latter. This kind of diversity makes it hard to prescribe what every organization's cloud journey will look like.

That said, there are common patterns across virtually every business we have worked with, and we offer specific action steps in nearly every chapter in the first half of the book before moving onto the technology knowledge we believe all leaders need to be equipped with to survive and thrive:

PART 2—Business and Strategy. Helping you work through the trends of enterprise IT, the KPIs, and how you make a decision whether to buy, build, or use technology.

PART 3—Culture and Organization. We cover in some detail the Amazon culture and the best patterns we have seen to bring about a pivot, principles to affect this, and how to get going the right way with your cloud journey.

PART 4—People and Process. How do you reskill everyone for the cloud, and what on earth should my Target Operating Model look like?

PART 5—Architecture and Migrations. A chance to dive deep into the foundational technology trends that are shaping our world and how to migrate your systems effectively.

PART 6—Data and Intelligence. How can I truly get the most out of my data?

PART 7—Security and Governance. Security is Job Zero at AWS

PART 2
BUSINESS AND STRATEGY

2.1 STRATEGY AND THE BOLD LEADERSHIP GOAL

"Hope is not a strategy."

– PRESIDENT BARACK OBAMA

In our meetings with customers, we often discover that businesses recognize that they need to change and that leveraging cloud can be a fundamental enabler of agility and growth. Leveraging cloud allows them to focus on what makes their business, their business, but they often struggle when it comes to articulating the precise way how to do it.

The unfortunate truth is that we see many leaders failing to grasp the holistic change that is required.

Most executives we speak with acknowledge that their IT strategy and business strategy are not aligned. In reality, they should be the same! There can only be *business* strategy—all other considerations should be details of how you execute against that business strategy. Leaders can resolve this dilemma by providing clear and concise direction. The ability to provide clarity of purpose separates great leaders from the merely good ones.

Some of the executives of the 2,000+ enterprise customers our team members have met with over the past two years have focused change on small, incremental improvements. While this is not wrong, strictly speaking, incrementalism does not create disruptive opportunities for your business. Creative destruction does not derive from investing in safe bets or in incremental change. Transformations are fueled by passion, by a strong belief in a better future. And this is where the bold leadership goal comes in.

Enel is an Italian multinational power company and a leading integrated player in the world's power and gas markets. In 2015, Enel decided to migrate 5,500 of their 9,500 servers to AWS and to close all of their data centers except one. Astonishingly, they were able to execute this ambitious goal in just nine months! Such accomplishments are simply not possible with the incrementalistic mindset. Enel's executive leadership created what seemed to an impossible goal, and then galvanized the entire organization, with the help of partners, to move the majority of IT systems into the cloud in record time.

While this might be looked upon as just another migration to cloud, Fabio Veronese, Head of ICT Solution Center Infrastructure & Networks, says that the move was both "massive and fast." According to Veronese, it was successful because Enel didn't view the move as an IT one but rather as a company one.

Several years ago, the CIO of GE Jamie Miller decided that she thought it was critical that GE moved to the cloud to move much more quickly. She got her top technical leaders together and said "We're going to move 50 applications to AWS in the next 30 days". For the next 45 minutes they told her what a dumb idea that was and how it was never going to work and she listened to them very patiently and said "I hear you but we're going to do it, so let's go". Over the next 30 days they got 42 applications moved and along the way they figured out their security model, their governance model, their compliance model and they had success and built momentum. All of a sudden, ideas started flowing in on what else they could move and they're now about three quarters of the way through moving several thousand applications to AWS.

Although Enel and GE cut their operating costs after migrating to AWS, this was not their primary goal. Instead, they wanted to eliminate the inherent limitations of their legacy systems. They decided to create virtual data centers that would provide the greatest flexibility and shortest time to market. Again, they did not approach this as a long-term, slow-rolling incremental-change process, but instead decided to go as fast as they could possibly go.

Time to market is key, speed matters. Cost of delay is a good metric to consider in this case. Had Enel or GE dallied in the execution of their ambitious goals, they would all have incurred extra costs—both in terms of operating costs and staff time. In addition, each of these businesses would have had to contend with the opportunity cost of missed revenue generation.

Yet, too many organizations fall into the trap of allowing well-meaning managers to defer action, to kick the can down the road. We're always shocked when we hear of companies that decide to build their own data center. The time and effort, and the inherent limitations, are no longer justified. What is now required are bold leaders who decide to close their data centers and embrace the opportunities of the future.

Our friend Stephen Orban once wrote that today's technology executives should consider themselves Chief Change Management Officers when leading their organization's journey to the cloud. In addition to handling the merging of business and technology, the CCMO is also responsible for providing clarity of purpose. That means being able to articulate your strategy, how your team fits into that strategy, where there is and isn't flexibility, staying determined, and staying patient. And above all, leading the change. Explains Stephen:

> *Early in my leadership tenure, I thought—naively—that just because I was the boss everyone would do what I said. I learned the hard way that this is, of course, not how leadership works. It wasn't until I*

started to clearly articulate what was important about our strategy that the behavior of my team started to change. Before presenting a new idea or goal to my team, I had to consider how everyone fit into this strategy and how it tied back to the business and everyone's careers. Then, I had to capitalize on every opportunity to reinforce these points.[2]

ACTION STEPS

Step 1: Remove ambiguity

Netflix declared a bold goal. Says Neil Hunt, Chief Product Officer, Netflix: "Our long-term goal is to let AWS do all the infrastructure work especially where it isn't Netflix specific. Our development team can focus on the features that are unique to Netflix so we can deliver the most compelling services to our members."

Step 2: Remove inertia

There are thousands, if not tens of thousands, of decisions that need to be made by everyone in the organization. Clear principles and the bold goal will clarify the direction to take. Any decision that is not aligned with the overarching goal is probably not important and should be deferred or eliminated.

Step 3: Remove the excuses

People are naturally uncomfortable with change, and left to their own devices, they will prefer the devil they know over the unknown and uncertain path toward the bold goal. Valid concerns must be addressed, but everything else presented as reason or evidence not to proceed is likely just an excuse to maintain the status quo. Excuses come in all shapes and form, including cost, security, compliance, lack of experience, and many more. Answer each excuse once and move on. In the words of Tim Brown, Cloud and Infrastructure Director at Inmarsat, "The biggest thing we fight every day is reversion."

Step 4: Measure progress

Define what the successful outcomes of the goal looks like. Make the outcomes known and make them measurable. Clearly articulate your motivations and goals to your team and your stakeholders, and hold everyone accountable for moving the needle in the right direction.

Step 5: Reward progress

Reward the behavior that drives attainment of the goal. Recognize victories along the way. Using a stand-up or all-hands meeting, recognize sincere positive progress.

2.2 THE FUTURE OF ENTERPRISE IT

"In the future, all the code you ever write will be business logic."
– *WERNER VOGELS, CTO, AMAZON.COM, INC.*

What will the future look like?

This is a frequent question we and many others at Amazon get asked, a lot.

When Jeff Bezos answers this question, he says it is far better to ask, "What's not going to change in the next 10 years?" As customers, we won't want slower delivery times, more expensive items, or less choice. So, focus your energy on innovating to improve these things as any improvements will be incredibly important.

What will the future look like in Enterprise IT?

Well, we will still want things that are delivered quickly and are cost effective, reliable, and secure. That is pretty straight forward.

But we also know that underneath this highly loaded question is the painful truth that what enterprise leaders are dealing with today are the challenges they created for themselves or inherited from yesteryear. As leaders, we know the amount of time we actually got to spend on imagining and enabling the future was directly constrained by the operational needs of our incumbent systems.

This "yesterday challenge" is encapsulated in the book, *The Day After Tomorrow: How to Survive in Times of Radical Innovation*, by nexxworks founder Peter Hinssen (who is currently working on a new book, *The Phoenix and the Unicorn*).

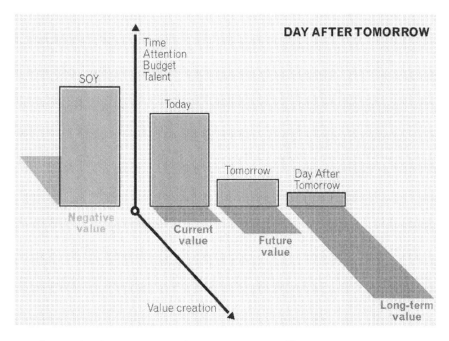

We focus the lion's share of our time and effort on maintaining the current book of business, since we cannot jeopardize our current revenue or contractual obligations. We also spend a great deal of time and money (and often blood, sweat, and tears) on the effects of decisions we (or our predecessors) made long ago. This "Ship of Yesterday" as Peter calls it (you can replace Ship with another word if you prefer), is the source of much unplanned work and requires painful work-arounds, duct tape, and bailing wire to keep it running (how many Cobol engineers do you have on staff?). Between these two sources of effort, very little time or resources remain to prepare for tomorrow and to create future value. And many of us have no time at all to work on the "day after tomorrow" for long-term value, putting us at risk of future disruption by nimble competitors without all of this baggage.

Getting future ready

One of the most requested Executive Briefing Sessions at AWS is titled "The Future of Enterprise IT" (FoEIT). The Enterprise Strategy team hosts this session, typically at the home of AWS in Seattle, but also around the world.

Leaders want to hear from other leaders and from their personal experience, lessons learned, and what works and what doesn't work.

Depending on the customer's needs, the session can cover many different aspects of enterprise IT. There are, however, some incredibly consistent enterprise issues that we hear, phrases like:

- Stuck between Agile and waterfall (WAgile).
- Being held hostage to software licensing.
- Security posture keeping me awake at night.
- Stuck between two worlds (digital and non-digital channels) and not enough funding to do either well.
- Talent focusing on the wrong things.
- Too many box checkers and not enough engineers or developers.
- Inability to attract talent.
- Intransigent middle management (we can do it, but only if I/we can control it).
- Technical pet projects (squirrel!).
- Wanting to innovate but scared to fail.
- Standalone innovation team doing something weird.
- Mainframe, please help me modernize.
- WebLogic, please, please help me modernize.
- ExaData, please give me some database freedom!

- How do I reskill my workforce for cloud?
- How do I deal with a workforce that is about to retire?
- Too many choices, argh!
- Where are you going? Where are we going?
- Stuck on the CAPEX-intensive hardware upgrade train, please help.
- Stuck on the never-ending operating system upgrade, please help.
- Data center lease expiring, how do we move everything by this date?

This list of course goes on. We are able to engage in these conversations with experiential empathy. We passionately believe that having the right business mission, goals (aligned to solving customers problems), and agreed principles (leadership and technology) in place can dramatically help improve the situation of each and every one of these pain points.

Inflection points

We also spend time with enterprises that are worried (rightly) about disruption. However, they have advantages that startups greatly covet, namely, deep knowledge of their markets. Skilled and committed employees. Financial resources. Customer base and brand equity. Operational processes and compliance certifications. Deep pockets of data.

Bringing these strengths to bear to fight disruptors to your industry is how you outmaneuver them. It's not actually the startups that are disrupting your organization, it's your customers' expectations! These sessions typically lead to some interesting inflection points.

First, that Software as a Service has been increasingly adopted by enterprises for its benefits of allowing you to focus more on your core business. The data center offerings that cloud brings enables you to double down on this strategy, using standard building blocks to remove a ton of heavy lifting, and to in effect level up your human resources to far more valuable work.

Second, that there is an important distinction to make between rapid idea failure (which is to be encouraged) and failure in production (which is never okay). How many times as leaders are you faced with a tsunami of well-intentioned business ideas from your business colleagues, but don't have the bandwidth to add in "one more project/epic?" Far better to have a team sprint for two weeks to test the hypothesis and either eliminate or double down on an idea with data. Having building blocks that you can either turn off or turn into production is the game-changing enabler here.

Third, not everything has to be Agile. If what you are offering as a business to your customers is highly commoditized and needs Six Sigma-type methodology, that is absolutely fine. If you are innovating on the edge, then a different operating model is fine. Agile worked extremely well for us.

The term Six Sigma originated from terminology associated with statistical modelling of manufacturing processes. The maturity of a manufacturing process can be described by a sigma rating indicating its yield or the percentage of defect-free products it creates— specifically, within how many standard deviations of a normal distribution the fraction of defect-free outcomes corresponds to.

Finally, bringing the IT and business together is of course crucial. Although as IT executives we may arm ourselves with all this knowledge of the new, unless our business colleagues can go on this journey with us and also adapt, then it is going to be a huge challenge. Typically, we see the journey of executive teams understanding what is required as a whole as being one of the hardest changes of all. For an excellent deep dive on this topic, we would strongly recommend the book *War and Peace and IT* by Mark Schwartz published by IT Revolution. Our teammate goes deep on bridging the gaps between IT and "the business" and executing Agile at scale as part of your Target Operating Model.

Moving to a high frequency that focuses on the right things

So, if we want enterprise IT to be "future ready," deliver things quickly, be cost effective, and reliable and secure, what do we see differentiating those enterprises that achieve this vs. those that don't?

Typically, today, you can compare and view the modern enterprise IT environment to that of an oscilloscope. At one end you have:

- **Low-frequency IT**—At this low tempo, change is infrequent. Any movement involves risk, instability, and lots of effort. This is typified by releasing three or four times a year, in a high-pressure cauldron of business system analysis, architecture, building of infrastructure, application, and finally logic, data, and UX development. Automation and trust are low, and as a result, documentation overhead is high. Handoffs are controlled events—the majority of human resources are devoted to planning and coordination of "the process." Command and control are the norm.
- **High-frequency IT**—At this high tempo, change is constant. With a flywheel of frequent value delivery, there's limited risk and a focus on customer benefit, not on ensuring change doesn't disrupt operations. Teams are guided by consistent principles and are rewarded for high automation and a focus on logic, data, user experience, resiliency, and security. Shifting technology right when a managed service is available is par for the course. (Easy, right? Of course, it's not!)

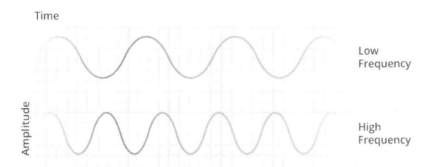

Cause of IT organizations leaning toward the low frequency of the change spectrum

Many times over the years, we have seen a catalytic event driving a kneejerk reaction (or suffering from a real jerk, the problem being people rather than situations or events) that then becomes bureaucratic behavior and part of the shared unspoken values. The trigger might have been a catastrophic event such as a failed launch, security event, or critical system outage that led the enterprise to a low-frequency cadence with fewer releases, more planning, reviews, and signoffs—*ad nauseam.*

Alongside this new embedded behavior, we normally see a complex customer and technical-support pyramid that accumulates layers of technical debt, in turn reducing velocity of creation activities. An attempt to focus on big vision without learning and practicing how to execute small then exacerbates the situation.

The "Death Star" program (we'll get it right this time, no...really)

Often, enterprises are focused on big vision but not on practicing how to execute small. So, projects are *big*—with bigger ambitions and a focus on lots of upfront planning. They create huge scopes of work. And even if they work in Agile sprints, releasing every sprint is not the focus. Instead, the focus is on assembling lots of work for a Big Bang release that requires more coordination and integration before anything is released.

The ever-squeezed testing cycle becomes more and more frantic as the countdown to the midnight go-live ticks down. This is typical because:

1. Big vision means big project, culminating in one big release (one long wavelength is the scope of the project), so everybody tries to get their pet project scoped in.

2. Before anyone can start, the enterprise writes extensive requirements documents, preplanning every phase of the initiative.

3. Without data to support the vision, the scope of the big vision is further bloated.

4. As blast radius for risk increases, enterprises try to plan risk away and impose gatekeepers and gatekeeping processes to limit risk and ensure projects are delivered as planned.

5. Security, testing, and integration signoffs are manual processes.

6. Launch heroines and heroes are required to put the puzzle together, meet deadlines, and salvage failing expectations of big vision. This leads to a symbolic and surreal death march to the finish line.

Move from low frequency to high frequency

Moving from the old matrixed and siloed resources, laden with technical debt, outsourced resources, and waterfall project delivery—which is mismatched to today's digital world—to high-frequency value creation is the goal. So, how do you move from a low-frequency (I'll birth a huge, risky project every two years) to a high-frequency world? A world where you can and will iterate quickly to identify customer problems, discover through testing whether ideas have validity, and decide whether to pivot or persevere (by using data) to solve customer problems.

ACTION STEPS

Step 1: Reduce the scope

Move from big bets that languish in development for extended periods to much smaller batch size of releases, think frequent value delivery, find what blocks this from happening, and remove the blocker.

Step 2: Move from HiPPO to data-driven decisions

HiPPO is an acronym that stands for the "highest paid person's opinion" or the "highest paid person in the office." HiPPOs are leaders who are so self-assured that they need neither other's ideas nor data to affirm the correctness of their instinctual beliefs. Relying on their experience and smarts, they are quick to shoot down contradictory positions and dismissive of underling's input.

Move from HiPPO-based decision making, moving instead to data-driven decisions where ideas and requirements are considered hypotheses to be tested and measured.

Step 3: Break down the silos

Break down the silos between IT and the business and then look to reduce the siloed technology teams. Bring teams together to focus on product or outcome.

Step 4: Maximize work not done

Carefully select when you are going to build, buy, or use technology. Don't waste time building something that is already a solved problem. See Chapter 2.3 Mapping Your Way Through.

Step 5: Build in security from the start

Don't bolt on security. If you need to, reduce the scope of the business outcome to ensure security is built in in every sprint or stage. Plan for the best case rather than unknown unknowns and relying on emergency responses to embedding checks that self-remediate assuming that attacks, failures, and flaws will happen. See Chapter 7.1 Security Is Always Job Zero.

Step 6: Invest in your workforce
This is covered in detail in Chapter 4.1 Becoming Cloud Fluent at Scale.

Step 7: Build in reliability from the start
This is covered in detail in Chapter 5.3 Resilience and Reliability.

Step 8: Pack the "Ship of Yesterday"
Migrate and over time refactor your incumbent workloads. This is covered in detail in Chapter 5.4 Migrating Your Applications.

Conclusion

The building blocks are available today to fundamentally transform enterprises and the products and services they deliver to customers while differentiating their business from the competition. This requires letting go of the decisions of yesterday that consume so much of our time, money, and other resources. For some IT executives, this is a very difficult thing to do, as change brings with it some amount of risk. However, the risk of doing nothing is typically far greater.

We want to give a very special thanks to Philip Potloff, Director and Head of AWS Enterprise Strategy for his help in writing this chapter. His material and experience were invaluable.

2.3 MAPPING YOUR WAY THROUGH

"You cross the river by feeling the stones"
– SIMON WARDLEY, RESEARCHER, LEADING EDGE FORUM

In business, we are constantly called upon to create strategies—plans for future initiatives that are important to our long-term success. This is certainly the case when it comes to taking your company to the cloud. A major migration effort like that requires planning, coordination, resources and effort to get it right. It requires a strategy. You can't just wave a magic wand one afternoon and declare your initiative done when you're just getting started.

The problem is that many business strategies never actually deliver their intended results. In fact, nearly a decade ago, a study of 163 CEOs and other top execs by Forbes Insights and Financial Dynamics revealed that almost one-third of all business strategies do not achieve their stated goals. Based on our own observations of today's increasingly fluid business landscape, we suspect that number is even lower now. According to the study, the top-five reasons for failure include:

- Unforeseen external circumstances (24 percent)
- Lack of understanding among those involved in developing the strategy and what they need to do to make it successful (19 percent)

- The strategy itself is flawed (18 percent)
- Poor match between the strategy and the core competencies of the organization (16 percent)
- Lack of accountability or of holding the team responsible (13 percent)

As you can see, these points of failure indicate a significant lack of situational awareness on the part of those who originally crafted the strategies. The environments in which they were doing business were not clear to them, the people tasked with executing the strategies were uncertain how to achieve them, and there were serious mismatches between the strategies and the purpose of the companies that deployed them.

Every great journey in life has both a beginning and an end—the destination you are aiming for. You start on the busy streets of New York City and you end up in a quiet lodge overlooking the Grand Canyon on holiday. Or you graduate college with a degree in art history, and one day—20 years later—you are COO of a fast-growing tech company with people and offices scattered around the globe.

The same is true in business. You begin, for example, with a customer desire for a solution to a long-standing problem, and you deliver a new product or feature that answers that customer desire (and perhaps sells millions of copies in the process). Or the growth of your business requires building out, opening, and staffing new offices in Atlanta, Phoenix, and London.

How do you find your way to your desired destination as quickly and efficiently as you can, with a minimum of wrong turns, crashes, and dead ends?

You use a map.

We are big fans of Simon Wardley and his approach to mapping strategies. Among other things, for four years Simon served as CEO of a company called Fotango, a UK-based photo sharing service. His idea for mapping strategies came from the realization he had at the time that he really had no idea whether the strategies he and his team were working to develop would work.

Perhaps of even greater concern, Fotango was growing, profitable, and healthy, and Simon could not explain why. Was it because of the company's remarkably well-crafted, insightful strategies (doubtful) or simply dumb luck (more likely)?

Simon explains the roots of his concern:

> I was that most senior of executives. The company would live or die by the strategic choices I made, or so I thought. I wrote the strategy or at least variations were presented to me and I would decide. But, something had gone terribly wrong in my journey. Somehow along the path to becoming a CEO, I had missed those all-important lessons that told me how to evaluate a strategy. I still had no means to understand what a good strategy was and it was no longer enough for me to think it "seems fine." I needed more than that as I was the experienced executive that the less experienced took guidance from.

Simon did what many other CEOs at the time did: he read lots of books about business strategy, he learned how to use SWOT analysis and 2x2 matrices, and he hired a consulting firm to improve communication within his team—hoping he would see the light and the right strategies would emerge as a result.

They didn't.

Plagued with self-doubt (and deathly afraid that he would soon be revealed as an imposter—a "fake CEO" not worthy of helming Fotango)—Simon happened to read Sun Tzu's book *The Art of War*. This book turned out to be the key that inspired his approach to mapping.

Summarized briefly, Sun Tzu explained in his book that when two opponents are in competition, there are five factors that matter: purpose, landscape, climate, doctrine, and leadership. As Simon considered this idea, he realized that maps—specifically, topographical intelligence—were one of the most important keys to developing successful military strategies.

What if maps could also be successfully applied to the development of business and the supporting IT strategies? What then?

Planning

Tools commonly employed in business and IT strategy are flow charts, 2x2 matrices, balanced scorecards, complex operating models, IT roadmaps, dependency diagrams, and the list goes on and on. While each of these tools may answer important questions, and may even be useful as a planning tool, all too often they are used as physical manifestations of handwaving—the equivalent of expensive consultant-developed PowerPoint presentations and spreadsheet models that look impressive at first glance, and then gather dust on the corporate bookshelf.

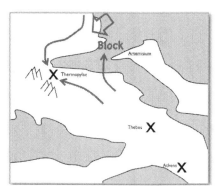

What is needed is a kind of map. Something that can help you get from point A to point B. Imagine you are strategic advisor to the commander of forces at Thermopylae (King Leonidas of Sparta). Which tool will you use to advise the king?

That's what we thought. You would of course prefer the map that is intuitive and conveys a great deal of information in a single glance. You need a sense of distance, of time and space, and an understanding of the terrain that dictate avenues of approach and show insurmountable obstacles.

What is needed is a mechanism for what in mapping is known as "wayfinding": a system that guides people through a physical environment and enhances their understanding and experience of the space in which they operate. Wardley maps provide this wayfinding system. They are organized by depicting activities needed to fulfill user needs (that is, the value chain) and an evolutionary axis. Things that are visible are located at the top of the map, and invisible things, such as "back-office" components, are placed toward the bottom. Such a system also requires a sense for how things evolve over time. Most successful companies started as innovators in their space—they create a unique and valuable solution for a particular problem set. This is what Wardley defines as the "Pioneer" period. Then as they build on their initial success, they optimize and refine their initial success—the period of the "Settler." And finally, over time, the solution or product, often under competitive pressure, evolves into a utility. This period is the managed by the "Town Planners."

The challenge is that many organizations have neither a clear sense of evolutionary time, nor a clear idea of the strategic environment in which they operate.

When a corporate board tells the CIO to be more innovative, but the company has been operating in the Settler or Town Planner mindset for a decade or two, then small wonder that innovation is relegated to an innovation lab. Here it might actually create something useful, but will likely never emerge in the marketplace because the COO will not know how to operationalize such an innovation.

Wardley maps are an excellent tool to both visualize where your business is at in a given moment in time and will help visualize the path forward. Wardley maps show value chains versus evolution. They are organized with a time dimension along the x-axis, starting with "Genesis" on the left, and then traversing the evolutionary path from "Custom Built, through "Product" (or "Rental"), and finally on to "Utility". If you think about a product or service you offer today, it will be generally found somewhere on this trajectory from original idea to fully commoditized offering.

The role of technology leaders to decide whether to build, buy, or use and understand technology that is now available is of critical importance. Why would you build something that is already available as a secure, scalable, and cost-effective service?

Using the discipline of a map allows you to figure out what you need to focus on and what is already a utility that you can leverage to remove work. It's amazing to us how many people continue to miss this step.

To build a Wardley map, you start with the user need at the top and then you add all the things that support it. The most visible things are also at the top, and you go deeper and deeper until, at the bottom of the map, you have such commodities or utilities as data centers, electricity, buildings, and so forth. At the top you might have a mobile app or an interface—something that supports a customer. Then there are all the bits in between.

Simon likes to point out that you start with something novel that you had to create from scratch and was hard to build. Think back 20 years or so—a data center was a custom thing that you would build from scratch. And if you had a better data center than your competitor, then you had a better product because your data center was faster.

The *idea* of building a data center is in the Genesis phase—on the left side of a Wardley map—then when you actually build one, that moves the data center to the Custom Built phase. Then you buy a cage in a colocation center and you prebuild it with some standard racks, which moves you to the Product phase. Finally, data centers become a Utility such as we have with the AWS Cloud. Today, the fastest way to open a state-of-the-art data center is to simply open an AWS account.

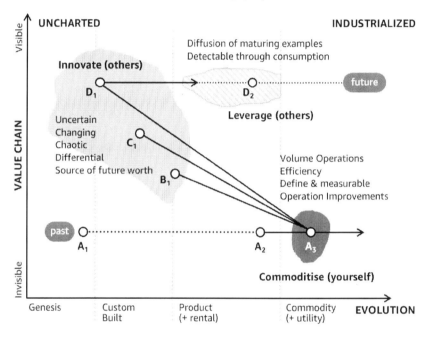

Since everyone now has access to leading-edge data center technology via AWS, you have to build something on top of that. So, the innovation moves up a level—to the upper left of a Wardley map, closer to the customer—while things that are lower in the value chain move to the bottom right.

On the left-hand side, you're doing full Agile development. You've never built it before—no one's ever built it before—it's startup land, it's a brand-new feature, you're experimenting, you're A/B testing, you're iterating incredibly rapidly, you're throwing ideas onto the wall to see if they stick.

On the right-hand side, it's very important to fine tune everything. It's Six Sigma—getting out all the variation—and it's cost optimization. We're familiar with this thing, it's a standard interface like electricity. There's a lot of innovation going on, for example, in the generation of electricity from renewable sources.

With the Wardley map, you're not just visualizing where you are—the current state of your technology stack—but how it's evolving over time. It shows position and movement.

Such a mapping can be used to drive toward meeting a strategic goal, or it can be used in imagining the future, and thinking about how you might create such a future.

In a presentation at AWS Palo Alto, Adrian Cockcroft, AWS VP Cloud Architecture Strategy, gave the example of how to apply a Wardley map to the development of a travel search product—using Simon Wardley himself as the subject.

Simon Wardley hates to fly coach—the cramped seats cause him great discomfort and back pain. So, he wanted to create a mobile search app that would help him find comfy flight options whenever he wanted to book an upcoming flight.

When you create a map, the first question to ask is this: What problem are you trying to solve? Let's say that users want faster, more personalized search. The business, on the other hand, wants faster feature releases and lower costs. The next question is: What does the value chain look like? You've got the user need at the top, followed by a search interface, some sort of travel data store, and compute and storage.

Here's a map of the starting point for Wardley's travel search product:

TRAVEL SEARCH: STARTING POINT

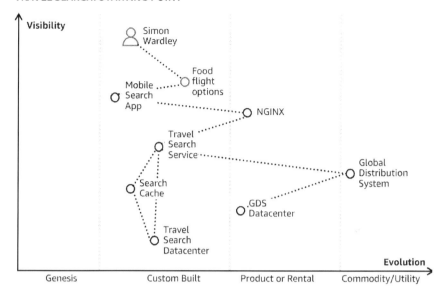

Wardley's user need—to find flight options—is at the top. He has a custom-built mobile search app that talks to NGINX—an API service that is a product which puts it farther to the right on the map—then there's a travel search service, a search cache for caching all the recent searches to make it more efficient, and a travel search data center—all custom built. Finally, there's a global distribution system (GDS)—for example, Sabre or Amadeus—that runs on its own data center.

As we run this app, we're caching a lot more data, costs are rising, and it's taking longer to do the searches. So, we'll take a look at our Wardley map to see what we can do with the stack to make it more efficient and cost less.

We'll take NGINX and rewrite it using AWS API Gateway, rewrite the travel search service using AWS Lambda, and run the search cache on AWS ElastiCache Redis. All of those things move to the right, which in cloud is a Utility. When we do that, we're no longer running these functions in our custom data center, which makes everything faster and cheaper to run.

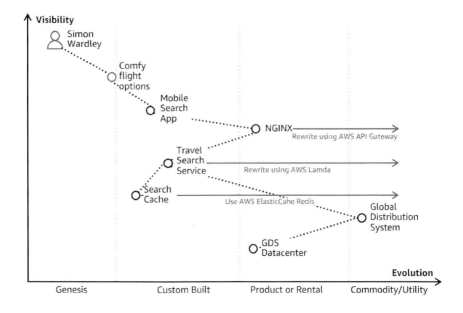

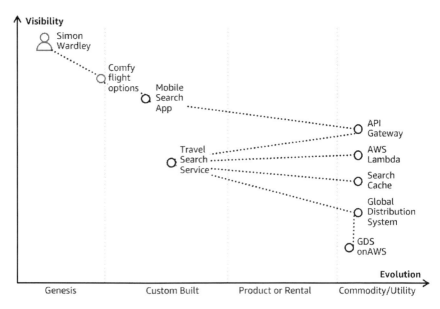

Finally we work with the GDS supplier to migrate their service to the same AWS region as the rest of the application, providing the lowest possible latency for searches.

Why does this matter with respect to cloud adoption?

There are two main areas that come to mind. First, Wardley maps make an excellent addition to help plan your approach to migrating to the cloud. And second, Wardley maps shine when mapping your product strategy.

Going deep on the mapping concepts

Genesis - This is the realm of testing hypotheses and of experimenting with new product ideas. This will include the outcomes of hackathons, as well as prototypes and minimum viable products. Teams quickly create new concepts based on business hypotheses and quickly test assumptions. These can be customer-facing user-experience tests, or core components of functionality in the back office.

> This represents the unique, the very rare, the uncertain, the constantly changing, and the newly discovered. Our focus is on exploration.

Custom Built - Applications that have passed muster during the initial hypotheses testing can be further enhanced and tested further. Product ideas are honed and optimized. As you deconstruct or "strangle" your monolithic applications, you will initially place your microservices in this column until they mature into a well-understood and rarely changing service in their own right. This is also where you have your offerings and services that you have built in house in a more traditional context. These are bespoke solutions, and hopefully, they are services that provide a unique value to your business and not things you have built simply because you can.

This represents the very uncommon and that which we are still learning about. It is individually made and tailored for a specific environment. It is bespoke. It frequently changes. It is an artisan skill. You wouldn't expect to see two of these that are the same. Our focus is on learning and our craft.

Product - Here you will place systems and services that are well understood and evolving more slowly through incremental improvement. You may have systems that are stable and will not change much. These can be migrated to cloud as is, without having to modify anything. These applications may be good candidates for the lift-and-shift pattern.

This represent the increasingly common, the manufactured through a repeatable process, the more defined, the better understood. Change becomes slower here. While there exists differentiation—particularly in the early stages—there is increasing stability and sameness. You will often see many of the same product. Our focus is on refining and improving.

Utility - Can you replace systems in your estate with SaaS or PaaS solutions? Have you built your own standards-based services that are easily maintained and are not likely to change? Then you have entered the Utility column on the map. The simplicity of standard building blocks allows higher orders of complexity.

This represents scale and volume operations of production, the highly standardized, the defined, the fixed, the undifferentiated, the fit for a specific known purpose and repetition, repetition, and more repetition. Our focus is on ruthless removal of deviation, on industrialization, and operational efficiency. With time we become habituated to the act, it is increasingly less visible, and we often forget it's even there.

ACTION STEPS

Step 1: Pick a product
Select a new product or revisit an existing product that you want to offer your customers.

Step 2: Map its current state
Break out the intended or existing components

Step 3: Understand the user needs
Follow the steps working backwards from the user down into the back office

Step 4: Bring the outside in
Validate your architectural assumptions based on what is now available as a service, with a focus on removing undifferentiated heavy lifting as possible by using elements that are on the right of a map in the Utility bracket.

Step 5: Build, buy or use
In design reviews, ensure the CTO is constructively challenging precisely when you should build, buy, or use a technology component.

Step 6: Execute
Execute, understanding that no map is ever perfect and is always changing based on the growth and availability of new services.

We would like to thank Simon Wardley for providing Wardley mapping under Creative Commons to the community, and Adrian Cockroft for enunciating it so effectively.

2.4 MEASURING BUSINESS AGILITY

"If you can't measure it, you can't improve it."
– PETER DRUCKER

It seems that most every executive we know wants their organization to possess *business agility*—the ability of an organization to sense environmental change and respond (proactively or reactively) efficiently and quickly. And for good reason. The more quickly an organization can respond to changes in the business environment, the more quickly it can capitalize on them.

But, while gaining and growing business agility is a laudable goal, how exactly can we accomplish that? And once we have some amount of business agility, how exactly do we measure it? John Doerr's recent book *Measure What Matters* provides guidance. Says Doerr, today's most effective organizations have "Acute focus, open sharing, exacting measurement, [and] a license to shoot for the moon..." Ultimately, to attain and maintain business agility, we must also engage in exacting measurement.

Business agility and your organization

What about you? Are you interested in increasing your own organization's business agility? If you are, you're not alone. As our colleague Zehra Syeda-Sarwat, Customer Solutions Leader, AWS, explains:

In most, if not all of my customer engagements, I heard technology executives repeatedly ask how they can gain business agility by adopting cloud, and how they can prove business outcomes to the board and CEO! To estimate the importance of this topic, I started counting the times customer executives used the term "business agility" in their discussions with AWS. I found that, on average, the term is repeated every six minutes in a given executive meeting. Achieving business agility is clearly important to our enterprise customers and therefore, it is important to us here at AWS!

And, what if we can prove that technology such as cloud services enables and enhances business agility? Does that help convert technology from a cost center into an innovation center? To this end, the AWS Customer Solutions team built a mechanism that helps enterprise customers measure business agility enabled by technology.

According to Peter Weill, Senior Research Scientist and Chair of CISR at MIT Sloan School of Management, business leaders are primarily interested in two specific benefits of business agility, illustrated in the figure below.

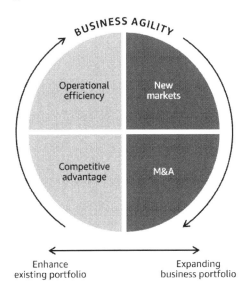

Enhance business portfolio

- Drive operational efficiency
- Increase competitive advantage

Expand business portfolio

- Enter new markets
- Execute mergers and acquisitions

First, they want to know how quickly and efficiently they can optimize their existing business portfolio by *increasing efficiency* and *competitive advantage* to ultimately drive profit and revenue growth. Second, they want to understand how quickly and efficiently they can expand their business portfolio by *entering new markets* and *executing mergers and acquisitions* (M&A).

Leaders need to identify how technology enables their businesses to achieve targets across each of these categories! Some leadership teams get stuck in analysis paralysis with no apparent pathway to escape.

ACTION STEPS

As leaders, we have spent many days in offsites—some useful, many not. As we reflect on the horrors of the latter, they were typified by drowning in minutia, fisticuffs over funding, pet projects, and praying for a better way to reach alignment within the leadership team. The AWS Customer Solutions team has developed a four-step approach to providing clarity, which we have used with customers to quickly focus on the few metrics that matter to your business.

Step 1: Executive alignment

In line with the working-backwards principle, the first step is to bring key executive stakeholders from business and technology together (yes, we know this alone is very difficult) for a one-day executive-alignment session. The purpose of this meeting is to agree upon a set of prioritized objectives with an associated high-level execution strategy, and to ensure alignment among attendees across the following items:

- **Prioritized list of technology objectives**—For the most part, enterprise technology teams should consider embracing business objectives as their own, instead of creating a new set of technology objectives! On the other hand, business executives should consider how technology can be a business driver rather than a cost center or a service provider.

- **Inhibitors**—Attendees collectively identify inhibitors that prevent the organization from executing objectives with speed and scale.
- **Alternate reality**—Teams explore innovative and "Think Big" ideas they would develop and run, including the results they would achieve given the existing capacity and market conditions if inhibitors didn't exist. For example, if inhibitors didn't exist, will go-to-market duration decrease from an average of two years to six months? Ask yourselves "What would you do, if you had no constraints?"
- **Path to alternate reality**—Now that we can see what the art of the possible looks like, the team discusses and collectively agrees upon a remediation strategy for inhibitors that are the biggest roadblocks. It is important not to overanalyze this, but instead to focus on the big-ticket items that will make the most impact.
- **Roadmap**—In a series of business outcomes or in Agile parlance, *epics*.
- **Owners**—An owner is assigned to each item and a cadence is established where the entire group comes together to continually re-prioritize. If you enlist the help of AWS or a partner, don't forget to list them as a co-owner for each item.

The outcome of the executive-alignment workshop is a list of prioritized technology objectives across the four categories of business agility, along with a high-level roadmap.

For example, a business objective of a technology company that develops software for clinical trials might be to increase revenue growth by 54 percent and increase EBITDA by 20 percent by 2021. The business objectives alignment chart will look something like the below:

Business Agility Category	Business Initiative	Priority	Technology Initiative	Inhibitors: Lack of experimentation	Slow Decision Making Model	Waterfall Business Process	Lack of Skills	Silo Teams	Risk Averse	Lack of CCOE	Analysis Paralysis	Trepidation to adopt new technology	Lack of security buy-in
Increase Operational Efficiency	Reduce operational Cost	1	Exit data center and reduce infrastructure cost	×	×	×	×	×	×	×	×	×	×
Increase Operational Efficiency	Enhance security	6	Reduce # of events/intrusion		×	×	×		×	×		×	×
Increase Operational Efficiency	Increase use of Automation through AI, ML, cloud native technology	3	Increase use of Automation through AI, ML, cloud native technology	×	×	×	×	×			×		
Increase Competitive Advantage	Enhance/digitize customer experience	2	Accelerate new customer/trial on-boarding from current 28 days to few hours.	×	×	×	×						×
Increase Competitive Advantage	Increase pace of innovation	5	Increase new feature and new product introductions per year	×	×	×		×	×	×	×	×	×
Increase Competitive Advantage	Increase revenue generated by existing products	4	Increase product Density (# of products used by customers)	×	×	×							×
Increase Competitive Advantage	Increase revenue generated by existing products	4	Increase product intensity (customer using existing product for multiple trials instead of 1)	×	×	×							×

Step 2: Measure what matters

The next step is to "metricize" the efforts and develop a scorecard that provides a performance temperature check across the transformation and technology initiatives. To do this, we align the respective initiatives with technology domains (for example, Security, Operations, Infrastructure, Projects, Change Management, etc.) and establish clear, relevant, prioritized, and measurable KPIs. Metricizing initiatives can be a daunting task, so AWS has built the high-level guide below to simplify the process. The guide is not set in stone, and while it helps get the efforts started, you will have to create list of KPIs that are most relevant to your target objectives.

TIER 1		TIER 2
BUSINESS AGILITY CATEGORY	**TECHNOLOGY DOMAINS**	
Operational efficiency	• Security and risk • DevOps and release management • Infrastructure and operations • Project and change management	
Competitive advantage	• Innovation • New product/services • Digital customer experience • Data and BI	**Time to value**
New market	• Experimentation • Innovation • Demand management • Security	**Cost to achieve**
Merger and acquisition	• Security integration • Operations integration • Business apps and DB integration • Infrastructure integration • Downtime	**Other**

We love this because we can take a red pen and quickly remove things that aren't relevant to our current business strategy. This helps to reduce the scope of KPIs to consider. We can then further drill down to the next level.

TIER 1		TIER 2		
BUSINESS AGILITY CATEGORY	TECHNOLOGY DOMAINS	Time to value	Cost to achieve	Other
Operational efficiency	• Security and risk • DevOps and release management • Infrastructure and operations • Project and change management	MTTD-breaches MTTR-tech debt MTTR-Sev 1 Duration-ideation to completion	Cost to resolve -breaches Cost to resolve -tech debt Cost to resolve-Sev 1 Cost per project-LOE	
Competitive advantage	• Innovation • New product/services • Digital customer experience • Data and BI	Duration-ideation to completion Duration-ideation to completion Duration to value Lead time-analysis	Cost per experiment Cost per unit Cost to implement Cost-analysis	# of experiments # of launches # of taps/clicks # of requests
New market	• Demand management • Security	Lead time-new environment Lead time-compliance		# of requests # of requests
Merger and acquisition	• Security integration • Operations integration • Business apps and DB integration • Infrastructure integration • Downtime	Duration-Integration Duration-Integration Duration-Integration Duration-Integration Duration-Integration	Cost integration Cost integration Cost integration Cost integration Cost integration	# of requests # of requests # of requests # of requests # of requests

There are hundreds of measurable KPIs under each technology domain and it is critical to select them carefully based on business objectives. It is imperative to only measure what matters. For example, if the business strategy is to increase pace of innovation, it makes sense to measure "throughput" and "flow metrics" that will ultimately help measure "innovation velocity." At the same time, it is important to ensure that, as velocity increases, the team is still headed in the right direction—otherwise, you may be moving fast toward the wrong destination. Taking an iterative approach and setting short-term destination targets mitigates this risk.

Let's look at competitive advantage as a Tier 1 example. It has multiple metrics, and these will differ slightly depending on industry vertical and business objectives. Most enterprises are looking to increase their pace of innovation and their ability to bring new products and services to market. Some enterprises limit innovation to new products and services only. In reality, innovation goes beyond new products and includes the ability to do something differently to make it better.

For an insurance provider, for example, customers might currently have to submit claims by phone and follow many onerous steps before they receive payments. Digital innovation can help revamp the entire process so that claims can be submitted through a simple and elegant online user interface. If an enterprise can expand the funnel of ideas that increases the rate of experimentation and process improvements, they are bound to increase the pace of innovation.

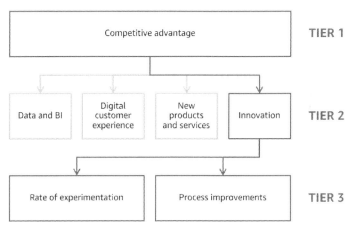

Below are a few KPIs an enterprise can measure to identify gaps around experimentation and implement strategies that will expand the idea funnel.

Rate of experimentation		
Time to value	**Cost to achieve**	**Other**
1. Average # of hours elapsed between ideation and approval	1. Average cost to experiment	1. # of experiments proposed
2. Average # of hours elapsed between approval and assignment	2. Total cost of failed experiments	2. # of experiments approved
3. Average # of hours elapsed between assignment and completion	3. Total cost of successful experiments	3. # of experiments completed
4. Average # of hours elapsed between ideation and completion		4. # of successful experiments
		5. # of failed experiments

Apply the same logic to all Tier 1 categories to create a list of KPIs. In order to ensure you only measure what matters, consider the following questions:

- Can you easily link this KPI to a business objective? If the metric is not linked to a business objective, should you spend any effort measuring it?
- Is the measurement mechanism directly linked to reality? It is important to choose the right metrics, and equally important to measure them correctly! How often have your teams followed the fallacy of counting lines of code as a measure of progress?

Step 3: Create a scorecard

Each Tier 1 metric decomposes into numerous KPIs and it is tempting for teams to want to measure everything. Instead, prioritize KPIs based on business objective priorities and then select the top 10 for ongoing measurement. Your scorecard should be a clear representation of business objective priorities. For example, you might focus heavily on operational efficiency for the next two years, and although you will need to continue to innovate, innovation itself has a lower priority! Hence the final business agility scorecard should have several KPIs that measure operational efficiency (you may select as many as five of the ten here) and the remaining KPIs will be distributed across the lower priorities.

Compare the scorecard against business objectives once per quarter to determine if changes are required, and reevaluate your top-ten KPIs.

Step 4: Measure, review, and close gaps

To keep things simple, the KPI status can be communicated using red and green indicators to show whether or not a target is being met. In our experience, a yellow indicator is redundant and is mostly used to sugarcoat the fact that a target is not being met. Teams often use the yellow indicator to show that they are "working on it," which is not a very helpful thing to know. As Jonathan calls it, "Red cloaked in amber."

On the other hand, if a KPI is red, then the scorecard should include a short root cause analysis and a plan to get to green. The team should also include any risks and unknowns to consider in light of this new information.

Ryan Hughes—VP Cloud Solutions, Nationwide Insurance—explains how he got clarity on Nationwide's KPIs using this approach:

Traditionally, IT and the business within an enterprise have a trans-actional relationship. Digital disruption across our industry is forcing a transformation where technology is more fully integrated across all areas of business planning and execution. This transformation stretches organizational and mental models and challenges the "art of the possible."

As we transformed, we found we needed a more effective way to communicate the importance of technology efforts that are funda-mental to the overall business transformation, such as cloud adop-tion, to ensure they are recognized and prioritized across our many lines of business.

IT-centric metrics such as infrastructure cost and uptime are not spoken in a language that makes the business really care or think about them as features that need to be prioritized. Our challenge was to quickly identify the right KPIs and implement efficient mea-sures that prove business value and benefits on an ongoing basis.

The AWS Customer Solutions Management team helped us take a simple, iterative approach by starting with a small set of key metrics that are relevant to our organization's business objec-tives. Emphasizing business value versus focusing on IT buzzwords enabled us to build a scorecard that established a common language between IT and business around metrics such as increased reliability, TCO, and speed of future feature delivery. By engaging with the AWS team, we were able to leverage their ideas, templates, and industry best practices which helped us avoid analysis paralysis."

Conclusion

There's an old saying, sometimes attributed to management guru Peter Drucker, "What gets measured gets done." Regardless of who first uttered these words, their sentiment is true. Metrics and data give you the clarity you need to make better decisions more quickly.

However, as John Doerr cautions, it's not enough to just measure—we must measure what matters. If you're measuring things that don't matter, then you're wasting valuable organizational bandwidth, time, and money. Not only that, but you will never achieve the business agility you seek.

Special thanks to Zehra Syeda-Sarwat, Customer Solutions Leader, AWS, for her help in writing this chapter.

2.5 BUILDING THE BUSINESS CASE

"If you wait until there is another case study in your industry, you will be too late"

– SETH GODIN, KEYNOTE SPEAKER, AUTHOR

In 2014, Thomas and his colleague Michael Kilander developed the detailed business case for cloud adoption at Experian Consumer Services (ECS). They decided against a business case based on cost reduction, and instead chose to focus on business agility and improving the customer experience as the dominant considerations. Business case in hand, Thomas and Michael went knocking on doors to start to build awareness if not consensus for what they were up to.

This approach paid off, and they were able to address most (but certainly not all) concerns raised by a variety of business leaders and stakeholders. We cannot overstate the importance of this important step in the process. It is possible that the original business case may miss the mark, because this is art and not science (contrary to what some people may tell you).

Thomas and Michael's business case was approved, although it certainly could have been better.

Why build a business case?

The business case is an exercise in quantified risk management. Investing time and effort to create a quality business plan is beneficial because it should serve to increase the likelihood of project success and so deliver a higher return on investment. It explains why one course of action is better or worse than another based on a series of tradeoffs. Stakeholders need to be assured that you have carefully examined whether the expected benefits of an investment can be realized and that you understand both the associated risks of proceeding and the risks of not doing anything. The business case is a due-diligence step that describes a path to success and enables multiple stakeholders to contribute their ideas and data within a given timeframe and build unity of purpose around the move to execution.

Depending on the level of ambiguity and risk faced by decision makers, the content of a business case could range from a highly detailed analysis to a short recommendation. The common baseline for a business case should be an explanation of why the investment is beneficial, a risk assessment, a list of decision options, and a rational method behind the elimination of poor options and selection of better ones.

The business case is an opportunity to double check whether the approach of the technology team is aligned with the wider needs of the organization. If current performance on cashflow and reputational gains are adequate, and there are few current or anticipated market disruptors, then a complex change program may not be necessary and a transactional approach to IT may suffice. However, if the organization is active in a market where new entrants have or are becoming disruptive, then the need for change may even exceed the organization's ability to transform, making action a matter of urgency. In these cases, where cloud is a change enabler associated with competitive advantage, a detailed business case can help speed up decisions and build the bridge between intention and action.

Cloud and cost reduction

Cost reduction is often cited as a key benefit of cloud adoption and many of the business cases for cloud are rightfully cost focused. However, cloud is a tool, and the outcomes obtained depend on how that tool is used. For example, cloud needs to be bought and used in a very different way than on-premise IT systems. The four core levers that determine cloud costs are:

- **Utilization**—Cloud spend should be optimized to reflect actual needs. Cloud costs and resources can be created and removed rapidly, avoiding the need to tie up capital in underutilized IT systems.
- **Pricing choices**—The decisions made are tradeoffs where cost reduction versus on-demand cloud pricing is the benefit. For example, use on-demand at higher cost versus committing capital for Reserved Instances for around a 70 percent discount. Use a high-powered instance versus saving 50 percent by using one rank of instance lower.
- **Cost-management culture**—Your goal is to create a sense of ownership with everyone on the team with respect to cost. In a pay-as-you-go cloud world, this needs a combination of tooling, training, the right leadership principles, and ideally, the allocating of budget to the lowest possible decision-making team unit.
- **Discounts**—Accomplish this by consolidating accounts and driving volume discounts.

In addition to these four levers, there are several other ways to use cloud to reduce cost. For example, retiring the assets that cloud replaces or refactoring applications to use serverless functions instead of instances. You might optimize storage based on the frequency of access or reduce database licensing overheads with AWS Optimized CPU. The cost analysis of cloud can be complex and is very different from on-premise IT. With cloud, for the first time ever you can actually have a detailed understanding of how you are spending your money. It's like shining a light in a dark corner for the first time.

The authors tried many times to allocate on-premise costs—it never worked. Your business partners would never agree with who should pay for which bit (certainly not *them*) and how much. With cloud that disappears.

Directional business case

A simple cloud business case may simply reflect financials, such as comparative running costs (that is, total cost of ownership) and an estimate of the costs of change (for example, how to move existing applications and workloads to cloud). In AWS, this is referred to as a "directional business case" and will typically include a high-level view of

- Migration costs
- TCO analysis
- A statement of measurable expected gain, such as economic or productivity

A directional business case can usually be completed in just one or two days. It utilizes low-fidelity data, it involves limited customer scope, and the output is generally just a presentation and an Excel spreadsheet.

The purpose of the directional business case is to help a team that already understands the benefits of cloud adoption to more rapidly access the funding needed to buy services that keep IT delivery aligned with business needs. This is ideal where the risk appetite is change friendly and the organization is already committed to change. The target audience for a directional business case is usually an IT Finance team.

Detailed business case

The detailed business case is more of a decision tool. It addresses the situation where a change vision needs senior-level endorsement for it to move from vision to funding and implementation. This is far more in depth and will likely include:

Decision summary: This is the initial framework for the business case. It is a 2-3 page summary that frames the decision to be taken so that stakeholders can be briefed and have a vehicle for providing feedback. No matter how detailed a business case is, unless it has buy-in from the people it impacts, it is unlikely to result in a successful project. By creating a short briefing document, the team that is driving change can drive proactive, early stage inclusion of stakeholders. By sending out a simple, nontechnical description of the decision to be made, consensus can be built, divergent opinions identified, and multiple perspectives included. A decision summary will usually contain:

- A summary of less than 50 words that describes the core problem that the business case decision is intended to address
- A list of the available decision options (i.e., the risk scenarios)
- A list of objectives describing how success would be measured in each
- A description of a target state and a current state
- A list of inhibitors and dependencies
- A list of the stakeholders that will be affected by the decisions

Financial model: One of the objectives is likely to be improved cash-flow (i.e., reduction of capital and operating expenses and liabilities). The financial modeling will cover three stages:

- Data: Discovery and assessment
- Analysis: Scenario modeling
- Outputs: Review and sensitivity testing

The output of the financial model should cater to some ambiguity and inaccuracy of data inputs. IT cost and usage may not be readily available in the time required. Data may be imperfect and perhaps incomplete, so the outputs of a cost model should be seen as reflecting scenarios and not as a single view of reality. By creating multiple "What-if?" scenarios, decision makers can view the output as a range based on assumptions and probabilities rather than as a single, fixed-value fact. Modeling the cost of cloud versus on-premise in a detailed analysis typically takes 4-6 weeks and includes:

- **Infrastructure costs.** Typically, on-premises compute environments are massively underutilized. According to a 2017 IDC study, the typical data center is only 45 percent utilized. Because of this overcapacity, infrastructure savings can be significant. Infrastructure costs include such things as:
  - Data centers
  - Connectivity
  - Servers
  - Storage
  - Network connectivity
  - Dependencies on other servers
  - Upcoming refreshes
  - Existing end-of-life plans
- **Application costs.** These costs are driven by such things as:
  - Number of application workloads
  - Workload dependencies
  - Upcoming application changes
  - Application migration patterns
  - Application maintenance costs
  - Licensing landscape
  - Application requirements
  - Regulation and compliance

- **Migration costs.** The costs of migration include such things as:
  - Planning and designing the migration
  - Development effort
  - Testing effort
  - Acceptance effort
  - Deployment effort
  - Landing zone configuration
  - Licensing
  - Data migration
  - Cut over
  - Rollback plan
  - Duplicate environment
  - Training and certification
  - Migration velocity
- **People costs.** There are two kinds of people costs to consider when building a business case: employees and contractors.
  - Direct people costs (employees)
    - Recruitment, retention, replacement, and retirement costs
    - Activity costs including understanding time and motion
    - Reskilling and development costs
    - Physical space, equipment, and services
  - Direct people costs (contractors)
    - Contracting costs
    - Cost per hour/day/week/month
    - Physical space, equipment, and services
- **Third-party costs.** These costs include such things as:
  - Contract-related costs (such as fixed costs for maintenance, variable costs for innovation and change requests, variation and early termination penalties, and lock-in deals)
  - Software licenses
  - Activity costs including understanding time, materials, and expenses.

You may need to manually obtain and reformat data for analysis. They may, for example, be buried deep in a financial report which requires you to go look for the data. In this case, **manual business case tooling** can be used to gather the necessary data in a variety of different ways, including:

- Migration cost estimator
- Simple TCO calculator
- Resource efficiency model
- Migration pattern analysis (see Chapter 5.4 Migrating Your Applications)
- Financial analysis
- Business value analysis

In the case of **automated business case tooling** for gathering the necessary data, there are a variety of tools for capturing data and performing analysis. Some of the tools we have used with customers include TSO Logic, Cloudamize, or Apptio.

A key benefit of using these tools is that they make it easier to manage cloud costs over time and ensure that the economic levers of cloud are working for you. We recommend you include budget for tools to more efficiently manage your cloud costs early. The business plan should also outline areas for potential improvement that may require process changes. For example, the ability to easily tag cloud resources with cost codes simplifies the work needed to identify operating expenses involved in creating assets as well as facilitating simple chargeback.

Decision model: Business models that focus exclusively on cost reduction assume that economic gain is the dominant objective. They encourage short-term thinking and are incomplete. Usually, cloud adoption is driven by a mix of objectives to drive improvements in cashflow, customer experience, and governance. Complex decisions have multiple objectives. Each choice will evidence those objectives in its own way and will require tradeoffs. The most common approach to quantifying decision options and managing tradeoffs is to use an additive utility scoring method such as swing weighting, which we have used extensively.

In swing weighting, the aspects that would evidence success in an outcome are ranked, weighted, and normalized. Then, along each aspect, a scale of measurement is created to reflect the value of one score relative to another. These two scales are then combined to generate a single numerical score for each decision option. This approach makes it possible to factor in the customer experience and governance value of agility, productivity, resilience, simplification, and so forth without attempting to convert all aspects of benefit into an estimated monetary value.

Risks and dependencies: Once the different options have been costed and the less beneficial ones eliminated through the decision model, a list of risks and dependencies should accompany the recommendation. For example, a move to cloud to replace on-premise IT needs to happen in parallel with a move to exit and remove the assets being replaced. Otherwise, double-running costs will be inevitable but can be smoothed with the AWS Migration Acceleration Program. Similarly, cloud adoption at scale will likely entail changes to the risk register and the effectiveness of controls, so there should be a note anticipating this step, the Cloud Business Office (discussed later) can own and help with this.

When to build a business case

A business case should be completed for any big decision in IT. Since cloud adoption is iterative and completed in phases, as capabilities increase it may well become part of the process that governs quality assurance and learning over a transformation program.

During the course of meeting with hundreds of companies at every level of maturity and progress through their digital transformation processes, our colleague Stephen Orban outlined four stages of adoption:

- **Project**—Experimenting with how to do IT differently using proof of concepts and development workloads, and learning what the cloud can do for the organization.
- **Foundation**—When organizations get serious about moving to the cloud and begin to make foundational investments in connecting internal business systems and internal IT to the cloud in a hybrid model running production both in the cloud and in on-premises data centers.
- **Migration**—When a commitment is made to a fast-paced, scaled-out migration to the cloud —moving servers to AWS while retiring accumulated technical debt to enable a greater focus on innovation.
- **Reinvention**—Optimizing IT costs and business capabilities as the organization's IT footprint is moved fully to the cloud.

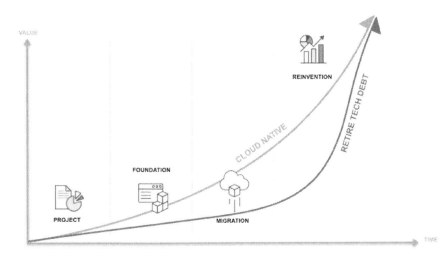

So, in which of these stages should you build a business case? That was a bit of a trick question, since the answer is in *every* stage. It's important to realize that each stage is a gating criterion for a business case. If, for example, you're going to move from Amazon EC2 in the migration stage onto a service environment, you need to be able to work out what it's going to cost you to run functions instead of code running on Amazon EC2 instances.

ACTION STEPS

Step 1: Gather your data

Step 2: Build a directional business case

Step 3: Create a detailed business case

Step 4: Revisit through each stage of adoption

Final thought

The business case is such an essential part of the journey that we recommend you employ the assistance of the AWS Cloud Economics team, or utilize a partner to help guide this process. Given the likelihood that this will become a part of the operating procedures, training members of the Cloud Business Office will be a wise investment.

We want to give a special thanks to John Enoch for his advice and invaluable assistance in the writing of this chapter.

PART 3

Culture and Organization

3.1 CULTURE

"Everyone thinks of changing the world, but no one thinks of changing himself."

– LEO TOLSTOY

Peter Drucker was famously quoted as saying that "culture eats strategy for breakfast," and he was right. Most leaders quickly realize that the technical implementation of cloud is not actually the most challenging part of the journey. It turns out to be culture and organization.

Geert Hofstede, Professor Emeritus of Organizational Anthropology and International Management at Maastricht University in the Netherlands, is well known for his pioneering research on cross-cultural groups and organizations. He defined culture as the "software of the mind." Culture encodes how we interact with one another. It has written and unwritten rules and norms that have evolved over time—whether in response to some problem or calamity, or simply based on what has worked in the past. While some cultural norms are explicit—for example, mission statements and codes of ethics—others are hidden. Regardless of how it manifests, culture is completely intertwined in how things are done in every organization.

And, as we all know, culture is remarkably powerful. Anytime someone tries to fiddle with culture, the corporate "antibodies" emerge to defend the corporate body from foreign influences. These defensive reactions can manifest in a variety of different ways—from public opposition, to political shenanigans, to outright sabotage. Some may simply adopt a passive-aggressive hope that the new endeavor will fail and go away. The only one of these responses we would consider to be healthy is public opposition. You can have a dialogue and an exchange with outspoken critics to sort out the issues. Critics probably have important concerns that should be heard and addressed, and incorporating this kind of feedback into the process invariably makes the outcome stronger. Be worried about the apathetic.

Successful leaders cultivate the culture they want for their organization, which requires employees to change and adapt. Humans have a natural bias toward maintaining the status quo—that which is perceived to be normal, traditional, and ordered. People naturally shy away from what they think of as "new-fangled ideas" that they often equate with uncertainty or even chaos. Better, they think, to stay with the familiar—even if it is less efficient or more expensive. Better the devil you know...

FUD—fear, uncertainty, and doubt—turns out to be a very personal affair. Whenever there is change in the wind, people naturally wonder how the change will affect them personally. People may, for example, worry about the long-term impact of cloud adoption on their careers, whether automation will eliminate their jobs, or if they are in danger of becoming somehow incompetent or obsolete in this new world. All of this contributes to doubt—whether the transformation will succeed, whether it is the right thing to do, whether it wouldn't just be better to leave things be.

This FUD is, as we've seen, one of the main sources of resistance to change. One way to deal with FUD is to understand the interests and motivations of key players in the organization. You will need to understand the obvious stakeholders as well as the non-obvious influencers. Stakeholders include all members of the C-suite, the board of directors, and business and IT leaders. The non-obvious influencers could be respected, long-tenured engineers—such as a senior network engineer, architects, senior developers, and many others. You can identify who they are simply by asking members of IT who the go-to people are in their respective disciplines. Sometimes influencers are well known, because they are not afraid to ask hard questions in public, but other times they are silent and influence IT through the expert power they wield in the organization. This dynamic is famously described by Brent, the indispensable IT expert in the previously mentioned novel *The Phoenix Project*. Brent is a human bottleneck who is essential to all important IT efforts. While this gives Brent strong job security, it is detrimental to the organization. Brent is not malicious in any way, but his role and influence puts the success of any transformation at risk.

To turn around a culture of fear, focus on success. For each stakeholder, you will have to think about how cloud adoption enables success. Can you help reduce cost for the CFO? Can you help drive desired cultural norms, such as hiring for diversity, for the VP of HR? Can you prioritize components or systems in the cloud journey to automate onerous tasks for the compliance team? If you think about these questions, you will find many opportunities to align the goals of the transformation with the individual ambitions of the key stakeholders. Find simple solutions that have a potentially high impact for the stakeholder to limit the impact on the overall roadmap. This cannot just be an IT-only initiative.

In the case of someone like the fictional Brent, you will need to train others to do and know what Brent knows, so that the resource constraint is removed on the one hand, and Brent's veto power is limited on the other. To sway the opinions of key influencers who command the respect of IT employees, you will need to spend time to understand their concerns. This is time well spent, because the years of experience they bring to any problem lets you anticipate challenges down the road. For every concern they raise, you will need to either dispel misconceptions by educating and clarifying, or you will have to mitigate concerns that are potential problems. Mitigation can be as simple as clearly articulating a plan, which you might even assign them to create directly so they have skin in the game.

Management, then, is not about enforcing control in a hierarchy of functional responsibilities. It is about gaining the power that the team-oriented approach offers by amplifying the teams' ideas, creating clarity around goals, removing impediments, and devising and allocating resources to support the teams' activities. You will have to engage the middle manager's ingenuity in accomplishing new goals where impact can be tied to business success and which collectively with other goals supports the new ways of working. An important task for leaders today is to creatively find ways to redefine the goals and incentives of their middle managers to align with transformation.

Cloud transformation is primarily a leadership effort based on influence and persuasion, rather than command and control or top-down authority. The cloud, DevOps, and today's other best practices for IT delivery can make heroines and heroes of everyone. They add so much value to the enterprise that there are more than enough super-powers to go around. The goal of transformation is to *empower* everyone across the organization—middle managers included—and make them successful. Mark Schwartz succinctly phrases it in his blog "The cloud, DevOps, and today's other best practices for IT delivery can make heroes of everyone."

Principles

All of your assumed constraints are debatable. We will strive to consciously and subconsciously debate our perceived constraints and not accept them at face value.

Keep the customer, employees, and company safe. However, we face a much bigger risk by doing nothing than doing something.

Don't fight gravity, the apple always falls. Moving to cloud is essential for our enterprise to get the cost, security, elasticity, availability, and flexibility benefits our business needs.

Use data to make decisions. We use data whenever possible, rather than opinions and conjecture, to drive measurable results.

Set a bold goal. Hands down the most successful transformations come from bold leadership combined with best-practice experience. The experiences of GE and ENEL are fantastic case studies in their own right—all have bold goals combined with superb tactical experience-led execution.

Unless you know better ones. This tenet list is always open to constructive challenge.

ACTION STEPS

Step 1: Define your leadership principles

Step 2: Dispel fear, uncertainty, and doubt

Step 3: Create quick wins

Step 4: Find complementary stakeholder objectives

Step 5: Deliver objectives

3.2 TEAMS

"If you can't feed a team with two pizzas, it's too large"
– JEFF P. BEZOS, FOUNDER AND CEO, AMAZON.COM, INC.

Much of Thomas's approach to cloud adoption stemmed from his military experience in the US Army. The US military is as hierarchical as an organization can be, yet small units are afforded a great deal of autonomy while they execute their mission. The US military organization is modeled on the organization originally deployed to great effect by the ancient Roman military. The smallest unit is a squad, usually comprised of 8-12 members, 4-6 squads form a platoon, and 3-6 platoons form a company. Companies are then aggregated into battalions, which make up regiments, which roll up to divisions, and then on to corps, and finally armies. While there are many reasons why this structure has proven itself to be effective over the past two thousand years, two aspects in particular are pertinent to our discussion: command and control, and local autonomy.

Squads are small because a small unit with fewer than 15 people can be effectively led by one squad leader. Trust and cohesion at the squad level are very important and are based on shared experience (sometimes hardship) and intensive training as a unit. It is relatively easy for a small unit to pull together and focus on achieving a particular mission (or outcome). Each team forms strong internal bonds, and team members identify with their squad. Each next level of command has a small number of direct reports (similarly, many business publications suggest a span of control of seven direct reports as optimal). Teams develop a broad set of common skills (such as first aid, marksmanship, or land navigation), as well as diving deep in their team and individual specialties. This ensures the team can operate largely autonomously in the pursuit of their mission while other units provide support when needed.

While the popular concept of military leadership is that leaders simply exercise command and control over their people, the reality is actually much more nuanced. Effective leaders earn the trust and respect of the men and women they lead. While certain decisions are not up for debate, many other decisions are debated and discussed by the whole team. The best leaders encourage and seek this kind of open, back-and-forth discussion to benefit from the experience and knowledge of all members of the team. Regardless, the final decision and responsibility for outcomes lie with the leader.

Team leaders and members receive orders from their command structure. When the command structure defines the mission and objectives, the commander will specify what is known as the "commander's intent," which is designed to enable disciplined initiative to empower agile and adaptive leaders. (Army Doctrine Reference Publication (ARDP) 6-0). A retired general framed it the following way: "Because tight centralized control of operations isn't possible or desirable... leaders must train their juniors to do the right things and then trust them to act independently."[3] This is a critical component as team leaders decide how to accomplish a particular objective. The commander's intent is not a free for all, however, as an accompanying statement called the "concept of operations" describes the principal tasks required, the responsible units (or teams), and how the principal tasks complement one another.

The commander's intent is deliberately sparse on execution details. This provides the team with the autonomy to react to local conditions and the tactical situation without having to constantly ask for guidance and detailed orders on how to proceed. The commander's intent was informed by the business vision, the strategic roadmap, and the epics for the next quarter or two, while user stories corresponded to the concept of operations for the sprint.

Here the similarity ends, however, since team leaders and managers do not have the same command authority as their military counterparts do, nor do they need it. There are no truly life-and-death situations, no potentially catastrophic emergencies, and no requirement to manage the health and welfare of each soldier.

So, what other benefits do small teams afford? First, they allow personal and human interactions to take center stage. Team members form strong bonds inside the team, which allows a team identity to form and team spirit to emerge. This is invaluable when weathering difficult times or traversing the "trough of disillusionment" (aka the "valley of despair") when a problem seems most intractable. Teams must have the mental toughness to persevere in order to experience a breakthrough to arrive at the solution. Team members must build trust, which can be strengthened by encouraging team-building exercises and fun team activities.

Consider this description of the book *Turn the Ship Around!* written by retired US Navy Captain David Marquet:

> *"Leadership should mean giving control rather than taking control and creating leaders rather than forging followers." David Marquet, an experienced Navy officer, was used to giving orders. As newly appointed captain of the USS Santa Fe, a nuclear-powered submarine, he was responsible for more than a hundred sailors, deep in the sea. In this high-stress environment, where there is no margin for error, it was crucial his men did their job and did it well. But the ship*

was dogged by poor morale, poor performance, and the worst reten-
tion in the fleet. Marquet acted like any other captain until, one
day, he unknowingly gave an impossible order, and his crew tried to
follow it anyway. When he asked why the order wasn't challenged,
the answer was "Because you told me to." Marquet realized he was
leading in a culture of followers, and they were all in danger unless
they fundamentally changed the way they did things. That's when
Marquet took matters into his own hands and pushed for leadership
at every level. Turn the Ship Around! *is the true story of how the*
Santa Fe skyrocketed from worst to first in the fleet by challenging
the U.S. Navy's traditional leader-follower approach.[4]

Second, small teams facilitate clear and consistent communication. This is simply a consequence of Metcalfe's law, which states that the effect of a (telecommunications) network is proportional to the square of the number of connected users of the system. So, the more users you add, the more you have to communicate.[5] Small teams can gather around a whiteboard and debate a particular technical problem by thinking out loud and by drawing out ideas on the board. Training within small teams can be accomplished peer to peer or by bringing in a coach for hands-on experiences. Learnings by individuals can also easily propagate through the entire team.

Third, small teams identify with their work and outcomes, which facilitates a huge sense of ownership. This ownership can be further cultivated to pursue something former Navy SEAL commander Jocko Willink calls "extreme ownership."[6] Team members and the entire team come to believe that they are entirely responsible for the success or failure of their mission. This means teams candidly discuss impediments they encounter, seek innovative solutions when they encounter an obstacle, and accept personal responsibility rather than looking for excuses or blaming others. This level of ownership must be carefully cultivated and is difficult to achieve. Teams that exhibit this level of ownership, however, are extremely effective and impactful, and can dramatically increase productivity and innovation within an organization.

There are, of course, other non-military models to examine, such as Amazon's Two-Pizza Teams or Henrik Kniberg's work with Spotify's tribes and guilds. That said, how you structure your teams ultimately depends on the needs of your organization, the desired business outcomes, and the culture you already have. We will cover this more in the Target Operating Models section in Chapter 4.3 Your Evolving Target Operating Model.

ACTION STEPS

Step 1: Define your target team size

Step 2: Evaluate moving from command-and-control to empowered teams

Step 3: Understand and address the impact on middle management

Conclusion

The aspiration in technology has long been to enable teams to deliver in this way. It has been hamstrung by the fact that many Agile teams were still dependent on siloed teams that only specialized in their technology or discipline and always ended up on another team's critical path. Cloud is the inflection point. It provides small teams with the ability to finally take ownership end to end and operate with commander's intent—aka guardrails—to deliver an outcome.

3.3 PRINCIPLES FOR YOUR CLOUD JOURNEY

"Obey the principles without being bound by them."

– BRUCE LEE

Tenet—*noun*—*a principle or belief, especially one of the main principles of a religion or philosophy. These tenets are held by the group. To be a member in good standing, you are expected to hold to its particular teaching.*

It's nice to think that everyone starts a transformation journey at the same logical time and place, and it's easy to assume everyone understands the *why* and the *how* behind the journey. Even leadership teams that are seemingly aligned (and we have sat on many) often think they are agreeing on the scope of the same problem, but never actually have the conversation to align properly and calmly on the why and the how. Sadly, good intentions don't work.

As a leadership team, how can you ensure your team—and the teams working for you—stay aligned and are able to make a majority of decisions autonomously, while still making decisions that align to your objectives?

One of the mechanisms in Amazon that deals head on with potential misalignment and ambiguity is the effective use of tenets. A team defines its own tenets. The tenets can be appropriately challenged by any member of the team, and if any member thinks they know a better one, then they own making a recommendation for change.

Taking just a small amount of time to define the tenets for your cloud adoption, and consciously allowing them to be challenged and amended as you know more, will save you incalculable time as you go forward. We have personally experienced and seen teams that have spent days, weeks, and months (and yes, even years) building software and infrastructure that to them seems important, only to find it's not used by anyone. One of the most common examples in our industry is the term *data lakes*. We have lost count of how many enterprises we have worked with where a team working away in a silo has constructed a thing of beauty around Hadoop and fast backend storage, only for no one to place their data in it or use it for answers. What a waste. A simple tenet constructed around data could have holistically prevented this. Even something as simple as, "Each team owns their data and makes it securely accessible on an as-needed basis by everyone via an API," could have solved massive wasted time and energy.

Unfortunately, it's not unusual to work with technology leadership teams that have spent the best part of two years working incredibly hard to build a fully featured automated new development model for their engineers. It is seen as a thing of beauty. Their CI/CD pipelines are deemed perfect, they tried to force a particular technology choice, and they had all the controls they thought they needed in place. There was just one problem. No one was using it, and they had no production workloads running.

In times like this, we find ourselves acting as cloud "shrinks," and it's our job to ask the challenging questions most folks in their respective companies would be too polite to ask. "What are your group tenets to building securely, operating, and migrating to the cloud?" They didn't have a single one, not even a business case they could agree on. This company is, sadly, not unique. We have found ourselves in our previous positions looking at the latest technology offering—thinking it was the best thing since sliced bread—only to get back to the office, discuss it with our engineers and developers, and then take the time to sincerely listen to why it was a terrible idea. In such cases, we were fortunately able to pivot and drop the whole thing, with nothing but a few hours' lost time. Wasting two *years* in today's economy, however, sends shivers down our spines.

A better approach is one of seductive adoption. What you are offering is so good, so easy, so compliant, why wouldn't you use it?

So, what is a good example of a tenet? The best ones we know of are the Amazon Leadership Principles (LP). These tenets drive every single Amazonian to use their judgment with a set of consistent principles. Our team is over 600,000 strong at the time of this writing, and we can have a conversation with any one of them about diving deep on a customer problem or not turning up for an internal meeting because LP1 (Customer Obsession) requires our undivided attention.

Amazon Leadership Principles

Customer Obsession—Leaders start with the customer and work backwards. They work vigorously to earn and keep customer trust. Although leaders pay attention to competitors, they obsess over customers.

Ownership—Leaders are owners. They think long term and don't sacrifice long-term value for short-term results. They act on behalf of the entire company, beyond just their own team. They never say "that's not my job."

Invent and Simplify—Leaders expect and require innovation and invention from their teams and always find ways to simplify. They are externally aware, look for new ideas from everywhere, and are not limited by "not invented here." As we do new things, we accept that we may be misunderstood for long periods of time.

Are Right, A Lot—Leaders are right a lot. They have strong judgment and good instincts. They seek diverse perspectives and work to disconfirm their beliefs.

Learn and Be Curious—Leaders are never done learning and always seek to improve themselves. They are curious about new possibilities and act to explore them.

Hire and Develop the Best—Leaders raise the performance bar with every hire and promotion. They recognize exceptional talent, and willingly move them throughout the organization. Leaders develop leaders and take seriously their role in coaching others. We work on behalf of our people to invent mechanisms for development like Career Choice.

Insist on the Highest Standards—Leaders have relentlessly high standards—many people may think these standards are unreasonably high. Leaders are continually raising the bar and drive their teams to deliver high quality products, services and processes. Leaders ensure that defects do not get sent down the line and that problems are fixed so they stay fixed.

Think Big—Thinking small is a self-fulfilling prophecy. Leaders create and communicate a bold direction that inspires results. They think differently and look around corners for ways to serve customers.

Bias for Action—Speed matters in business. Many decisions and actions are reversible and do not need extensive study. We value calculated risk taking.

Frugality—Accomplish more with less. Constraints breed resourcefulness, self-sufficiency, and invention. There are no extra points for growing headcount, budget size, or fixed expense.

Earn Trust—Leaders listen attentively, speak candidly, and treat others respectfully. They are vocally self-critical, even when doing so is awkward or embarrassing. Leaders do not believe their or their team's body odor smells of perfume. They benchmark themselves and their teams against the best.

Dive Deep—Leaders operate at all levels, stay connected to the details, audit frequently, and are skeptical when metrics and anecdote differ. No task is beneath them.

Have Backbone; Disagree and Commit—Leaders are obligated to respectfully challenge decisions when they disagree, even when doing so is uncomfortable or exhausting. Leaders have conviction and are tenacious. They do not compromise for the sake of social cohesion. Once a decision is determined, they commit wholly.

Deliver Results—Leaders focus on the key inputs for their business and deliver them with the right quality and in a timely fashion. Despite setbacks, they rise to the occasion and never settle.

These tenets are designed to be naturally contentious and to provoke a conversation. Every single day, every Amazonian reflects on and balances them. Sometimes we have to Dive Deep before showing Bias for Action, and sometimes we just need to make things happen. How we use the tenets requires judgment, and we recruit strongly for that judgment.

So, with the thought that tenets are a really good idea, what makes a good cloud tenet for your enterprise? In our own travels and journeys, we have come across quite a few. This list is by no means definitive— our goal is to present the best we have seen. Of course, "the best" is subjective and not objective.

Agility principles

Small multi-skilled teams (Two-Pizza)—We will organize ourselves into small teams no larger than 12. Wherever possible, the teams will be self-contained and have the ability to own their destiny and work schedule.

You build it, you run it—As the new, small teams create features, they will own the support of them 24x7x365. DevOps in its simplest form.

It's often at this point that we get asked about segregation of duty. Ultimately, you want all code deployments and operations to be highly automated, using code pipelines for everything. If you need to retain two-man control, then consider differing levels of this role within one team, and/or two-man automated approval roles for pipeline deployment.

The team we have is the team you need—We are always working first to reskill, retool, and promote our workforce with the best knowledge so they can execute our cloud vision, before trying to hire externally.

Teams choose—The team decides with their product manager how to build and what tools to use, so long as they meet the company's security and business objectives.

One size doesn't fit all—Our business is large and diverse. Use the right tool for the job. We do not assume one size (tool or product) fits all, but we do have strong opinions on how to solve commons problems. We automate and codify our opinions into simple, integrated experiences. We remove and deliberately avoid undifferentiated engineering effort.

Get out of the way—Allowing service teams to own their AWS adoption themselves, we decouple and decentralize development. We prefer to build guardrails, not gates. We automatically audit for compliance.

Publish your API—Each time will ensure their product and data is accessible securely via an internal, and if appropriate, external RESTful API.

Cost-saving Principles

Cloud First—To remove as much undifferentiated heavy lifting as soon as possible, all new development will be Cloud Native.

Cloud Native—Wherever possible, we leverage AWS features rather than build our own solutions. We build the thinnest possible control plane over AWS to leverage efficiencies of scale. We acknowledge that "perfect" is the enemy of "good enough." While we bias to using AWS features, when blocked, we will innovate with our own temporary solutions.

Run less software—If a component has become a utility, you shouldn't be spending precious development time maintaining it. Instead, you should be consuming it as a service.

This can be a hard shift for technology professionals. They want to build their "own" thing. But even containers are now run and operated as a service. If your engineers are no longer building data centers, why are they building container platforms? This will only lengthen time to value and create technology debt for you to manage in perpetuity.

Focus on customer data, logic, UX, and security—We strive to build and support the company's data and business logic, not systems that do not differentiate our product.

Primary public cloud partner—We will select a cloud services provider (CSP) that will allow the focus for our organization to get to an expert level rapidly with a chosen platform across people, process, and technology paradigms—avoiding the distractions that come with too many platforms.

Minimum likeable product/cloud—We will investigate the appropriate security, availability, and efficiency objectives to get the first production workload to the cloud. We will expand our research to other tools as customer features demand it.

Close the data centers by a set date (burn the ships)—We will have migrated or found the right homes for all our systems to enable the close of our data centers by a specified date.

Save as you earn—The team and product manager are accountable for their cloud spend. If a means to an end justifies the use of something that delivers material fiscal benefit to the organization, they are allowed to reinvest it.

Frugality matters—Being prudent and owning your cloud spend is important—teams should strive to continually lower their costs. Money spent on wasted resources could have been better spent on customer features.

Elasticity principles

Everything fails all the time; design for it—Design and test for failure to levels appropriate for the customer problem we are solving. Use reliability engineering principles as we go.

Fail in production—Be bold and use reliability engineering in a controlled way to deliberately fail components running in production.

Production always runs in multiple Availability Zones—Production services and their data are always run in more than one Availability Zone.

Auto-scaling rules—We will leverage auto-scaling as appropriate to mitigate potential bottlenecks occurring in production.

Innovation principles

Everyone is a security engineer—Everyone focuses on appropriate security every day.

Pair programming works—For both training and development of production code and support, we will frequently practice this using two developers working side by side on a single machine. The sum is greater than the parts.

Tooled correctly for continual learning—We will ensure developers have the tools they need for the job. And we will put in place mechanisms to encourage and reward continual technical self-development.

Certification rules—We will encourage, recognize, and reward those engineers and developers who attain AWS certified status.

Get to 10%—Getting 10 percent of all engineers and developers certified is our goal. Read Chapter 4.1 Becoming Cloud Fluent at Scale to learn why.

Recruit for alignment with our tenets—Ensure that the folks you want to hire have demonstrable experience aligned to your tenets.

Recognize what motivates engineers and developers—Motivation comes from autonomy, mastery, and purpose. This can be nurtured by allowing people to run with their own ideas, master, and have impact with them.

Bad ideas should fail fast, production should not—We encourage people to test ideas and fail quickly, not in production.

Going global principles

Trust, but verify—We will intrinsically trust our leaders, engineers, and developers to make the right decisions to protect our data and systems, but will have mechanisms in place to verify that trust.

Source code security—All code will be securely held in an enterprise repository, and access will be monitored.

Policies matter—While teams have autonomy to choose their tooling, the tools and solutions must comply with security and availability objectives.

Credential blast radius reduction—We will appropriately reduce access to the minimum.

Assume the enemy knows your code—Dance like no one is watching; encrypt like everyone is.

Radically restrict and monitor human access to data—Drive people to use tools to access data rather than by hand.

Immutability rules—The authoritative data source and logs will be immutable.

This list is by no means exhaustive. These are just a small selection of tenets you can copy and paste and adapt as you see fit for your own business and teams. Hopefully, you can see a long thread of Agile and innovation at the edge (i.e., from the teams themselves). Trust that your teams will be accountable and responsible for the *how* and *why*, while making sure you verify that this is the case.

At their very heart, principles and tenets such as these are a reflection of an organization's culture and most deeply held values.

ACTION STEPS

Step 1: Agree on your principles
Be sure that your principles and tenets reflect your actual organizational culture and values. If they are out of alignment, employees will pursue less-than-optimal activities and inefficiencies will emerge.

Step 2: Challenge and update
Don't just set and forget your principles and tenets. Publish them clearly and embed them into your design reviews at every stage. Continually revisit them to ensure they still reflect your organization's culture and values.

Step 3: Publish and use them everywhere

As Amazonians, we have seen the power of well-crafted principles and tenets, and we live them every day of the week. Make them a vital and important part of your organization too.

3.4 CREATING THE CLOUD LEADERSHIP TEAM

"Tell me and I forget. Teach me and I remember. Involve me and I learn."
– BENJAMIN FRANKLIN

Enterprises on this journey can stall. We have seen this on our own journeys and on the journeys of the customers we work with. Having an aligned leadership team that feel ownership in the journey and empowered to exercise their ability to question and get answers to those questions is vital. When this alignment has not occurred it very often then materializes itself in what is called the "frozen middle," where chief executives, engineers, and developers can clearly see the benefits of cloud adoption and actively want to move that way, but managers, directors, and junior executives are concerned about the impact on their role. So, the conscious and unconscious desire of this latter group is to try to block or control such a move.

Nearly every enterprise cloud journey will suffer from this frozen middle at some point, and it can be fatal to transformations. At times, both of us felt like we were stuck in parts of our own journeys. It's frustrating and akin to walking through a room filled with treacle (molasses), while everyone is shouting from the sides for you to go faster.

So, what mechanism actually works to remove these stalls? Time and again we see customers moving at pace when they have a Cloud Leadership Team (CLT) in place.

What does a CLT do?

The Cloud Leadership Team ensures the effective governance for the organization to adopt and accelerate public cloud use across the business. It does this through the holistic representation of key stakeholders from across the business who form a quorum, who commit to be broadly educated on key cloud differentiators across security, reliability, availability, cost, and time to market. It will establish and agree bold objectives and principles to the same, and act positively to encourage the enablement of the workforce to adopt cloud at scale and address and remediate any risks or blockers that arise in its course.

Ultimately, the CLT exists to ensure alignment of the cloud goals to the business's goals and the strategic and tactical execution of them across elements of people, process, and technology in a well-governed and inclusive way.

Getting the right leadership team together

Cloud Transformation Leader - The most effective individual has the implicit authority to accept and/or mitigate perceived risks in line with the board's risk appetite and sets controls appropriate in this regard. The position works best when either the CIO or CTO themselves— or at the very least, a direct report of these two roles—assumes it. The Cloud Transformation Leader has an expansive role in leading the CLT, and indeed for taking everyone on the journey across people, process, and technology in congruence with the board's risk appetite. This is a senior executive role.

Chief Information Security Officer (CISO) - Having either the CISO themselves in this position—or an empowered direct report—is crucial. This person has multiple roles within the group: First, to educate themselves in the Amazon Shared Responsibility model, with clear understanding of which parts AWS handles and which parts customers are responsible for. Second, to educate others in the new security paradigm that now exists. Third, to ensure potential blockers are scrutinized appropriately. And, finally, to ensure the security objectives for the organization's move to cloud are clear and appropriate. We cover security in depth in Chapter 7.1 Security Is Always Job Zero.

Legal and Procurement - In the old world of business, supplier contracts were heavy with CAPEX decisions and guesstimates of as-yet-unknown required capacity. The contracts would take months or even years to negotiate and were often packed with a multitude of SLAs that were pretty much just so many words on paper when an actual outage occurred.

By default, supplier contracts in hyperscale public cloud are appropriately different, with no committed spend and pay-as-you-go consumption, along with a high security bar and the natural requirement to protect every customer from every other customer. This means it's important that Legal and Procurement are involved from the start and have a chance to understand these differences.

Risk and Audit Representation - Ensuring the Risk and Internal Audit teams (if appropriate for your organization) are present within the CLT is important. As you look to adopt the profound benefits to your business that public cloud brings, these functions will help ensure that frontline leaders are raising, accepting, or mitigating risks across these areas.

Head of Infrastructure and Operations - The Head of Infrastructure and Operations will typically command 51 percent of the vote for any decision that comes to the CLT regarding cloud. And from their perspective, this makes some sense. This is the team that probably gets called at 3:00 a.m. when things fail, and that has to maintain critical operations 24x7x365, as well as patching, availability, and DR—and all the infrastructure in between—so it will always have a powerful voice in the CLT quorum. Of course, an element of "Wait a minute, I build infrastructure—what do I do when we move to cloud?" can also be a very large elephant in the room.

In our experience, the infrastructure engineers who previously built, ran, and continually upgraded data center-based infrastructure have a crucial role in cloud migration and growing the business. Their inherent ability to understand infrastructure as code—through their experience with Linux/Network/Storage/Windows/Database command-line subsystems of legacy data centers—is of profound advantage. This is particularly the case when it comes to using those same command line interfaces skills to configure scripted API calls as AWS CloudFormation Templates to build not just servers or networks of servers, but entire Regions of servers, data services, and everything in between as continuous integration/continuous delivery pipeline code (CI/CD). We will cover CI/CD more in Chapter 4.2 Enterprise DevOps.

The boost in motivation (covered more in Chapter 4.1 Becoming Cloud Fluent at Scale) as they become skilled AWS experts who are ready and able to perform scripted wizardry across any of the AWS Building Blocks ensures that they will always have an important place within Agile teams. Helping engineers through this profound change curve is the job of leaders.

Head of Delivery and/or Line of Business Representation - By far the most-rapid transformations are when business leaders demand to leverage the new tools that AWS Cloud brings to transform the ability of their lines of business to deliver different and better results for customers.

We've seen for ourselves that it's potent stuff when business leaders can clearly articulate a vision of value, leverage the new building blocks of the digital age, and then rapidly engage with teams to deliver this change. In more times than we can count, the idea of being able to use their data to make better automated customer decisions in the areas of credit risk, decisioning, fraud reduction, cross-sales opportunities, and more is far more impactful.

Having their representation, critically for the first workloads, is literally like jumpstarting your journey to AWS Cloud. It provides a problem catalyst, funding, and goal. Everything else follows.

Human Resources - As you move to reskilling your current and future employees at all levels for public cloud, the place of Human Resources to act as trusted advisors to ensure you are engaging effectively and appropriately with your workforce is required. This is especially the case as you look to continually adapt and transform your workforce and job roles.

CCoE Leader - We will delve deeper into the prerequisites of the Cloud Center of Excellence Leader and the role they play in the next chapter. Suffice it to say they have a crucial role as both leader of the CCoE and a trusted advisor to the CLT.

The Head of Architecture - Historically speaking (the last few decades), the role of enterprise architecture has been vaunted, and at the same time derided, in equal parts. Its role in waterfall execution of projects was a key early stage and ongoing governance function that would often make or break a business case and project in equal measure.

We would respectfully argue that technology architecture has never been more important (see Chapter 5.5 Using the AWS Well-Architected Framework). But the *way* in which this role is performed has changed beyond measure, with the powerful move to Agile and teams that now build and support in this API-based pay-as-you-go cloud model.

The enterprise architects of today can no longer sit in their ivory towers and act as the authoritarian old guard. The role has changed. The current expectation is that architects can code just as well as any developer. They are now expected to operate as Senior Principal Developers/Engineers who have significant experience across a multitude of technology disciplines and can effectively technically lead and mentor engineers and developers in their product/Agile teams to ensure they consider all of the inter-relational components that modern architectures need. In their teams, they groom all the architecture assets for their fit for purpose and adapt them in line with the product managers to effectively manage technical debt. That said, their role in the CLT is crucial to ensure a controlled move to cloud.

The CLT has a long list of actions they can take. Here are the ones we have consistently found to be **most important:**

Action Steps

Step 1: Set a bold goal
Covered in PART 2, Chapter 2.1 Strategy and the Bold Leadership Goal.

Step 2: Ensure goals align to business objectives
Covered in PART 2, Chapter 2.4 Measuring Business Agility.

Step 3: Catalog and eventually answer all the questions
Everyone will have questions—you can count on it. Most senior executives are consciously curious, and this curiosity materializes in the form of questions. Do not simply give these questions lip service; capture every single one. Each question is important to the person who asked it, and if left unanswered will act like a sea-anchor with a negative drag force on your transformation. The word "eventually" answer is really important here. If the CLT tries to get the answer to every question before it does anything, it will never achieve anything. Don't

let this stop you from getting started! For example, it's natural for an organization to not let customer data exist in the cloud until the CISO and their teams quite rightly thoroughly understand the AWS Shared Responsibility Model. But that doesn't preclude a team starting to work toward a first workload. Think just-in-time answers and eventually answer everything rather than needing to answer everything before getting going. An Executive Briefing Session held locally (in country), or ideally at AWS in Seattle, can answer whole swaths of questions and can be both highly educational and enable rapid building of executive relationships.

Step 4: Agree on your principles
Covered in PART 3, Chapter 3.3 Principles for Your Cloud Journey.

Step 5: Remove roadblocks
Rapid removal of roadblocks builds and maintains momentum and neutralizes large team ambiguity around commitment to the change.

Step 6: Agree on the first production workload
Pick something important. It's got to matter to your business peers, it has to demonstrate value, and it must define a new way. A simple microservice for your production website can work really well and is still important to your business. We don't encourage proof of concepts—nobody really cares about science projects.

Step 7: Establish the Cloud Center of Excellence (CCoE)
Discussed in PART 3, Chapter 3.5 Creating the Cloud Center of Excellence

Step 8: Assist in the contracting process as required
Pay-as-you-go public cloud contracts are obviously different than capital expenditure-intensive, fixed-term contracts. It is of course

important for leaders to be appropriately informed and supportive of the differences.

Step 9: Ensure funding is available

Specifically, for the assignment of dedicated resources and the grooming of priorities. This becomes especially important for business case establishment and migration decision points.

Step 10: Agree, execute, and monitor migration of applications and data

Ensuring congruence, priority, and awareness of *what* and *when* to migration is a key role of the CLT. Migration is discussed in detail in Chapter 5.4 Migrating Your Applications.

Step 11: Communicate broadly and consistently

Unless you communicate, the information vacuum will be filled with fear, uncertainty, and doubt.

Step 12: Establish broad reskilling program

Covered in detail in Chapter 4.1 Becoming Cloud Fluent at Scale

Step 13: Establish regular review cadence

Meeting weekly or every day to check progress and ensure consistent progress is made and perceived risks are appropriately decisioned is crucial to maintain momentum.

3.5 CREATING THE CLOUD CENTER OF EXCELLENCE

"Give me a lever long enough and a fulcrum on which to place it, and I shall move the world."

– ARCHIMEDES

One of the key principles of AWS from the very beginning has been to level the playing field for every customer by ensuring that they have access to world-class technology, that had previously only been available to the largest and wealthiest businesses.

No longer.

Anybody can start using AWS Cloud with just a few simple clicks on the AWS website and a credit card. The self-service nature of this process has enabled hundreds of thousands of customers to make the journey to cloud quickly and autonomously. But what is the right way for an enterprise to start?

Well, of course, enterprises can also start with just a company credit card. But if you want to learn from those that have gone this way before, and are looking to develop a holistic AWS Cloud experience that can scale across your business—and subsequently allow you to extract the maximum benefit from the cloud—then you should start by creating the Cloud Center of Excellence (CCoE).

What does the CCoE do?

A CCoE team coalesces all applicable technical and business product expertise into one team to bring the first production Cloud-Native workload or migrated workload to the cloud. In the process, it establishes the technical objectives, reusable architecture patterns, and associated code for the organization's use of cloud across the paradigms of security, reliability, scalability, cost, and time-to-value differentiation. Its members commit to become intensely and consciously curious about AWS Cloud and aspire to set the technical bar of Cloud Expert.

We both started our own journeys by bringing together the right engineers and developers with the right leaders and goals.

Of the many important steps you'll take in your journey to cloud, creating the Cloud Center of Excellence Team—the first technical team of performers you bring together—is one of the most important. Not only will this team have a tremendous impact on your positive momentum, but it can also have a disproportionally positive impact on the outcome of your journey to the cloud. The team that executes your first cloud workloads and sets the first design patterns will set the bar for everyone who follows (and they should keep raising it). The efforts, actions, standards, and engagement of this team with other teams is crucial.

Similarly, the nature of the relationships of the people you assign to the Cloud Platform Engineering team will have a direct impact on its ultimate success—or failure.

The purpose of the CCoE is there to be a beachhead, a leading light, a fulcrum of technical change for your cloud transformation. Then, as you scale your talent transformation (Chapter 4.1 Becoming Cloud Fluent at Scale), by the very circumstance of success the requirements and nature of your CCoE will change.

Over time, the team should right size as you automate more and more of your processes, and if you so choose (we would argue you should), transfer much of the responsibility—not just build, but also run—to the product teams. In effect, a CCoE team should be working hard to make its function unnecessary, as cloud simply becomes the way you deliver IT. We discuss this more in Chapter 4.3 Your Evolving Target Operating Model.

Where can this go wrong?

Sadly, we have seen customers who are on the second or third incarnation of creating a CCoE. Why does this happen? How can you avoid this?

First, failure can result because they are trying to implement a significantly different technology platform within legacy on-premise thinking that is not appropriate for the new business models that cloud enables. In the words of Dr. Werner Vogels "Thou shall not use old IT concepts for new applications." Your AWS Solutions Architect is your very best friend here.

Second, we see this failing when the CCoE team is at risk of becoming a bottleneck because they try to build (and own) everything centrally for their organization rather than working toward team empowerment within guardrails.

Third, they want to boil the ocean and create the perfect platform, taking the approach "I will create the perfect gold-plated platform," and spend years getting there.

Fourth, because they have created a central and divisional CCoE team model. But the central teams want to approve everything rather than enabling the defining principles that can be followed globally.

Finally, when an organization is treating cloud as a side project, or worse, a side-of-desk project that doesn't have the support of the leadership team to provide clear goals and principles, and remove roadblocks.

If any of the above are true, watch out!

The CCoE is sometimes described as a Cloud Enablement Engine, with various configurations depending on your situation. This is something that AWS Professional Services has an approach for. And it is for these reasons that we see the creation of a CCoE morphing to that of a Cloud Enablement Engine.

What is the right mechanism to establish a continual process of scaling your entire organization to be Cloud First? It starts with putting the right team in place.

Getting the right team together

First of all, the CCoE is a team that needs to be dedicated to the task. As we previously mentioned, but it's worth stating again, side-of-the-desk or matrixed resourcing is not going to work. It's a dedicated team with complementary skills that allow them to overcome each technical hurdle they may encounter during the journey to cloud, without seeking much, if any, external technical assistance from other teams.

The second key element is to consciously acknowledge you are blending multiple skills together. While many organizations aspire to "do" DevOps, so many we work with forget the "Ops" bit of the equation. Our goal is to bring together diverse skillsets that can overcome any and all potential technical roadblocks.

Creating a diverse team helps increase performance. Researchers Brian Uzzi and Jarett Spiro studied the relationships of collaborators (composers, directors, lyricists, producers) from nearly 500 musicals produced on Broadway between 1945 and 1989. Using a ratio for density of past working relationships they called "Q," the researchers found that musicals with a low ratio of existing working relationships among the collaborators (low Q) were not likely to be a commercial or critical success. Maybe not surprising, but Uzzi and Spiro also discovered that so-called "A-teams"—teams that had very strong connectivity or a track record of working together (high Q) on other musicals—were not a good indicator of success either. It turns out that Broadway teams with a good mix of new and existing relationships (mid-range Q) were three times more likely to achieve box office success. Put simply, they found that most successful musicals were by teams that had a good balance of people who had worked together in the past and knew how to pull off a top production, as well as new blood that brought in a steady supply of new ideas.

Also, worth noting from painful personal experience, with the diversity of complementary skills you are going to pull together in your CCoE team, the virtual team construct is initially very important. If you try to walk into the fire of changing reporting lines (which is always emotional for everyone at some level) this will definitely slow things down, potentially terminally so. You can revisit this important organizational topic in Chapter 4.3 Your Evolving Target Operating Model.

The more-effective teams have a broad and deep set of technology skills. For this first team, permanent employees may be preferable to outsourced or out-tasked resources. It's okay to recognize that initially the foundational team almost certainly won't have the AWS Cloud skills they need from the outset. We will get to this later.

Below is the *ideal* list of CCoE team members. It's not necessarily the number of people who comprise this team that is important. It's entirely possible for a single builder to do all of these tasks, and thousands of startups get going this way!

Many organizations will not have these individuals in discrete roles but will have great engineers and developers who do one or many of these tasks. That is perfectly fine. Also, we fully recognize that assigning some of your most-effective individuals from the organization to put into this team can be itself be a huge challenge. These individuals are likely already allocated to critical work elsewhere, and they can't always be easily replaced with contractors due to budget constraints. This is why the involvement of the Cloud Leadership Team is crucial to ensure resources and tradeoffs can be made if they are required.

CCoE Leader - The individual that leads this team has a deep responsibility. The performance of the individual in this role can (and often will) make or break journeys. When we designated CCoE leaders on our own journeys, we chose individuals who over-indexed on empathetic people skills and who had a firm collaborative bias for action. While strong technology appreciation is required, emotional intelligence is more important here. Consider this description of emotional intelligence from the great book *The EQ Edge* by Steven J. Stein, Ph.D. and Howard E. Book, M.D.:

> *It's a set of skills that enables us to make our way in a complex world—the personal, social, and survival aspects of overall intelligence, and the elusive common sense and sensitivity that are essential to effective daily functioning...Emotional intelligence also encompasses our ability to read the political and social environment, and landscape them; to intuitively grasp what others want and need, what strengths and weaknesses are; to remain unruffled by stress; and to be engaging and the kind of person others want to be around.*

This role is best enacted with an individual who has an appropriate level of seniority that is both explicit and implicit.

Security Engineer - Security is Job Zero for us all. Everyone, but especially the Chief Information Security Officer (CISO), will want to ensure that the right security decisions are being made. Having a hands-on, code-centric, security engineer or developer who has a healthy constructive attitude towards outcomes and who has a reporting line into the CISO will be crucial. This individual will be responsible for ensuring the first cloud components you choose align with your security objectives.

Carl "CJ" Moses, Deputy Chief Information Security Officer and VP of Security Engineering at AWS, puts it well here: "The Security group should not be the group of no, if your security team is the group of no, you have got the wrong security team." He goes on: "Security should be an enabler, and we should be part of the process all the way through."

Network/Firewall Engineer - Ensuring you can securely design and connect your existing enterprise network to AWS Cloud with Virtual Private Network and/or AWS Connect Direct—while ensuring harmonious IP address ranges, adequate bandwidth and latency calculations, Domain Name Server integration, and network routing—will be critical. Having a network engineer on board who can do this while working with the rest of the team on a shared outcome is critical.

Ensuring you can appropriately set firewall ports as required from your on-premises infrastructure to the AWS Cloud, and to enable correct routing of any network segmentation you have in place, will likely mean having an individual with firewall expertise on the team.

Automation Engineer - All AWS engineers and developers learn the importance of using AWS CloudFormation or the AWS Cloud Development Kit to ensure repeatable and well-managed "infrastructure as code" as a foundation for DevOps. If you are going to build on Amazon EC2, you'll need an expert-level engineer who is not only familiar with AWS CloudFormation but is also able to assist with automating those elements crucial to secure, scalable Amazon EC2 operation across a variety of operating systems required by your enterprise. Having someone who can do this from the start will save you a lot of time and rework later. Whoever this is, he or she will likely be drawn into maintaining AWS Amazon Machine Image Design, which will be an ongoing process for as long you want to use Amazon EC2s rather than running AWS Serverless. To this end, the Automation Engineer will probably specialize Chef Automate or Puppet Enterprise (as you so choose) to assist with your automation efforts and create the right guidelines to ensure consistent infrastructure as code. The goal is to automate everything possible. Everyone needs to learn intrinsic infrastructure as code automation.

Operating System Engineer - Whether your preferred operating system is Windows or Linux, having an experienced engineer who can understand the breadth of critical OS interdependencies that exist in a corporate OS landscape is crucial. It's a position similar to, but potentially different from, the Automation Engineer. Engineers who are very familiar with UNIX/LINUX and its fundamental elements typically have a shorter learning curve with AWS Command Line Interface (CLI).

Software Development Engineer (SDE) - You'll need experienced developers who are actually able to create business logic in whatever language your teams prefer. They are, of course, going to create the business logic required for your first production instance. Putting them onto the team is therefore crucial and will lay down a constructive path toward Build IT/Run IT, if that is a principle the leadership team chooses.

Software Quality Engineer (SQE) - As you move toward CI/CD and DevOps practices, testing what you do does not go away—in fact, it becomes a core part of the cycle. If you want to move to small DevOps teams, then getting your testers to move toward test-driven

<u>development</u> is an important step in CI/CD. Test-driven development is a software development process that relies on the repetition of a very short development cycle, whereas previously defined "requirements" on a waterfall process are now turned into specific minimum test cases as part of an Agile sprint where the software developed must pass tests defined in the sprint. SQEs help the team break down their story steps into the test cases that are going to be needed and take input from all members of the team, especially security.

Operations Engineer - How infrastructure and applications are monitored, where logs go, and how the existing ITIL processes integrate are important. Although mature DevOps can indeed automate many of the ITIL functions, you might not be there yet. Having an individual who knows how to get the important application/database/infrastructure telemetry data and have access to some sort of performance baseline will ease the integration of existing systems and processes appropriate to use in the cloud.

Data Engineers - Having engineers who know where your data is, how to access it, how to move it appropriately, and how to establish the first cloud data stores can accelerate your journey. This individual might be a System Database Administrator—normally responsible for the underlying database engine, performance, operations, backups, and upgrades. Or this person might be an Application Database Administrator—normally responsible for writing and debugging complex SQL and understanding the best ways to incorporate database requests into application programs and performance tuning. Alternatively, you might also enlist a Data Scientist in this role who typically creates various machine learning-based tools or processes within the company, such as recommendation engines or automated lead-scoring systems and statistical analysis. Regardless of who you assign, one of these individuals can help reduce cycle time for the team. The topic of databases and analytics is covered in far more detail in Chapter 6.1 Cloud Databases & Analytics.

AWS Solutions Architect & Partner Resource - Finally, and crucially, involving both your AWS Solutions Architect and approved AWS Partner or AWS Professional Services resource to accelerate the learnings and to actually help develop your infrastructure as code—allowing you to grow your knowledge—is a real catalyst for development time.

Removing blockers

Ensuring a regular cadence of daily stand-ups and the appropriate escalation of blockers to the CLT, especially in the first workloads, is crucial. The CCoE Leader—and ideally another member of the CLT who is empowered to remove blockers that arise for this team—should be in attendance as required.

ACTION STEPS

Step 1: Help establish security objectives
Refer to Chapter 7.1 Security Is Always Job Zero.

Step 2: Oversee the creation of AWS Landing Zones
Establishing the right AWS Landing Zone is of crucial importance for the Cloud Platform Engineering team to consider. And the team should work with their AWS Solutions Architect, an AWS Approved Partner, or AWS Professional Services and ask the following questions:

- What is your plan to ensure that your cloud/AWS environment is set up properly for your organization?
- What best practices for account setup do you plan to use to help secure your environment?
- How do you plan to get visibility across your entire organization for what all your teams are doing?
- As more teams start using AWS, how will you make sure that all of them set up their accounts with the security baselines applied?

The answers to these questions will guide the decisions you make regarding how you should build different pathways, whether that is to use AWS Control Tower, AWS Landing Zones, or something more bespoke. To save time in the long run, being thoughtful about this choice is strongly advised.

Step 3: Ensure consistent code repository
You will, of course, already have existing code repositories in one form or another. However, over the last few years, the *de facto* standard has become Git. This is a code version-control system for tracking changes and coordinating work on those files among multiple people. Having a consistent mechanism for code sharing is crucial, especially as everything becomes infrastructure as code.

Step 4: Establish initial availability objectives
Covered in detail in Chapter 5.3 Resilience and Reliability

Step 5: Help establish training and reskilling program
Covered in detail in Chapter 4.1 Becoming Cloud Fluent at Scale

Step 6: Ensure resilient and secure network connections
Review and select the right connectivity patterns to ensure you can route and secure networks from your existing on-premises environment to AWS Cloud in a scalable and efficient way.

Step 7: Conduct quick-win analysis with business partners
While we, of course, always aim to create strategic change, quick tactical wins generate "wins" that can materially demonstrate success.

Step 8: Complete first production workload
If you don't yet have anything live in AWS, you should aim to get to live in 12 weeks. This is your goal. Use the mechanisms in this book

to accelerate your journey. Choose something that gets you live and generates positive news internally. Speed in business matters.

Step 9: Establish initial billing/payment process review

Getting your first AWS bill is like throwing sunshine in a dark corner. It is your pinnacle point of truth in what was used and when it was used. Ensuring the right mechanisms are in place so that teams or product owners are accountable for their spend and budget can really help the right decisions to be made.

Step 10: Establish user access management

Refer to Chapter 7.1 Security Is Always Job Zero.

Step 11: Establish initial run books

Setting the patterns for effective support 24x7 as you approach production and establish monitoring canaries is needed for today's systems. Although you have built infrastructure as code and via CI/CD pipelines, does the team understand how to gain bastion host access should it be required? Do appropriate on-call individuals have the right access? Do you have an on-call rota? The AWS Well-Architecture Framework is an excellent reference framework to cross check against in this regard.

Step 12: Initiate effective communication of Technical Patterns and feedback

If the CCoE team operates in a vacuum, expect the rest of the organization to be clouded with FUD. Establishing an internal wiki site and push communication of what the team is doing week by week—and being humble in its engagement with other teams and ideas—is of crucial importance. Even more so as you approach production and start to scale the teams.

3.6 CREATING THE CLOUD BUSINESS OFFICE

"A year from now you may wish you had started today."
– KAREN LAMB

Getting and keeping the show on the road is not something the leadership team can do with good intentions. There needs to be a mechanism to do so.

Typically, we have found there is a Project Management Office (PMO), an Office of the CIO, a Chief of Staff function, or elements of all three typically in place with enterprises we have both worked in and engaged with in our travels.

What mechanism can join the strategic oversight of the CLT, understand the tactical build that the CCoE is doing (that needs to scale), and handle the other significant moving parts, track all the action items, relationships, and interdependencies, and be there to scale and communicate the new?

For that we need a Cloud Business Office (CBO).

What does a CBO do?

The Cloud Business Office is a body that guides and informs cloud adoption. It acts on behalf of the CLT—ensuring their intent is well managed. It tracks progress, identifies blockers, architecture alignment, vendor relationships, delivery methodology, migration tracking, reskilling, communication, budget, governance, risk management, and compliance.

Because of the significant governance, risk management, and compliance focus in highly regulated businesses (typically financial services institutions, health care and government) we have also seen the CBO take on the name Cloud Governance Office (CGO). There is no hard or fast rule here. Bottom line, you need to name this function as you see appropriate and its composition will likely form from a contingent of folks from existing PMO, Office of the CIO, or Chief of Staff function(s). It will need a Single-Threaded Leader, and will of course work best when the personnel assigned to it are working there on a permanent basis.

Ultimately, the CBO exists to ensure alignment between the thousand-and-one elements that need to be coordinated as you execute any change program, which of course needs to be well managed. And if you don't have a team alongside—helping address not just the technology, but the complementary processes and mechanisms with which the rest of the organization leverages—you run a significant risk of the "great stall" caused by being stuck in the frozen middle.

Getting the right team together

Architecture Alignment - While, as we discussed in the CLT chapter, the role of Enterprise Architect is going through a seismic change, it's still important that reference architecture alignment, work decomposition, and engineering support is provided. The CBO is the place to corral this effort and change.

Product Management and Delivery Management - Most organizations have long obsessed on a backlog of projects, and what can and can't be funded. As such, this topic is always a charged one. The Project Management Office has always been a lynchpin of such a function. As you move to a product/outcome Agile-based way (if that is appropriate to you) of delivery versus project management, management of the change is absolutely crucial. Being able to ensure demand management, that functional work is decomposed and prioritized, and that a product roadmap strawman is available for account executives to groom, is still required. This is alongside Agile execution support and overall status reporting.

Financial Management and Cost Optimization - Budget management has always been a focused effort in technology. The ability for the first time to get the clarity on infrastructure when you use cloud is, as we have previously mentioned, a revelation.

AWS's breadth of services and pricing options offer the flexibility to effectively manage your costs and still keep the performance and capacity your business requires. You can easily right size your services, leverage Reserved Instances, and use powerful cost-management tools to monitor your costs so you can always be on top of how much you're spending.

By following a few simple steps, you can effectively control your AWS costs: 1) Right size your services to meet capacity needs at the lowest cost, 2) Save money when you reserve, 3) Use the spot market, 4) Monitor and track service usage, and 5) Use AWS Cost Explorer to optimize savings.

Establishing both principles and mechanisms for your organization as you scale your use of AWS will help with speed and execution and keep the CFO on your side.

On-Boarding - The ability for new employees to get up to speed effectively with the right knowledge and appropriate access is critical to your success. Alongside this, existing employees need to know how they can access the new platform. Make sure this role has an effective content creator assigned who can work hand in hand with the communications output. As you build more capabilities in this space, and as this grows, it will change. That needs to also be clearly and continually communicated.

Training/Reskilling - We discuss this in detail in Chapter 4.1 Becoming Cloud Fluent at Scale.

Organizational Change Management - Organizational change management and strategy execution is the role of the leadership team. However, the delivery of the change at a macro level, and appreciation of the complex independencies that make up the modern enterprise landscape, have it typically handled by a function in the office of the CIO. As your own organization moves to small teams, focusing on what differentiates the business from others and having a way to holistically present the pros, cons, and risks of different possibilities should come through the CBO to the CLT.

The other critical role is, of course, clear and timely communication of what is happening, why it is happening, and when it is happening. Ensuring both push- (email) and pull-type information (website) is available and digestible is absolutely key.

ACTION STEPS

Step 1: Identify the leader for the CBO
As we have previously mentioned, having balanced EQ and IQ is going to be crucial for this role. Also identifying that the CLT have the final say on execution and working hand in glove with the CCoE leader to establish and scale the *how* is going to be crucial for this individual.

Step 2: Helping the CLT
Tracking actions, identifying blockers, ensuring cadence of stand-ups and tracking everything else we have mentioned throughout the CLT,

CCoE, and CBO chapters (and indeed this entire book) will likely form into the tactical responsibilities of the CBO. The scope is of course very, very broad. Ultimately, it comes back to helping the CLT and keeping the wheels on the train.

Step 3: Building the team
Building the right team with the balanced complimentary skills set as you adopt cloud and engage with adjacent teams across the enterprise is going to be crucial to this team's success.

Step 4: Establish an OODA loop or equivalence
The role of the CBO is so varied that it is best to incorporate the practice of the OODA loop.

> *The OODA loop is the cycle observe–orient–decide–act, developed by military strategist and United States Air Force Colonel John Boyd. Boyd applied the concept to the combat operations process, often at the operational level during military campaigns. It is now also often applied to understand commercial operations and learning processes. The approach explains how agility can overcome raw power in dealing with human opponents. It is especially applicable to cyber security and cyberwarfare. (Source: Wikipedia)*

Thus, observing what is going on and then adjusting accordingly is very good advice for the CBO leader. Things will change, curve balls will come in. You of course need to handle them.

Step 5: Communicate
Establishing and maintaining both push comms (email, town hall meetings) and pull communication (intranet, self-help channels) is crucial to success. As we have said before, unless you fill any communication vacuum, folks will fill the vacuum for you. So, communicate!

PART 4
People and Process

4.1 BECOMING CLOUD FLUENT AT SCALE

"A leader takes people where they want to go, a great leader takes people where they don't necessarily want to go but ought to be."
– ROSALYNN CARTER

We all know the importance of learning—it's how we are able to keep up (and perhaps even stay ahead) of all the change swirling around us. Becoming cloud fluent is primarily about education and learning. However, as leaders, we know from our own (sometimes painful) experience that it's easy to oversimplify gaining cloud fluency as "teams just need a little classroom training." This is not the case at all. Training, while very useful, is just a tip of the iceberg, as our own journeys can attest.

There are a multitude of factors at play here. Your business may be a complex mixture of divisions, outsourcing, siloed resources, some Agile practices, some waterfall practices, some DevOps, operations teams, and third-party vendors that have their own project delivery processes. In this case, the challenge of actually leading people to upskill so we can remove the thankless tasks and release people to be able to innovate can become daunting.

It's daunting because people need to be motivated—ideally, *self*-motivated—to want to learn something in the first place. This is difficult enough, let alone getting people to unlearn ways and methods they may have used at least somewhat successfully for decades, especially when they yielded traditional results. In his book, *Unlearn*, Barry O'Reilly explains, "We must unlearn what brought us success in the past to find continued success in the future."

As the old saying goes, "You can lead a horse to water, but you can't make it drink." In the same way, you can't force reskilling. People have got to be motivated to do so. And some people are inevitably going to tenaciously hang onto their previous way of working while remaining passionately wedded to incumbent technology skillsets.

As a leader, it's worth deeply reflecting on the fact that your strategy is about to be impacted by three human drives—autonomy, mastery, and purpose—that are all typically deeply personal to our professional identity. These lead us to perform a role and receive an income, which ultimately allows us to pay our mortgages and live our lives. For as long as the cloud remains a mystery to people, they are going to be fearful of it. As humans, we naturally fear the unknown.

Fear is a fickle thing. We are not poets, so we are not going to wax poetically on the topic. But we know from personal experience that fear can lead to all sorts of irrational decisions—nearly all of which will delay your transformation in one way or another. And delays in business can, of course, be costly or even fatal.

Ok, let's reset for a second. At this point in the journey, it's important to remind you that this emotion—fear of the unknown—is going to occur. It's a natural thing. You can't avoid it, but you can lean into it by sparking motivation, interest, and a crushing honesty from all leaders so that we can learn together.

Getting this right is so very important. If you get the reskilling part correct, everything else will largely solve itself, because people will understand how to solve the challenges on the other side of the reskilling coin for you. We see this being true with customers the world over. Successful reskilling needs understanding (and support) of motivation (especially of engineers and developers), a mechanism (the 12-step process detailed later in this chapter), and funding—both with time and money to allow your business to become cloud fluent at scale.

Tackling motivation

Motivation—and what motivates us—is an incredibly nuanced topic. As individual contributors, managers, and then leaders, we have both had to learn what actually motivates one person may not motivate another person at all. As a result, you need multiple motivational levers in place to support different people.

In his book, *Drive*, Daniel Pink argues that human motivation is largely intrinsic and that the aspects of this type of motivation can be divided into autonomy, mastery, and purpose. He argues against old models of motivation driven by rewards and fear of punishment, dominated by extrinsic factors such as money.

- **Autonomy**—Our desire to be self-directed. It increases engagement over compliance.
- **Mastery**—The urge to get better skills.
- **Purpose**—The desire to do something that has meaning and is important. Businesses that only focus on profits without valuing purpose will end up with poor customer service and unhappy employees.

Having gone through tremendous reskilling journeys ourselves, and from working with customers around the globe, we would agree that Daniel Pink has a significant part of the motivation formula nailed here. Certainly, when you look at what motivates *builders*. And today's builders are not just engineers or developers, they are product managers, entrepreneurs, and leaders in all walks of life. The idea of being able to act autonomously, leverage your mastery, and execute in a purposeful way—without having to build massive capital expenditure-intensive data centers has of course enabled thousands upon thousands of startups to challenge the status quo in a way never before seen. From Pinterest, to Lyft, to Monzo, to Peloton, the list goes on and on.

Therefore, everything you do as a leader should focus on the short-term fear that reskilling for cloud is going to cause for your engineers. They are going to have to slow down to learn before they can go fast—faster than they ever thought possible. In the 2018 Accelerate: State of DevOps report, the authors go into detail: "How you implement cloud infrastructure matters. The cloud improves software delivery performance and teams that leverage all of cloud computing's essential characteristics are 23 times more likely to be high performers."

However, there is a complication. When it comes to reskilling—particularly with engineers, developers, managers, and a whole host of business functions—autonomy, mastery, and purpose are not the only elements to contend with. People are actually going to have to *unlearn* what they have done previously to then learn the new. A Linux engineer who has racked, stacked, cabled, installed, configured, and maintained servers from the hardware up probably has a high level of autonomy, mastery, and even purpose with the status quo! And you are about the introduce the fear of the unknown with your Cloud-First and Cloud-Native principles.

According to Barry O'Reilly, the Cycle of Unlearning is a three-step process: (1) Unlearn—why and what specifically do you want to unlearn? (2) Relearn—as you unlearn limiting but ingrained methods, behaviors, and thinking, you can take in new data, information, and perspectives (3) Breakthrough—as you break free of existing models and methods, you can achieve extraordinary results. You then use what you learn from your breakthroughs to tackle bigger and more audacious challenges, starting the Cycle of Learning all over again.

You already have the people you need to succeed with the cloud

Stephen Orban has written convincingly about this in his post, "You Already Have the People You Need to Succeed with the Cloud." We often see many organizations that think they need to recruit new builders for cloud. While it's always important to be onboarding new folks that align to your culture and expertise requirements, having a reskilling mechanism that scales and addresses the motivational needs of the different types of people and the different ways they like to learn is especially important. With the benefit of hindsight from our own experience and working with customers around the world, here are 12 steps that have been proven to work.

ACTION STEPS

Step 1: Acceptance through the art of doing

Your engineers need to realize the fact that they have the ability to learn AWS Cloud skills and become experts (mastery) operating (autonomy) in a far more valuable way (purpose!) building a customer product. This is far more exciting than building and endlessly refreshing hardware. It's also important for technology leaders within your organization to accept this. Realize when the way you have been doing things is having diminishing returns and needs to change. Spending time discussing this in town hall meetings, team meetings, and in water cooler one-to-ones is all going to help. Engaging in humble, but confident communication that we are going to learn together is incredibly important.

Step 2: Training

The ability to work in a classroom environment with an instructor is a safe space for many people and important to their learning. It's also excellently facilitated by AWS's own training team on site, at an approved training center, or via an Approved Training Partner. The AWS Cloud Practitioner, AWS Technical Essentials, and AWS Associate

Architect are all excellent starting courses depending on the knowledge level of different engineers and developers.

This classroom course is an eye-opener, and a delightful peek into the art of the possible. It will also radically change your perspective on where you are wasting time with previous practices. The AWS website has hundreds of videos that provide online training on a whole range of technical topics, from novice to advanced.

We would recommend offering training immediately prior to a team coming together to use AWS. Resist trying to compel people to attend training without offering the time and goal for them to apply and reinforce what they have learned.

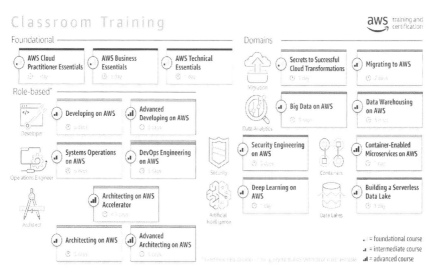

Step 3: Hands-on time

There is no compression algorithm for experience. So, safe hands-on time is now required. Consider offering an AWS sandbox account to your engineers to reinforce how you do things—a place that will never host production, has a billing alert set on it, and ideally the engineers and developers have the ability to configure everything from an account's Identity Access Management (IAM) through to a Virtual Private Cloud (VPC) and associated Internet Protocol (IP) address space. Thomson Reuters explained on stage at re:Invent 2017 that they were giving their engineers and developers a safe sandbox account in which to learn. Understand that, at this point, it feels like there are a million ways to accomplish the possible with cloud. It can all be a little overwhelming. Your engineers can get both very excited by the possibilities and slightly disillusioned. Recognition of the normal change curves everyone goes through (some are short, some are long—it's personal) is absolutely critical. Continual encouragement is the key!

Step 4: Create your Two-Pizza Team

As we explained in the preceding chapter (3.5 Creating the Cloud Center of Excellence), the first engineering team you put together should ideally consist of a holistic set of core skills—network, database, Linux server, application, automation, storage, and security. The team will make some progress—it will probably look at tools like Terraform and others. It will also develop AWS CloudFormation templates.

Step 5: Bring in some experts

Now, you should bring in some real experts. Indeed, adding some expert-level engineers who have the right attitude when it comes to sharing their learnings and best practices is essential at this point. Both of us found that embedding engineers from AWS Accredited Partners into the CCoE team was a significant and material accelerator for our teams' journeys. Enabling engineers to pair program and go from a bash shell on their laptop, to installing the AWS command line interface, working with a code repository, and actually building and executing AWS CloudFormation code is a proven way to accelerate learning. It has a transformative effect. Humans learn from other humans by watching, asking questions, and repeating. Even better, engineers like to learn from fellow engineers. Working in small teams, they get the chance to ask questions and try things they wouldn't be able to in a timebound classroom course. The jumpstart via pair programming can often take, initially, no longer than a day and can be repeated to enable the learning of more-advanced configurations. This method of pairing a new engineer with an expert when they join the team scales very effectively—radically reducing the lead time for an engineer to be effective and understand how your CI/CD pipeline operates.

Step 6: Make it real
At this juncture, the goal of the Agile Two-Pizza Team should be to build something real and in production. This can be your foundational Amazon Machine Image (AMI) to host a small app and associated network setup. The objective is to find something important that solves a business challenge you have. Set the goal of getting it done in weeks, not months. Track progress. Show an interest. Set a demo deadline. And be there to see progress as well as the end results. A word of advice: don't let the team boil the ocean here. Only work with the AWS building blocks you need. (You don't need to master all 175+ building blocks from the get-go.) There will be plenty of time later to expand into the others as you need them for your solutions. The advantage of experimentation is key, and the ability to discard and start again as many times as required to learn becomes as natural as walking with AWS.

Step 7: Scale the learning with cellular mitosis
As this first team achieves a level of AWS proficiency and delivers a product, you now need to oversee the team's cellular mitosis. This requires gently but consciously splitting this first team of up to 12, which has gained experience and best practice, into two new six-person teams—introducing up to six more engineers into each team. This will be difficult and should be handled with care. Being honest with the team members and positively acknowledging their collective achievement will be crucial. Also, ask for their help in passing on the learnings and best practices to their new teammates. Keep splitting and reforming teams in this mitosis-driven approach until all engineers rotate

into a team. Of course, the precise composition and mix of heterogenous skill types should be appropriate to the task in hand.

Step 8: Certification

Following on from the training, peer programming, and hands-on time, people can now start down the path to AWS certification. Ensuring everyone can prepare themselves in their own way for the certification is important. Having resources available for your team so that they can self-service their learning is incredibly helpful. In the AWS Marketplace, you will find the ability to procure an enterprise license from ACloudGuru—allowing anyone with an email suffix from your company to access excellent preparatory training material for the exams. This provides engineers with a process that enables them to pass the certification in their own time and at their own pace. We suggest starting with the Associate-level certification and building up to the Professional-level certification.

As you can see from the table below, your certifications are broad and deep—allowing real mastery to be developed. This becomes a powerful circle of reinforcement and learning for all engineers.

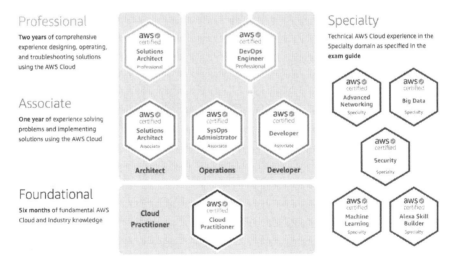

There are many side benefits of certification. We have seen some enterprises cleverly use AWS certification as a driver's license to achieve a particular level of account access. We've also seen it built into graduate-induction courses.

Step 9: Scaling the certification and associated leadership

Experience with many of our customers—plus scientific study[7]—shows that you need to reach a critical mass of just 10 percent of employees advocating a platform before the network effect takes hold. So, scaling this learning and certification to 10 percent of your engineers is a major milestone in your journey. From here onward, you get a compelling *halo effect* which starts to influence how your company is seen externally and not just internally. Those engineers external to your organization, who only want to work with Cloud-Native companies, will start seriously considering working for you. In turn, the pace of your transformation increases exponentially as you attract or convert more talent to be cloud literate. And at this point, few internally will want to be left behind either, further increasing the pace of reskilling. Some may want to coast to retirement rather than relearning. This can be fine, since these individuals can then manage the sunset period of remaining legacy systems.

Step 10: Recognize and reward expertise (in a very loud and proud way!)

Your goal as an IT executive is to shout from the rooftops the name of every person who passes each certification exam. Reward and recognize technical progress in any way that you can. That means meals, vouchers, drinks, special team chair, novelty awards, you name it. Many large customers establish a global roster of every person and every AWS certification that they obtained. Certification was viewed as a tangible and visceral achievement. Nearly every engineer we've ever met craves peer respect, and certification—combined with what you build—contributes to community kudos. This goes a massively long way to addressing the mastery part of motivation.

Step 11: Take the challenge yourself

When Jonathan was standing at a town hall meeting in his previous role, recognizing and rewarding the engineers who had progressed thanks to certification, one of the sharper sparks in the audience spoke up loudly: "If you believe so passionately in certification, when will *you* take the exam?" That stopped Jonathan pretty squarely. He hadn't taken an industry exam for a long while. But, as somebody who likes to practice what he preaches, he stepped up to the plate—passing his AWS Associate Architect certification exam. He could proudly stand on that stage, too! Taking the exam acted as an excellent forcing mechanism, ensuring that Jonathan gained a broad, yet sufficiently detailed, overview of the key AWS building blocks.

Step 12: Create a unifying job family portfolio

Finally, and at the right time, you will need to offer a concrete job family track for your technical employees.

National Australia Bank Case Study

For almost 160 years, National Australia Bank (NAB) has been helping customers with their money. Today, NAB has more than 30,000 employees servicing 9,000,000 customers at more than 900 locations in Australia, New Zealand, and around the world.

In November 2017, NAB launched an ambitious digital transformation and decided to adopt a public Cloud-First strategy. Part of this transformation included an ambition to recruit 2,000 employees with new skills, such as cloud engineers, developers and architects. They also realized that, in addition to bringing in new skills, they must invest in the development of their current workforce to help them with the journey. This was the catalyst that led to the creation of the NAB Cloud Guild.

As this journey began, NAB had just seven AWS-certified employees. NAB initially started by running a 12-week course with one-hour, focused deep dives on cloud, and soon attendance started to grow significantly. To cater for the significant demand, NAB moved to daily deep dives with 24 people in each session. Here they hit a scaling limit on instructor time. So again, they pivoted to build a community of practice and instead of just AWS speaking, they shone a light on their own employees to present about cloud. (As Richard Feynman once wisely said, "If you want to master something, teach it).

By March 2018, 150 employees had been trained, but only 15 were AWS certified.

At the April 2018 AWS Sydney Summit, NAB officially announced the launch of their Cloud Guild and a bold goal of having 3,000 people trained (a crucial 10 percent), including an aim to also accelerate the rate of AWS certifications. Within 24 hours, 1,900 employees had registered in Guild training sessions. Within 48 hours, 3,000 employees had registered for training.

Says NAB's Paul Silver, "If you imagine a lake and a pebble, and you drop the pebble in the lake, you'll make a splash that ripples outward across the lake's surface. That's your 10 percent, the ripple effect that continues afterward when everyone starts talking the same language."

By November 2019, more than 4,500 NAB employees have been trained on AWS with 817 employees AWS certified and together holding 1,134 AWS certifications. NAB now has the most AWS-certified people in Australia and New Zealand outside of AWS itself.

NAB's Paul Silver goes on "We moved from an ad-hoc cloud organization, where it was hard to move and move quickly, to one where people can clearly see the benefits and a path on how to do it. After we trained all of those people, we moved to a can-do mindset organization when it came to cloud and its potential."

Verizon Communications Case Study

Verizon Communications generated $130.9 billion in 2018 revenues.[8] The company operates reliable wireless and all-fiber networks and delivers integrated solutions to businesses worldwide. Its Oath subsidiary reaches about one billion people around the world with dynamic media and technology brands. To gain agility and scalability for its development teams and workloads, Verizon began to explore options for deploying Cloud-Native software solutions and applications on AWS.

Verizon knew that underpinning its ability to transform on the cloud would be the ability to drive a culture shift within the organization to embrace cloud development and focus on ongoing learning. So, they engaged with AWS Partner Network (APN) Advanced Consulting Partner A Cloud Guru to help the team drive such a shift.

In the words of Chivas Nambiar, executive director of cloud engineering at Verizon:

> Our incentives were primarily focused on the ability to achieve industry-recognized certification and internal bragging rights. Certified employees were called out and employees with multiple certifications were recognized and highlighted by senior leadership. We started with very few public-cloud-aware architects, while these few early adopters were enthusiastic and learned on their own, it was evident that we needed to target the larger mass of the IT organization to drive meaningful progress.

Verizon set an ambitious goal of having 10 percent of all IT employees certified with AWS. Getting 10 percent of your technology employees AWS certified is a key goal and enabler of cloud transformation success.

Verizon exceeded its initial training goal—more than 1,300 IT employees received their AWS Certified Solutions Architect - Associate certifications in just seven months. Verizon also achieved a cultural shift within its engineering organization, encouraging and rewarding learning in a new and continuous way.

Final thought

Breaking some ceilings if you haven't already. As you follow this path, it's important that some glass ceilings get broken. In particular, it's essential that engineers who don't manage people now have the ability to get to very senior levels—including that of Director and above—and still not be managing people. These promotions should respect technical depth and associated competency development, as well as technical leadership maturity as it broadens.

As a leader, seeing your employees scale new heights and attain hard-earned promotions is always the most rewarding part of the role. Establishing VP-level individual contributors who have EQ, IQ, and technical leadership skills sends an extremely powerful message to your technology workforce. In addition, how you compensate all of your technology staff should be reviewed closely to match the market. The competition for outstanding technology talent is not slowing.

4.2 ENTERPRISE DEVOPS

"DevOps is not a goal, but a never-ending process of continual improvement"

– JEZ HUMBLE

Atlassian, a company whose products we have both used in the past, describes DevOps the following way:

> *DevOps is a set of practices that automates the processes between software development and IT teams, in order that they can build, test, and release software faster and more reliably. The concept of DevOps is founded on building a culture of collaboration between teams that historically functioned in relative siloes.*[9]

Of course, there is a bit more to it than that. We think of DevOps as a continuation of an evolution to simplify software development and IT operations, while continuously driving towards higher and higher quality, security, and compliance—all the while continuously removing or optimizing things that slow us down. DevOps is a philosophy based on the lean principles of continuous improvement combined with respect for people aimed squarely at increasing velocity.

These are not new ideas, although we like to think they are. DevOps is on a continuum of principles that have emerged based on the experience of several generations of software developers, engineers, and technologists. In 1986, F. Brooks enthusiastically spoke about "growing systems organically," building on earlier work by Harlan Mills from 1971. Brooks writes:

> *Harlan Mills proposed that any software system should be grown by incremental development. That is, the system should first be made to run, even though it does nothing useful except call the proper set of dummy subprograms. Then, bit-by-bit it is fleshed out, with the subprograms in turn being developed into actions or calls to empty stubs in the level below.*

Brooks also stated that:

> *Much of present-day software acquisition procedure rests upon the assumption that one can specify a satisfactory system in advance, get bids for its construction, have it built, and install it. I think this assumption is fundamentally wrong, and that many software acquisition problems spring from that fallacy.*[10]

(1971! We are a slow lot, we are.)

Our software development methodologies, our project management approaches, and our operational processes have been in need of improvement for decades. We are still undergoing the much-needed evolution that the automotive industry pursued in the 1980s when it adopted the lean production principles of Toyota. These principles started with Sakichi Toyoda, who had invented textile looms that stopped themselves when a thread broke, implementing the principle he called *Jidoka* (autonomous automation) in the mid 1920s.

Agile Manifesto revisited

In 1994, a group of 17 software development professionals got together to re-imagine what software development (already a

30-year-old profession by then) could become. At the time, the Standish Group found that only 16.2 percent of all MIS projects were completed on time and within budget according to something appropriately called the CHAOS report. Another 52.7 percent were late and over budget, and 31.1 percent were outright cancelled.

In the past 25 years, the rate of completion of traditionally managed projects had increased to a 29 percent completion rate. While nearly double, it's still certainly not something a prudent investor would put money against. Compound this with the behavior of product managers who are necessarily convinced that they must create new stuff in order to stay competitive.

Even if that is true, are you building the right stuff? According to more Standish Group research, only 40 percent of projects had high to very high value, 46 percent had average value (will that differentiate you from the competition?), and 15 percent had low or very low value. So, 60 percent of projects may not be worth doing at all. Are you focused on the right things for your business?

Based on these insights, in 1998 Ron Jeffries described a principle called YAGNI—"you aren't going to need it." He gave two reasons for this:

1. You save time, because you avoid writing code that you turn out not to need.

2. Your code is better, because you avoid polluting it with "guesses" that turn out to be more or less wrong, but stick around anyway.

Which brings us to DevOps. In 2008, at the Agile Conference in Toronto, Andrew Schafer posted an offer to moderate an ad-hoc "Birds of a Feather" meeting to discuss the topic of "Agile Infrastructure." Only one person showed up to discuss the topic: Patrick Dubois. After watching a video session titled, "10+ Deploys per Day: Dev and Ops Cooperation at Flickr" by John Allspaw and Paul Hammond,

Patrick became inspired to organize a new conference dedicated to these topics called DevOpsDays in Ghent, Belgium. With that, the term was born.

The core concern voiced by Dubois and others was that those who write code have been organizationally and functionally apart from those who deploy and support that code. To this end, the philosophy of DevOps (because that is what it really is), unites Agile, autonomous automation, test-driven development, continuous integration and deployment, and a culture of collaboration—squarely aimed at value creation and measured by time-to-value.

At its simplest, DevOps is about removing the barriers between two traditionally siloed teams: development and operations. In some organizations, there may not even be separate development and operations teams; engineers may do both. With DevOps, the two teams work together to optimize both the productivity of developers and the reliability of operations. This bears repeating: They work together to optimize both the **productivity** of developers and the **reliability** of operations! They strive to communicate frequently, increase efficiencies, and improve the quality of services they provide to customers. They take full ownership for their services, often beyond where their stated roles or titles have traditionally been scoped by thinking about the end customer's needs and how they can contribute to solving those needs. Quality assurance and security teams may also become tightly integrated with these teams. Organizations using a DevOps model, regardless of their organizational structure, have teams that view the entire development and infrastructure lifecycle as part of their responsibilities.

These teams use practices to automate processes that historically have been manual and slow. They use a technology stack and tooling which help them operate and evolve applications quickly and reliably. These tools also help engineers independently accomplish tasks (for example, deploying code or provisioning infrastructure) that normally would have required waiting for work to be completed by other teams, and this further increases a team's velocity. In our previous organizations, we each leveraged a centralized "platform" team to create shared resources, frameworks, and tooling to provide continuous software integration and continuous delivery capabilities to the development teams.

Let's reset for a moment.

It is normally at this point that leaders state that, while they understand they need to reconstitute their teams to work in a different way (there is no such thing as a DevOps team), and while they want to trust their people to work in this new way, they worry about a perceived lack of control and the tradeoff of empowerment that is needed in this model. For a leadership team that is used to command and control methods, this is understandable. To quote President Ronald Reagan, you need to "Trust, but verify."

> *Trust, but verify is a rhyming Russian proverb. The phrase became internationally known in English when used by President Ronald Reagan on several occasions in the context of nuclear disarmament discussions with the Soviet Union. (Source:* Wikipedia*)*

The "verify" part in DevOps comes in the form of *guardrails*, which serve as a means to allow engineers to move faster (and with permission) as long as they stay within the defined policy. We are going to deep dive on this topic in Part 7 of the book.

How to adopt a DevOps model

Transitioning to DevOps requires a change in culture and mindset. Traditional IT service management—based on ITIL or similar frameworks—is chiefly concerned with managing risk, governance, security, and compliance. Certainly, these concerns retain their importance, however, these are achieved using DevOps approaches which are squarely focused on speed (of development, delivery, and to market), leveraging automation to quickly iterate solutions and enable innovation. Embracing DevOps is an enabling approach and mindset for existing IT infrastructure, as well as supporting migration to the cloud and operating IT in the cloud.

For example, you will still have a change record when new code is pushed into production, but you can automate the creation of a change ticket each time this is done.

The approach to adoption is the same one we have described elsewhere. Identify individuals on your staff who have the ability or the aptitude for process improvement and automation by using scripting. Look for infrastructure engineers who have a background in Unix or Linux system administration or software development engineers who understand how to troubleshoot problems from the command line—they quickly grasp and embrace DevOps principles. Ask your engineers what the recurring processes or problems in your infrastructure are that are manually addressed, and then have them script solutions to automate them. This will free up time, which they can use to solve other problems with automation.

In parallel, have a team develop a continuous integration/continuous delivery (CI/CD) pipeline for and with your software development teams.

Continuous integration is the practice of routinely integrating code changes into the main branch of a repository, and testing the changes early and often.

Continuous delivery is an approach where teams release quality products frequently and predictably from source code repository to production in an automated fashion.

Source https://www.atlassian.com/continuous-delivery

Continuously improve these automations and tools.

Note that you can and should do this to support your on-premises environments as well as for your cloud workloads. To truly succeed in the cloud, DevOps is a must-have capability. Be thoughtful to balance the time required to focus on building the new cloud DevOps capability versus continually being drawn back into optimizing the old.

There are many excellent tools you can use to accomplish this, including an ever-increasing suite of AWS services for DevOps.

Benefits of DevOps

Speed - Move at higher velocity so you can innovate for customers faster, adapt to changing markets better, and grow more efficient at driving business results. The DevOps model enables your developers and operations teams to achieve these results. For example, microservices and continuous delivery let teams take ownership of services and then release updates to them quicker.

Rapid Delivery - Increase the frequency and pace of releases so you can innovate and improve your product faster. The quicker you can release new features and fix bugs, the faster you can respond to your customers' needs and build competitive advantage. Continuous integration and continuous delivery are practices that automate the software release process, from build to deploy.

Reliability - Ensure the quality of application updates and infrastructure changes so you can reliably deliver at a more rapid pace while maintaining a positive experience for end users. Use practices like continuous integration and continuous delivery to test that each change is functional and safe. Monitoring and logging practices help you stay informed of performance in real-time.

Scale - Operate and manage your infrastructure and development processes at scale. Automation and consistency help you manage complex or changing systems efficiently and with reduced risk. For example, infrastructure as code helps you manage your development, testing, and production environments in a repeatable and more efficient manner.

Improved Collaboration - Build more effective teams under a DevOps cultural model, which emphasizes values such as ownership and accountability. Developers and operations teams collaborate closely, share many responsibilities, and combine their workflows. This reduces inefficiencies and saves time (e.g. reduced handover periods between developers and operations, writing code that takes into account the environment in which it is run).

Security - Move quickly while retaining control and preserving compliance. You can adopt a DevOps model without sacrificing security by using automated compliance policies, fine-grained controls, and configuration-management techniques. For example, using infrastructure as code and policy as code, you can define and then track compliance at scale.

Business Impact

In 2019, Nicole Forsgren, Jez Humble, and Gene Kim published fascinating research about the impact of DevOps on technology companies, called "Accelerate: The Science of DevOps – Building and Scaling High Performance Technology Organizations." Their research demonstrated that high-performing organizations (using DevOps in the cloud) have:

46 times more-frequent code deployments

2,555 times faster lead time from commit to deploy

2,604 times faster mean time to recover from downtime

7 times lower change failure rate (1/7 as likely for a change to fail)

Final thought

What could you accomplish with a more than 100 or 1,000 times faster organization? What would it mean for your customers and your business to experience a failure only 15 percent of the time you do today? In our experience, DevOps is rocket fuel for organizations, and we believe it is essential for yours.

4.3 YOUR EVOLVING TARGET OPERATING MODEL

"If you dislike change, you're going to dislike irrelevance even more."

– GENERAL ERIC KEN SHINSEKI

If you have skipped ahead to this chapter first, many of the topics you encounter may be alien to you. That said, we're going to guess you skipped ahead because you're hungry for an answer to this burning question: "What does my Target Operating Model need to look like when I use AWS?"

This is a completely valid and natural question, and as we have learned during the course of our own careers—and from the many executive conversations we have had all around the world—it's where many executives start. Hiring and developing a team is job one for every leader because leaders are only as good as the people they have working with them.

Here we must insert a health warning. The operating model(s) we are about to discuss are likely to provoke an emotional reaction—you will probably agree or disagree with parts or the whole. This is fine. There is no such thing as a perfect operational model, and you need to do the right thing as you see fit with regards to your operating model. Even in Amazon, the learning never stops and leaders are always iterating from feedback loops and adjusting accordingly. That said, in Amazon, there are very strong principles and mechanisms in place to guide and ensure leaders have the visibility they need.

Ultimately, the best operating model is one that is owned and accepted by the teams.

That said, we rightly get asked repeatedly what works, and we do see questions and opportunities as customers are migrating and trying to understand their new model. Having an operating model framework that is congruent to keeping mission-critical technology running, meeting the needs of your business colleagues, and moving to adopt and migrate to cloud will of course help significantly.

Are current models failing?

For decades, generally only one operating model was broadly accepted within enterprises. And this model—*waterfall*—has had a cult-like following with armies of certified Project Management Professionals (PMP), Information Technology Infrastructure Library (ITIL) folks, Business Solution Architects, and Enterprise Architects.

When we read this last sentence back, one thing that strikes us is how few of these people actually touch the keyboard and develop real technology solutions for our customers.

Typically, it's the engineers and developers who have been siloed into different areas (and are actually the bottleneck) and we have then applied matrixing resourcing to slice them to many different projects. This has necessarily led to many tradeoffs, handoffs, and ever-escalating attempts to prioritize their time. It's an ongoing source of conflict as technology executives routinely have to make tradeoffs for which engineers and developers are working on which project on any given day.

We believe strongly that the folks that have previously been the "organizers" often have underused technical skills that can have a newfound life in a different model.

On the whole, we are personally against matrix resourcing (there are a few exceptions we discuss later in this chapter). Escalations around matrixed resourcing have previously dominated our calendars in unproductive ways. And we have lost count of how many developers and engineers have complained that, "It takes me hours to focus in on a problem, and I have been allocated to 10 projects today!"

Typically, in waterfall operating models, we have seen technical resources siloed into buckets of infrastructure and applications with either engineering or operations specialties.

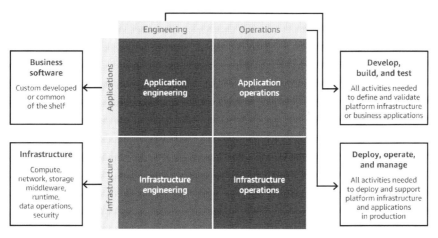

As we discussed in Chapter 3.2 Teams, humans have for millennia worked best when they are in small teams dedicated to solving a task for which they have heavy influence over the *how*. One of the templates to this effect that has gained significant interest and intellectual following in our travels is Spotify's engineering model, which is built around squads and tribes. While we are always cautious about customers attempting to emulate another company's culture and organization, you can see human-driven elements of why this has been so successful for Spotify.

Business complexifiers

Ok, let's reset. When we look back at the four principal areas that executive committees are focused on (PART 2 of this book), the KPIs on which you choose to focus, and the principles you adopt to power them, two factors will ultimately determine what your organization needs to look like. If it doesn't positively aid those metrics, you are probably going to fail.

At the same time, many of the modern-technology practices in this book that executives aspire to achieve—high-frequency DevOps, for example—are nigh impossible to apply backwards. You can't wave a wand and DevOps away your 30 years of technology debt while you still have your siloed infrastructure teams and segregated application and support teams. At the same time, you do not have an infinite pot of investment money at your beck and call. In our experience, that precious investment line item is one of the most contentious executive topics in an organization, and we are certain it will always be hotly contested.

So, how do you move forward?

You keep it simple while offering a path forward for everyone.

Target Operating Models

We have found three Target Operating Models that work hand in glove with both your migration targets and the aspirations of your business partners.

The first thing to point out is that these new operating models are intrinsically linked to *how* you migrate. Why is this the case? Well, as we just mentioned, no business we have ever worked in or with has an infinite pot of money to go back and DevOps their legacy technology stack. This technology debt is your metaphoric ball and chain. And unless you are a startup, you are not going to start with a clean sheet of zero technology debt. Even then, startups can acquire technology debt at a frightening rate as they continually make tradeoffs to get things over the line and grow as fast as possible.

Before we go further, we need to briefly talk about how you migrate, which is going to be relevant to this chapter. Migration is a very deep topic, and we have dedicated an entire chapter to it later in this book. For the purposes of Target Operating Model decisions, you need to know there are seven patterns of migration we have seen to be effective.

Relocate—The ability to extend your VMWare hypervisor into AWS and vMotion your virtual servers to run on AWS.

Rehost—The ability to lift and shift the existing on-premise server and its host operating system with installed software/database over to a new host in cloud.

Replatform—The ability to replatform an existing application or database from the existing on-premise operating system over to a new operating system on cloud.

Repurchase—The ability to move your existing workloads to software from the AWS Marketplace or a SaaS provided service.

Refactor—The ability to refactor the existing application to be fully Cloud Native by rearchitecting the application and data to your desired target.

Retire—Self-explanatory.

Retain—Workloads you may need to keep in place for a variety of reasons.

Next, you need to carefully pick your application targets for refactoring legacy workloads (or, of course, your Cloud-First/Cloud-Native applications can be built this way) and determine which targets are the best for your business to apply investment money. This is driven directly from your business goals and the KPIs you want to materially impact. Focusing on what makes your business your business—your secret sauce, as it were—is the thing that normally directly equates your most powerful revenue and income generators.

From our own experience, and from diving deep with customers, the following three Target Operating Model constructs can align broadly with your business objectives and the KPIs with which you measure outcomes—progressively transforming your organization to an evolving target where high-frequency delivery is constant:

1. **Sustain**—Traditional operations (undifferentiated or commodities with minimal investment)

2. **Optimize**—Distributed DevOps (and run core business functions)

3. **Grow**—Decentralized DevOps (market share or enter new markets)

Within Sustain, Optimize, and Grow it's possible to map your existing technology landscape and operating model based on your business priorities, while bringing the new elements you need to run on the cloud. This can be accomplished in parallel with developing the cloud fluency to be able to fully focus on what differentiates your business and not what is already a solved problem.

This model explains an evolutionary approach to moving from traditional, on-premise technology to a high-frequency model where your precious human resources are focused on solving customer problems using business logic, data, interfaces, and security. When you reach this state, you are continuously improving and you are making data-driven decisions that are tested and measured. There is no longer a distinction between the business and IT—it's just the business.

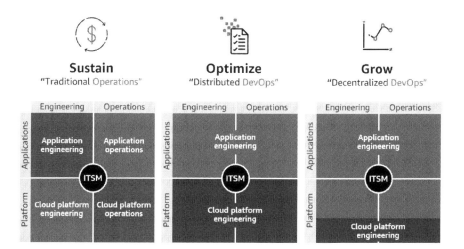

* Target Operating Models

Sustain - The Sustain model is keeping your existing support, development organization, and run books the same for the applications that are mapped to this bracket. It primarily maps to the rehost migration option, and as the graphic above shows, this is a transitional state. The goal is to eventually optimize the application stack in this category, then move into the Optimize or Grow categories depending on the business need. There are certainly going to be elements of your existing organization that are not going to move to DevOps modes.

Optimize - Many organizations do find that they want to replatform or repurchase applications to gain the benefits that having infrastructure as code gives as discussed later in Chapter 5.3 Resiliency and Reliability. So, they perhaps decide to change out the operating system and package the application for automatic deployment. When you take this path, you can break the traditional dependencies of custom crafting the OS and having the application installed and managed from infrastructure teams. You can instead start to empower the early DevOps team to operate within your defined guardrails—configuring their infrastructure as code and potentially utilizing a centrally provided CI/CD pipeline and Golden Amazon Machine Image provided by a divisional or central Cloud Platform Engineering team.

Grow - With this Target Operating Model, you move to DevOps teams that are both heterogeneously skilled and empowered to utilize, configure, and support the AWS building blocks (within guardrails) to meet the business goals. They will likely still rely on a divisional/central Cloud Platform Engineering team for operating system images, if those are required, network configurations, or—for when the need arises—to execute a command for which there is a preventative control in place. This is the strategic target for nearly every enterprise we work with.

Mapping the TOM to migration targets

Now that you have familiarity with the models, you can see how they map onto the 7 R's from Chapter 5.4 Migrating Your Applications.

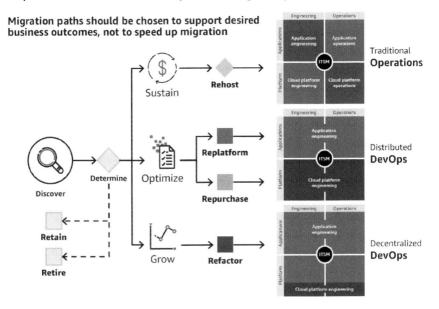

Having a technology migration target is symbiotic with the operating model. Aligning an operating model to each of the R's provides clarity and helps you prioritize next steps to reach your desired business outcome.

Technology complexifiers

Let's out the on-call elephant. In the split, traditional enterprise waterfall delivery world of support-versus-delivery organization, we have seen more organizational and us-versus-them tension than anywhere else.

Delivery just wants to throw things over the fence to support, and support just keeps adding people support 24x7 and then blaming delivery for poor-quality builds not to their standards. We have some news for you: This world is doomed to be disrupted by other organizations and startups that have moved away from this dysfunctional approach.

In the small-team Optimize and Grow modes, the team supports its own software 24x7. This can, however, produce nothing short of outright mutiny within some organizations. We know from personal experience that dealing with critical incidents—and the mental impact they have at all levels—makes IT easily one of the most stressful roles out there.

Candidly, some engineers don't want to be on call, and this is the elephant in the room that must be addressed. In the small, empowered team model, there is no one else to call when your stuff breaks. The team has to sort it out, which means putting folks on call with a rota, and having secondary on call and escalation to team leaders and upward if necessary. There's no way of sugarcoating this—it can be a tough conversation. Again, this is where having a CLT with declared principles that will be followed holistically is crucial. All Optimize and Grow teams will need to be on call. Period.

But, believe us, the effort is worth it. When everyone on the team owns the result of their work 24x7, the care and fortitude with which they deliver will increase. Multiple human factors come into play here and lazy workmanship will be quickly called out. If your team colleague is woken up at 3:00 a.m. because you didn't click "Auto Scaling" in that new Amazon DynamoDB database, you are sure to hear about it the following morning.

Exceptions to the rule

The small-team model works, in particular, when dealing entirely with software configurability. You are moving and scaling that way. Does the small-team, empowered, skill-mixed, self-contained model work absolutely everywhere? For a modern organization in a Cloud-First world, it does for the absolute majority. But we have experienced exceptions, including:

- **When a team has to deal with physical hardware support and maintenance.** Examples include an end-user support team dealing with personal computer deployment and maintenance—for large organizations, this could be a large global team. However, the 3rd line desktop support team will likely deal entirely with software, and thus the small-team model works well. Another example would be a network team, which is probably dealing with 10s, 100s, maybe 1000s of network devices—from corporate Wi-Fi to routers and switches. Again, a mixture of a large team and perhaps 3rd line/4th line engineers in smaller, software-only teams will do the trick.
- **When dealing with a physical construction line.** If you are a highly mature team that is moving an item to utility for your customers, then using lean methodology and maturing that element to the nth degree is entirely appropriate.
- **Certain operational processes to ensure consistent holistic monitoring and security.** Ultimately, keeping some teams

central/divisional will just make sense. Examples here include critical service teams, a central Cloud Platform Team (responsible for operating systems images, preventative control exemptions, best practice), batch operations, network operations center/security operations center, vendor management, Agile management office, security teams, and others—this list is not exhaustive. Again, the model that works and is accepted is the best.

The key differentiator we see is whether or not a team can entirely use APIs to bring solutions to accomplish their work and configure their business logic to achieve their outcomes. If yes, then great—the small, decentralized DevOps model will work. (Of course, appropriate security and governance guardrails are mandatory.)

Aligning teams to outcomes

Experience has shown—both from our personal experience, and around the world with a multitude of organizations—that, as you start building your small teams, aligning them to an executive owner of a particular product is indeed the most appropriate way forward. Over time, changing reporting lines—whether they be dotted or solid—is almost certainly going to be the right way forward. This will create an interesting challenge for your business partners as they are now faced with managing development teams directly. And engineers and developers respect leaders who have a very strong appreciation of what they do, how they do it, and what it takes to achieve desired outcomes.

In this tech-driven world in which we live today, the business leader who doesn't understand that technology and their business outcomes go hand in hand is not going to survive the disruption wave that has been sweeping the planet.

This can be very intimidating for executives who are not naturally inclined toward technology, and when threatened as humans, our most natural reaction is to fear that change. Yet again, this is why the CLT—and the principles agreed there—are so utterly crucial to this changing paradigm.

How many teams to support an outcome?

Aligning teams to an outcome is empowering stuff. Some learnings here though. The question is this: How many teams can be aligned together to an outcome and still remain manageable by a single executive?

Our own experience is that, just as the Two-Pizza Team model comprises 6-12 people per team, aligning 6-12 teams to an outcome also turns out to be a good number. Go beyond that and keeping track of the Agile epics becomes a challenge for a line of business.

Release trains

The Scaled Agile Framework can be a useful guide when adopting Agile, although we are always cautious of adopting things verbatim (books never have the context of your business, including this one!). While each organization needs to adopt its specific working practices as it sees fit, one of the concepts that we have seen work well in practice is the cadence of sprints and release trains.

Typically, SAFe release trains run in three-month increments, bringing all the empowered teams together with leaders to sense check dependencies between themselves and ultimately ensure their outcomes align to the executive goal. Sometimes, a holistic need to align something will have to be spread across all teams. An example of this could be alignment to publish a user interface in multiple languages that requires all teams to work in support of this goal.

In the release train model, considerable planning and forward-thinking work is required from leaders and the accountable line-of-business (LOB) executives—it is inescapable. You will look pretty silly if you stand up at a release-planning session and can't clearly explain what the business and priorities are and the *why* behind them (as one of the authors found out, you cannot "wing this bit"). This will lead directly to engineers and developers doubting your ability to lead, making attrition a definite risk. It's a seller's market in software development talent, after all. Ensuring team leader alignment and deeply understanding the technical practicality of what is needed (in what sequence AÐBÐC things could be dependent) is a modern leadership key skill and a true differentiator for modern business leaders. Whether it's a two-day quarterly offsite before the actual release team presentation, or workshops in the office, find a leadership communication and alignment method that works for you.

The ability to pivot

As an executive, you are always juggling 85 balls on top of that things come at you out of left field all the time—whether it's a new business opportunity or the aforementioned 3:00 a.m. "problem" phone call. The ability to pivot and refocus work while keeping to a consistent quality cadence is utterly crucial.

In the release-train model, you are essentially sense checking every 12 weeks that what the teams are doing is still driving you toward your goals. If it isn't, then you need to make changes. We strongly suggest not messing with the two-week sprint cycles your team is running during a release train because this a sure way to ruin their motivation.

A 12-week sprint check-in also gives you the ability to make certain talent skill movements/changes between teams. If, for example, you need to move a resource from x to y, then it is easy so long as you don't change the nucleus of the team and the software it is supporting is safe to do so.

Mixing the team skills but not the location

The ability to resource and skill up teams with different resources is key. There is no hard-and-fast rule that says all have to be "permanent" employees. If you need to leverage out-tasked resources, partners, or contractors to resource the team, then by all means do so. In the same way that a Formula One team is a mix of different employees from multiple companies—they all share a common goal and wear the same shirt.

The common element—proven time and time again—is the actual location where this team sits. While we absolutely believe we are approaching a zenith of when virtual reality will make full-time working a reality, we are not quite there yet.

In fact, we haven't seen it work for this small-team model yet. Life is going to be very difficult when folks can't pair program, work a whiteboard problem, or even go out for lunch together. Putting folks together in one location works. The hours that teams choose to collaborate (9:00-5:00 is dead), or whether they collectivity decide to work from home Monday and Friday, should be the team's decision. Again, the importance of principles to allow this comes through here. But, in our experience, coming together in one location for at least 60 percent of the time, can be a key factor to success.

Action Steps

Step 1: Review your business agility metrics
Be clear on what and where you want to see improvement and why, as we discuss in Chapter 2.4 Measuring Business Agility.

Step 2: Understand your current operating model

An obvious step maybe. But do you truly understand where the human risks are right now across your organization, where the skill pinch points are? Where are the key service challenges right now? Doubling down on help for those areas as/before you change will alleviate stress all round.

Do you truly understand the needs and career aspirations of the entire leadership team? Who is the right person to lead the Cloud Leadership Team and who is best to lead the Cloud Center of Excellence? Both roles are going to be crucial.

Step 3: Identify the migration pattern that best supports your business objectives

Which pattern of Sustain, Optimize, or Grow is going to be right for which system and part of your organization? See Chapter 5.4 Migrating Your Applications for a deep dive on migrations. Have you produced a straw man for mapping the 7 R's to your systems yet? This can be incredibly insightful for identifying which teams move first and when.

Step 4: Determine your short/medium/long-term resourcing plan

Do you have the right resources in every role? No, of course not. We have yet to meet any enterprise with all the roles filled with all the skilled folks they need.

But do you understand the mix of partners that can go on this journey with you? Which partners do you wish to move away from? Where do you want to increase/reduce permanent headcount? Hiring for your core business and selectively using suppliers for utility is important. Having a tactical and strategic plan for this is crucial.

Sadly, we have seen some customers who have been badly advised by their incumbent providers, leading to significant discontent. We would strongly encourage you to discover the AWS Partner status of any partners you work with and make an informed decision from then on.

Step 5: Start with one team to execute in a selected Target Operating Model

We discussed in Chapter 3.5 Creating the Cloud Center of Excellence and Chapter 4.1 Becoming Cloud Fluent at Scale how to bring new cloud-fluent teams together, especially if you are moving to Agile teams that are going to be refactoring or building new Cloud-Native applications directly. You can scale this model as we discussed through a process of cellular mitosis.

It is well worth noting that if you are migrating for cost reduction and are opting to "optimize" this could mean leaving a team exactly as they are, because you are going to rehost an existing workload to cloud, and the team is going to stay (for now) in the Optimize operating model. The team will need some training on AWS as their workloads are now running on cloud, and as such, their run books will have changed accordingly.

Step 6: Select the next workload and map another team to it

In effect, you are going back to Step 1 here. You must be continually grooming all of your workloads and their current service status, location, risk status, and technology debt, and reviewing them in light of the business goals and their current resourcing levels. You should be aiming to establish a flywheel of momentum for all your workloads to move with a migration plan around the 7 R's.

Final thought

We are never done. There is no such thing as a perfect operating model. The truth is that your operating model is never done and it needs to evolve as your business objectives, capabilities, and organization change. People are always leaving, always joining, and always being promoted.

PART 5

ARCHITECTURE AND MIGRATIONS

5.1 COMPUTE, CONTAINERS, AND SERVERLESS

"Serverless will fundamentally change how we build business around technology and how you code."

– SIMON WARDLEY, RESEARCHER, LEADING EDGE FORUM

Always solving problems and moving up

There is a very good reason that, for the most part, humans no longer live in caves. Caves bring problems and problems mean hard work—much of it tedious and dangerous. Caves are hard to heat, hard to secure, damp, un-comfy, and sometimes filled with bats, spiders, and other creatures. You get the picture. Most of us no longer live in caves, and on the main, our dwellings are getting better all the time. Central heating, air conditioning, refrigerators, gas fireplaces, automatic lights, security alarms. Alexa anyone?

Of course, the analogy—with ever-increasing performance (and abstraction)—is exactly the same in enterprise technology.

From 1952 into the late 1960s, IBM manufactured and marketed several large computer models, known as the IBM 700/7000 series. The first-generation 700s used vacuum tubes, while the later, second-generation 7000s used transistors.

IBM initially sold its computers without any software, expecting customers to write their own. Programs were manually initiated, one at a time. Later, IBM provided compilers for the newly developed higher-level programming languages Fortran, COMTRAN, and later COBOL. The first operating systems for IBM computers were written by IBM customers who did not wish to have their very expensive machines ($2M USD in the mid-1950s) sitting idle while operators set up jobs manually. As with this first compute machine and the first operating system that was produced for it, humans have been abstracting away and automating the layers of human-intensive technology operations ever since.

We would humbly submit that, although the technology industry has been prone to hype cycles, no inflection point in the world of technology has and is being as transformational as the one we have been going through during the last 13 years—that of public cloud. This is a very special inflection period we are living through, a once-in-a-career event.

Amazon Elastic Cloud Compute (EC2)

As our wise, purple-haired evangelist teammate, Jeff Barr (VP & Chief Evangelist at AWS), pointed out to us recently, the very first public service that AWS launched in beta was the Amazon Simple Queue Service on November 3, 2004. This was followed by the Amazon Simple Storage Service (S3) on March 14, 2006. A month later, on August 24, 2006, AWS launched Amazon Elastic Compute Cloud (EC2) in beta, and the world of IT has never been the same since.

Since that first Amazon EC2 service, as of December 2019, there are:

- 90 General Purpose instance types
- 30 Compute Optimized instance types
- 74 Memory Optimized instance types
- 25 Accelerated Computing instance types
- 23 Storage Optimized instance types

It's an understatement to say that you have a lot of choice.

The Amazon EC2 service is leveraged by thousands and thousands of customers including Netflix, Expedia, Airbnb, NASA JPL, General Electric, and Cathy Pacific to name but a few. The ability to bring online any of these types of compute instances in the Regions where they reside—on demand in minutes, billed to the second (after the first minute of use)—has been and continues to be a gamechanger for enterprises all around the world. You can start a single instance, hundreds of instances, or even thousands. You can use Amazon EC2 Auto Scaling to maintain availability of your fleet and automatically scale your fleet up and down depending on your customers' needs and their demands on your applications. You have complete control of your instances including root access and the ability to interact with them as you would any machine.

We have witnessed what is possible with this type of compute from our own executive journeys, where we were able to test and scale production on these new compute instances in enterprises. And we have witnessed this even from the experiences of our children with this new paradigm of possibility, playing games like Fortnite, the runaway blockbuster developed by Epic Games. Fortnite incorporates special scheduled in-game moments where millions of players simultaneously experience a global in-game synchronous event, collectively. This was simply not possible before cloud—all hosted and made possible by Amazon EC2 compute. Epic Games is rightly breaking new ground and making history with these in-game experiences.

And it's not just in gaming that these records are being set. On October 19, 2017, the Children's Hospital of Philadelphia (CHOP) and Edico Genome set a new scientific world standard in rapidly processing whole human genomes into data files useable for researchers aiming to bring precision medicine into mainstream clinical practice. By deploying on 1,000 Amazon EC2 F1 instances using Field

Programmable Gate Arrays (FPGA) on the AWS Cloud, 1,000 pediatric genomes were processed in just two hours and twenty-five minutes. Not only were they able to analyze genomes at high throughput, they did so averaging approximately $3 per whole human genome of AWS compute for the analysis. For comparison, the first human genome sequence cost hundreds of millions of dollars.

In traditional enterprises, this highly scalable compute ability to host hundreds, thousands, or tens of thousands of compute instances covering the entire spectrum—from small web servers hosted on highly horizontally scalable General Purpose EC2 T3 instances, through to the Memory Optimized instances that host intensive SAP HANA services used by the likes of Kellogg and Brooks Brothers, to name a few—is radically changing how these companies can operate.

Of particular importance to enterprises and startups has been security, reliability, and crucially in this regard, the ability to auto scale (and only be charged when you need to scale). The speed with which you can actually scale the compute when needed—and place your operating system (Amazon Machine Image, or AMI), patching, applications and anything else—actually itself starts to become the speed bottleneck. This, along with the developer need/ability to package all code dependencies locally, and test locally on a laptop, has led to the rise of the container.

The rise of the container

"The speed at which you can tolerate auto scaling will define what technology you should use." – Adrian Hornsby, AWS Principal Technical Evangelist

When most enterprises start using Amazon EC2, one of the first things they do is to launch a new instance and have scripts (bash, Puppet, or Chef) do the software configuration whenever a new instance launched. Needless to say, this can work extremely well. However, over time, the speed to auto scale the complexity of the configuration "recipe," especially with developers shipping code very frequently (multiple times a day), can become a serious bottleneck in its own regard.

Normally, the next step is to create custom AMIs that are preconfigured (known as *golden AMIs*) enabling enterprises to shift the heavy configuration setup from the instance launch to an earlier, "baking" time, built within a continuous integration/continuous delivery (CI/CD) pipeline.

It is often difficult to find the right balance between what is baked into an AMI and what is done at scaling time. In some cases, particularly if you're smart with service discovery, you don't have to run or configure anything at startup time. This should be the goal because, the less you have to do at startup time, the faster your scaling will be. In addition to being faster at scaling, the more scripts and configurations you run at startup time, the greater the chance that something will go wrong.

Finally, what became the holy grail of the golden AMI was to get rid of the configuration scripts and replace them with Dockerfiles instead. That way, you didn't have to maintain Chef or Puppet recipes, which at scale were tricky to manage. With Docker (and containers in general), isolation is done on the kernel level without the need for a guest operating system. Containers are much faster, more efficient, and lightweight—allowing for applications to become encapsulated in self-contained environments. Developers and engineers can test the applications from the laptop all the way to production systems, using the same container, in a predictable way, and do so quickly.

Enter Amazon Elastic Container Service (ECS). Which was made generally available in April 2015—allowing you to run containerized applications in production without the manual heavy lifting of having to manage the container orchestration service yourself. ECS is a highly scalable, high-performance container orchestration service that supports Docker containers and allows you to run and scale containerized applications on AWS. It eliminates the need to install and operate your own container orchestration software, manage and scale a cluster of virtual machines, or schedule containers on those virtual machines. In addition, it is deeply integrated with the AWS Services you need, such as Elastic Load Balancing, Amazon Virtual Private Cloud (VPC), AWS IAM, Amazon Elastic Container Registry (ECR), AWS Batch, Amazon CloudWatch, AWS CloudFormation, AWS CodeStar, and AWS CloudTrail.

Like all AWS services, with simple API calls you are able to launch and stop Docker-enabled applications and query the complete state of your application. The attraction to migrate both Linux and Windows applications from on-premises to the cloud, and run them containerized using Amazon ECS, has led to incredible growth of this service.

And then along came Kubernetes

Kubernetes (commonly called **K8s**) is an open-source container-orchestration system for automating deployment, scaling, and management of containerized applications. It was originally designed by Google and is now maintained by the Cloud Native Computing Foundation (CNCF), of which AWS is a Platinum member. Kubernetes is incredibly popular and has a high residency on Amazon EC2. According to a survey completed by the CNCF, 51 percent of Kubernetes running on the cloud runs on AWS.

There is, however, a lot of manual work required to run it at scale. You have to deploy a Kubernetes master and Kubernetes workers, and then if you want high availability, you have to configure those components across multiple Availability Zones. You also have to configure the network and have yet another credentials store that didn't use AWS IAM.

To address this, the Amazon Elastic Container Service for Kubernetes (EKS) was released and was made generally available in June 2018.

Amazon EKS runs the Kubernetes management infrastructure across multiple AWS Availability Zones, automatically detects and replaces unhealthy control plane nodes, and provides on-demand upgrades and patching. You can provision worker nodes and connect them to the provided Amazon EKS endpoint. Secure and encrypted communication channels are automatically set up between your worker nodes and the managed control plane. It runs upstream Kubernetes and is certified Kubernetes conformant, so applications managed by Amazon EKS are fully compatible with applications managed by any standard Kubernetes environment. And, crucially, it is integrated with AWS IAM and the AWS networking.

As cool as Amazon EKS is, it's important that we are always abstracting and looking to remove as much of the heavy lifting as possible from the setup. No container cluster is easier to manage than no cluster at all. And many engineers and developers just want to operate at the container task and task definition levels, and let AWS manage the containers for them. For that we have AWS Fargate, which was made generally available on April 24, 2018.

> A task is the instantiation of task definition. Tasks can be run individually or as part of a service definition.

> Task definitions are blueprints that define what containers to use, their resource specifications like memory/CPU, the ports that need to be exposed, the volumes that will be used, permissions of containers using IAM role, and networking details.

With AWS Fargate, you only have to think about the containers— enabling you to just focus on building and operating your application. AWS Fargate eliminates the need to manage a cluster of Amazon EC2 instances. You no longer have to pick the instance types, manage cluster scheduling, or optimize cluster utilization. And you no longer have to worry about provisioning enough compute resources for your container applications. After you define your application requirements in the task, AWS Fargate manages all the scaling and infrastructure needed to run your containers in a highly available manner.

The leap to light speed—serverless

Ensuring your precious human resource is continually focusing on the right things is crucial. Recruiting, retaining, and continually reskilling great engineering and development talent is very hard. (See Chapter 4.1 Becoming Cloud Fluent at Scale). The unfortunate truth is, it is only going to get harder. This, as Marc Andreessen said in 2011, is because "Software is eating the world."

As we have talked about previously, having your technology talent focused on your business logic, data, and the UX for the same—as well as being closely aligned to customer and product management—is what will differentiate your business from that of your competitors. Especially if your competitors are out there focusing on building undifferentiated infrastructure, and then maintaining that infrastructure for years, if not decades, and spending both CAPEX and human time for the lifespan of said maintenance.

> *"If enterprises or startups are going to win, they have to go faster than their competitors."* – Stephan Orban, General Manager, AWS

So many of the conversations we had as executives when we were customers ourselves, and so many of the conversations we have in our current roles, pivot around an organization's ability to get to market ever more quickly. Yet, few if any enterprises measure time-to-value (TTV) metric or cycle time in Software Delivery Life Cycle parlance as part of their business agility metrics. Few enterprises or even startups have a principle to maintain or *increase* development velocity over time.

> *"Development Velocity," to be specific, means "the speed at which you can deliver an additional unit of value to a customer." Velocity is a metric for work done, which is often used in Agile software development.*

Retrospectives are crucial in today's world and have come to the fore with Agile practices. The specific activity of actually looking back and thinking and being very honest with ourselves is extremely useful. Where are we spending too much time? What hasn't added value? What worked? What did not?

Today's Agile software development teams are rightly a heterogenous mix of skill types, including Software Development Engineer, Security Engineer, Software Quality Engineer, and Data Scientist. The tools they have to use to deliver solutions, even with microservices, can be diverse. It's not just the application code that you have to consider, it's the surrounding elements. Identity management, telemetry tracking, logs, security groups, databases, management information systems—the list goes on. Engineers and developers spending their time maintaining those tools (even Amazon EC2 or Amazon ECS or Amazon EKS) is time they could have spent pulling forward user problems to solve them by applying logic, data, or a better UX experience. Removing the work (and continuing to abstract even higher and more efficiently) is where serverless comes in. And it has, and continues to have, a profound impact on development.

While serverless is very often championed as a way to reduces costs and scale massively and on demand, there is one extraordinarily compelling reason above all others to adopt a serverless-first approach. Simply, using serverless is the best way to achieve maximum development velocity over time and remove vast amounts of undifferentiated heavy lifting.

The serverless landscape

In the same way the term "cloud computing" does not mean that there are server farms operating in airships flying continually at 35,000 feet, the term "serverless" does not mean that aren't servers operating still. There are servers there, you just don't care about them at all. Not the hardware, not the hypervisor, not the operating system, not even the software execution engine. This is all taken care for you.

Let's explore the serverless landscape.

Compute execution framework. AWS started the serverless movement in 2014 with a *serverless compute* platform called AWS Lambda. You can use it for nearly any type of application or backend service, and everything required to run and scale your application with high availability is handled for you. You pay only for the compute when a function is activated (Function as a Service)—there is no charge when your code is not running. Lambda@Edge allows you to run Lambda functions at AWS Edge locations in response to Amazon CloudFront events. As already discussed, AWS Fargate is a purpose-built serverless compute engine for containers, and is considered part of the serverless compute execution framework.

AWS Lambda natively supports Java, Go, PowerShell, Node.js, C#, Python, and Ruby code. And with Custom Runtimes, you can use nearly any Linux-compatible language, for example, AWS shared open-source runtimes for C++ and Rust, and AWS partners added the possibility to use platforms such as Erlang, Elixir, PHP, and even COBOL.

An AWS Lambda serverless architecture allows you to write code and place that code into a "package" to be run by AWS. The package is referred to as a "function" by AWS Lambda. This ability to package code into small, single-purpose functions has led to the rise of the term FaaS (Function as a Service). The ability to carefully create your functions and enable them to interact and use other functions—like AWS Cognito (user authentication) or Amazon Aurora—is where the massive time saver lies.

Storage. With Amazon Simple Storage Service (Amazon S3), using simple PUTS and GETS, you are able to read and write objects at speed. Amazon Elastic File System (Amazon EFS) is built to elastically scale on demand, growing and shrinking automatically as you add and remove files.

Databases. Amazon DynamoDB is a NoSQL database service for applications that need consistent, single-digit millisecond latency. Amazon Aurora Serverless is an on-demand, auto-scaling configuration for Amazon Aurora (MySQL-compatible and PostgreSQL-compatible editions), where the database will automatically start up, shut down, and scale capacity up or down based on your application's needs.

API Proxy. Having an API gateway function for both internal and external control of your business's API has become a crucial need in today's digital businesses. Why spend many months having a team build and then support an API gateway service on Amazon EC2 when you can leverage Amazon API Gateway? This is a fully managed service that makes it easy for developers to create, publish, maintain, monitor, and secure APIs at any scale. It allows you to process hundreds of thousands of concurrent API calls and it handles traffic management, authorization and access control, monitoring, and API version management.

Interprocess messaging, or "message busses" to use the common enterprise vernacular, has been another perennial source of frustration and bottlenecks. In the early days of Amazon, they were also a challenge, which is why Amazon SQS was one of the very first services offered by AWS. It is a fully managed message queue service, with guaranteed message delivery and optional first-in, first-out (FIFO) messaging capability. Sitting alongside this is the Amazon Simple Notification Service (SNS) which is a fully managed pub/sub messaging service that makes it easy to decouple and scale microservices, distributed systems, and serverless applications.

Many AWS customers also make great use of SaaS (Software as a Service) applications. For example, they use Zendesk to manage customer service & support tickets, PagerDuty to handle incident response, and

SignalFx for real-time monitoring. While these applications are quite powerful on their own, they are even more so when integrated into a customer's own systems, databases, and workflows. In order to support this increasingly common use case, in July 2019, AWS launched Amazon EventBridge. Building on the event-processing model that forms the basis for Amazon CloudWatch Events, it makes it easy to integrate AWS applications with SaaS applications. The SaaS applications can be hosted anywhere, and simply publish events to a specific event bus. The publisher (SaaS application) and the consumer (code running on AWS) are completely decoupled, and are not dependent on a shared communication protocol, runtime environment, or programming language. You can use simple Lambda functions to handle events that come from a SaaS application, and you can also route events to a wide variety of other AWS targets.

Orchestration with AWS Step Functions makes it straightforward to coordinate the components of distributed applications and microservices using visual workflows. Building applications from individual components with each performing a discrete function lets you scale and change applications quickly. AWS Step Functions is a reliable way to coordinate components and step through the functions of your application.

Analytics, of course, is a crucial component for nearly every service you construct. Amazon Kinesis is a platform for streaming data on AWS, offering services to make it easy to load and analyze streaming data, and also providing the ability for you to build custom streaming data applications for specialized needs. Amazon Athena is an interactive query service that allows you to analyze data in Amazon S3 using standard SQL.

By combining these different serverless elements, you can build very powerful applications, massively change TTV for the teams, and now just focus on the business logic.

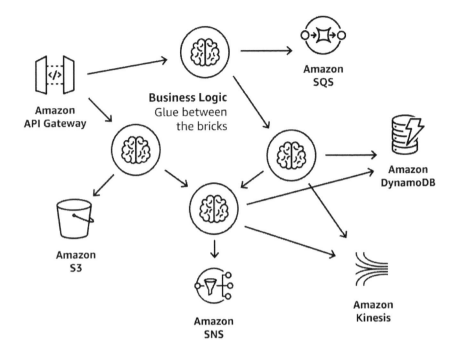

How much does it cost? An example

AWS Lambda is an order of magnitude cheaper than leaving a server running and waiting for code to run. AWS Lambda counts a request each time it starts executing in response to an event notification or invoke call, including test invokes from the console. You are charged for the total number of requests across all your functions. Duration is calculated from the time your code begins executing until it returns or otherwise terminates, rounded up to the nearest 100ms. The price depends on the amount of memory you allocate to your function. Let's take look at a quick example.

If you allocated 128MB of memory to your function, executed it 30 million times in one month, and it ran for 200ms each time, your charges would be calculated as follow:

Monthly compute charges

The monthly compute price is $0.00001667 per GB-s and the free tier provides 400,000 GB-s.
Total compute (seconds) = 30M * (0.2sec) = 6,000,000 seconds
Total compute (GB-s) = 6,000,000 * 128MB/1024 = 750,000 GB-s
Total compute – Free tier compute = Monthly billable compute seconds
750,000 GB-s – 400,000 free tier GB-s = 350,000 GB-s
Monthly compute charges = 350,000 * $0.00001667 = $5.83

Monthly request charges

The monthly request price is $0.20 per 1 million requests, and the free tier provides 1M requests per month.
Total requests – Free tier request = Monthly billable requests
30M requests – 1M free tier requests = 29M Monthly billable requests
Monthly request charges = 29M * $0.2/M = $5.80

Total compute charges

Total charges = Compute charges + Request charges = $5.83 + $5.80
= *$11.63 per month*

While users have to increase their server size if they hit a capacity constraint on Amazon EC2, AWS Lambda will scale more or less infinitely to accommodate load without any manual intervention. And, if an Amazon EC2 instance goes down, the developer is responsible for diagnosing the problem and getting it back online, whereas if an AWS Lambda dies, another AWS Lambda can just take its place. The business logic runs on extremely cost effective, near infinitely scalable infrastructure, thereby eliminating the need for servers altogether.

Herein lies the magic of using serverless AWS components and complementing them with managed service offerings from partners like Twilio, SendGrid, and PagerDuty. Enterprises and startups alike get the benefit of using the providers' offerings as a strategic asset.

Serverless principles

Be responsible for only business logic code—As you as you write code, you create debt. Write only the code you need.

No server management—There is no need to provision or maintain any servers or storage. There is no software or runtime to install, maintain, or administer.

Flexible scaling—Your application can be scaled automatically or by adjusting its capacity through toggling the units of consumption (e.g., throughput or memory) rather than units of individual servers.

Pay for value—Pay for consistent throughput or execution duration rather than by server unit. We only want to charge you for something when you use it. If the code is there but not used, you do not pay for it.

Automated high availability—Serverless provides built-in availability and fault tolerance. You don't need to architect for these capabilities since the services running the application provide them by default.

A recent CNCF survey has started to track the usage of serverless technology: 41 percent of survey respondents currently use serverless technology, while 31 percent do not. An additional 28 percent have plans to use it within the next 12-18 months. Of the respondents currently using serverless technology, 70 percent are using AWS Lambda.

ACTION STEPS

Step 1: Upskill the workforce for serverless

Step 2: Use mapping to evaluate the applicability of serverless to new applications

Step 3: As you migrate and refactor applications, evaluate serverless technology to remove the creation of unnecessary software/systems

Step 4: Move to put in place principles to reinforce the use of serverless to remove undifferentiated heavy lifting

Step 5: Use the AWS well-architected Framework to ensure best practice usage

Final thought

Friends, not rivals. Serverless has often been measured against containers since both technologies provide similar benefits in terms of rapid development. However, it is important to note that both serverless computing and containerization do not actually negate each other—they can work in tandem to build modern applications.

As leaders, it would be easy to make a declaration like "We are now a serverless shop!" The stark reality is that, in today's customer-driven world where product managers focus on always improving cycle time, security, reliability, and costs, you will need to use all three. But the key is to have the right principles (to continue to abstract up the stack), and encouraging (and rewarding) engineers, developers, and partners to do so. In particular, when they can leverage a technology like serverless, which gives you a profound ability to improve velocity, you should always evaluate and look to make the move—before your rivals do.

This is, of course, easier said than done. Even for startups.

One of the anti-patterns we have seen some startups make is staying just on Amazon EC2 and believing that, because they are on AWS, they can rest on their laurels. No, you can't. The journey is never done. We are always abstracting up the stack and grooming our technical debt to increase developer velocity.

We want to give a special thanks to our AWS colleague and author of the book *AWS Lambda in Action,* Danilo Poccia, for his advice and invaluable assistance in the writing of this chapter.

5.2 API'S AND MICROSERVICES

"The whole is greater than the sum of its parts."

– ARISTOTLE

Everyone is talking about microservices lately. But why? Have we been doing it wrong all these years? Well, yes and no. There are distinct benefits to monolithic applications, but time to market and (development) agility are not among them. The ideas behind microservices have actually been around for quite some time, summarized in a paper from 1978 (but arguably much older even than that) called "UNIX Time-Sharing System" by M. D. McIlroy, E. N. Pinson, and B. A. Tague. In their paper, the authors made the following observations (emphasis ours):

> *A number of maxims have gained currency among the builders and users of the UNIX system to explain and promote its characteristic style:*
>
> *1. **Make each program do one thing well.** To do a new job, **build** afresh **rather than complicate old programs by adding new "features."***
>
> *2. **Expect the output of every program to become the input to another,** as yet unknown, program. Don't clutter output with*

extraneous information. Avoid stringently columnar or binary input formats. Don't insist on interactive input.

*3. **Design and build software,** even operating systems, **to be tried early, ideally within weeks. Don't hesitate to throw away the clumsy parts and rebuild them.***

*4. **Use tools in preference to unskilled help to lighten a programming task,** even if you have to detour to build the tools and expect to throw some of them out after you've finished using them.*

We've bolded the most important parts because these ideas directly manifest themselves in microservices and APIs.

1. A microservice is a program that does one thing really well!
2. Inputs and outputs are clearly defined in the API (a kind of contract).
3. Microservices are small enough that they can be developed, modified, or re-written in weeks (and in many cases even hours or days). This by the way, aligns rather elegantly with having small teams.
4. Teams have the freedom to choose the best tool to address a specific problem within their microservice.

So, at the risk of stating the obvious, APIs—application programming interfaces—represent a contract between a requestor (a user or a program) and a responder (a service that answers requests). This is an important point, since API contracts need to be agreed upon and should then become essentially immutable. Since other services will expect a particular, well-defined response to a request, it would break the architecture if someone suddenly changed the contract. Contracts can be expanded, and the implementation details inside the service can and do change (Amazon S3 has been continually improved since its original implementation, while maintaining backward compatibility).

But the original API contract must not change, although new functionality can be added. An API is for life, not just for this month or this year! Luckily, there is a growing body of practices, patterns, and tools that make designing APIs easier.

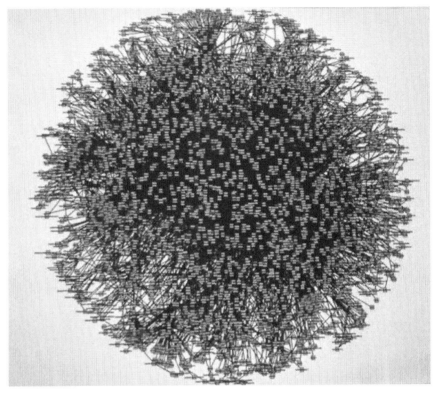

* Real-time graph of microservice dependencies at Amazon.com in 2008

Microservices are thus small, independently managed building blocks that can be assembled in myriad and often unexpected ways to create sophisticated systems. A simple analogy is that of a child's building blocks. Each building block is simultaneously simple and versatile. Building blocks can be assembled into simplistic models by inexperienced parents (typically their kids can create true marvels), or by experienced builders to create something as "cool" as a replica of the *Millennium Falcon*! Another analogy is swarm logic, which states that intelligent-seeming behavior can emerge from complex systems that are composed of simple, "non-intelligent" agents. An ant has only two simple ganglia, which give it all the intelligence it needs to navigate its six legs across a truly complex environment. Another level of abstraction higher, individual ants work together to make the highly complex and sophisticated ant colony thrive.

Microservices and velocity

In our view, microservices are one of the keys to increasing business velocity, as well as improving your ability to innovate. Your product managers don't lack for ideas. They lack the ability to try them out without looking into their crystal ball and picking a winner. This has been necessary, but rarely successful, in order to secure funding for the upfront investment. This investment used to be necessary in order to purchase new infrastructure capacity across multiple build, test, and production environments *before* starting to develop the new product or service or thing. Small wonder then that it takes most organizations months or years to create any new value. Of course, that is assuming that you guessed correctly and created the right thing in the first place.

Imagine instead a world where your product team can try an idea in a matter of days or weeks (or in some cases, hours), by building a very simple version of the product. This minimum likeable product (MLP), interacts with your existing systems via APIs. In this world, the MLP can interact with existing services and components in a loosely coupled way that prevents an inadvertent mistake from crashing your cash cow. In such a world you could try ideas—maybe one new idea per sprint (per day?)—and learn from the ones that miss the mark while scaling up the ones that hit the bullseye. If a microservice fails, applications can detect the failure and gracefully degrade rather than causing a complete outage, as is typically the case with component failures in monolithic applications.

General description of microservices pattern on AWS

How then does AWS help with this approach?

The general pattern of a microservice on AWS consists of using an AWS Application Load Balancer (ALB) together with Amazon EC2 Container Service (Amazon ECS) and AWS Auto Scaling, and one of several data storage services, such as Memcached or Redis—both part of the managed Amazon ElastiCache service—or a NoSQL service such Amazon DynamoDB. The only way to communicate with the microservice is by way of the API, typically a RESTful web services API. This means there is no way to access data from the data store, except via the API!

The AWS Application Load Balancer distributes incoming requests to Amazon ECS container instances running the API and the business logic. Container instances are automatically added or removed depending on the number of incoming requests, which helps keep costs down to the bare minimum. The data store is used to persist data needed by the microservice. Data cannot be stored on the local instance because that instance is ephemeral and will suddenly disappear—taking your precious data with it to oblivion.

So far, this sounds fairly simple, and it is. Complexity arises, however, in managing APIs. Access management of APIs is an important consideration, as is throttling the volume of requests (to protect the backend), caching, transforming request and response, and managing and documenting API definitions. The AWS API Gateway Service was designed to help developers create, publish, maintain, monitor, and secure APIs. It also handles routing of requests to the nearest Amazon CloudFront Point of Presence or Regional Edge Caches to minimize latency.

Amazon CloudFront is a fast content delivery network (CDN) service that securely delivers data, videos, applications, and APIs globally with low latency and high transfer speeds. Amazon CloudFront can be used to secure and accelerate your WebSocket traffic as well as API calls. Amazon CloudFront supports proxy methods (POST, PUT, OPTIONS, DELETE, and PATCH) and is already integrated with Amazon API Gateway by default. With the content-delivery network, TLS connections with clients terminate at a nearby edge location, then Amazon CloudFront uses optimized AWS-backbone network paths to securely reach your API servers.

You might further reduce the operational efforts to run, maintain, and monitor microservices by using a fully serverless architecture. In this case, when using AWS Lambda, business logic execution can be triggered by calls from AWS API Gateway without the need to manage any server instances whatsoever. Done properly, this eliminates the architectural burden of designing for scale and high availability and eliminates the operational burden of running and monitoring the microservice's underlying infrastructure.

Challenges with microservices

Critics of microservices argue that the challenges and complexity associated with a monolith are replaced by cross-service challenges and challenges inherent to distributed systems. There are definitely a few important things to consider when employing a microservices architecture.

Eventual consistency - One of these is that you might have many instances of the same microservice running in parallel. A monolithic application usually has a single, massive database where all data is stored—allowing for consistency of data at all times. Let's say you have a microservice for shipping orders that needs to reduce the available inventory after the order has been shipped. How do you manage consistency in such a case? Enter the world of "eventual" consistency. Basically, your distributed application needs a little more time (we're still working in microseconds here) than a monolithic application does to ensure all associated data changes everywhere it needs to be changed.

In effect, this means your data store selection for each service will depend on whether your user can tolerate short-lived inconsistency or not. Most services will work just fine with eventual consistency. The CAP (consistency, availability, and performance) theorem states that, in the presence of a network partition, one has to choose between consistency and availability. This is where the notion of eventual consistency stems from.

Service discovery - Another challenge we encountered during adoption of this pattern in 2015 was service discovery. How do I know what microservice is available, and how do I know (or can a system programmatically "know") how to interact with the API? How can I know the health of a service? If it exists, is it available? Again, there are well-understood architectural patterns one can employ, namely DNS services, which have been around since 1985. You can leverage the AWS Application Load Balancer here as well since it automatically provides health checks and can be configured with either path- or host-based routing. Or you can implement a solution based on Route 53.

AWS services for microservices

AWS offers a variety of services that can help you with the development, management, and deployment of microservices. Here are some of the most commonly used.

AWS Cloud Map - Developing a small number of microservices is straightforward. However, as you add more and more microservices to the environment, it can become challenging to manage all the dependencies and resources used by your environment.

AWS Cloud Map is a cloud resource discovery service that allows you to define custom names for your application resources, and to maintain the updated location of these dynamically changing resources.

This increases your application availability because your web service always discovers the most up-to-date locations of its resources.

Modern applications interact with a variety of other resources, such as databases, queues, object stores, and customer-defined microservices, and they need to be able to find the location of all the infrastructure resources on which they depend in order to function. Manual resource management becomes time consuming and error-prone as the number of dependent infrastructure resources increases or the number of microservices dynamically scale up and down based on traffic. You can also use third-party service-discovery products, but this requires installing and managing additional software and infrastructure.

AWS App Mesh - When you start building more than a few microservices within an application, it becomes difficult to identify and isolate issues. These issues can include high latencies, error rates, or error codes across the application. There is no dynamic way to route network traffic when there are failures or when new containers need to be deployed.

You can address these problems by adding custom code and libraries into each microservice or by using open-source tools that manage communications for each microservice. However, these solutions can be hard to install, difficult to update across teams, and complex to manage for availability and resiliency. AWS App Mesh (based on an open-source proxy called Envoy) implements an architectural pattern that helps solve many of these challenges and provides a consistent, dynamic way to manage the communications between microservices. With AWS App Mesh, the logic for monitoring and controlling communications between microservices is implemented as a proxy that runs alongside each microservice instead of being built into the microservice code. The proxy handles all of the network traffic into and out of the microservice and provides consistency for visibility, traffic control, and security capabilities to all of your microservices.

You use AWS App Mesh to model how all of your microservices connect and AWS App Mesh automatically computes and sends the appropriate configuration information to each microservice proxy. This gives you standardized visibility and traffic controls across your application.

Amazon SQS - Amazon Simple Queue Service (SQS) is a message-queuing service that enables developers to decouple and scale microservices, distributed systems, and serverless applications. It eliminates the complexity and overhead associated with managing and operating message-oriented middleware, which we have both experienced. You can send, store, and receive messages between software components at any volume, without losing messages or requiring other services to be available.

If your application requires queues that preserve the exact order in which messages are sent and received, then you have the option of using FIFO (first-in-first-out) queues. FIFO queues also ensure "exactly once" processing, which means that each message is delivered once and remains available until a consumer processes it and deletes it. This extra convenience comes with a slower performance, so your specific requirement will determine which tradeoff makes the most sense for you.

The following are common use cases for messaging:

- **Service-to-service communication**—You have two services or systems that need to communicate with each other. Let's say a website (the front end) has to update a customer's delivery address in a customer relationship management (CRM) system (the backend). Alternatively, you can set up a load balancer in front of the backend CRM service and call its API actions directly from the front-end website. You can also set up a queue and have the front-end website code send messages to the queue and have the backend CRM service consume them.
- **Asynchronous work item backlogs**—You have a service that has to track a backlog of actions to be executed. Let's say a hotel

booking system needs to cancel a booking and this process takes a long time (from a few seconds to a minute). You can execute the cancellation synchronously, but then you risk annoying the customer who has to wait for the webpage to load. You can also track all pending cancellations in your database and keep polling and executing cancellations. Alternatively, you can put a message into a queue and have the same hotel booking system consume messages from that queue and perform asynchronous cancellations.

- **State change notifications**—You have a service that manages a resource, and other services that receive updates about changes to that resource. Let's say it is an inventory-tracking system that tracks products stocked in a warehouse. Whenever the stock is sold out, the website must stop offering that product. Whenever the stock is close to being depleted, the purchasing system must place an order for more items. While those systems can keep querying the inventory system to learn about these changes, the inventory system can instead (better and with lower cost) publish notifications about stock changes to a topic and any interested program can subscribe to learn about those changes.

Which brings us to publish/subscribe messaging.

Amazon SNS - Publish/subscribe messaging, or pub/sub messaging, is a form of asynchronous service-to-service communication that can be used in serverless and microservices architectures. In a pub/sub model, any message published to a topic is immediately received by all of the subscribers to the topic. Pub/sub messaging can be used to enable event-driven architectures or to decouple applications in order to increase performance, reliability, and scalability.

Amazon Simple Notification Service (SNS) is a managed pub/sub messaging service that enables you to decouple microservices, distributed systems, and serverless applications. It provides topics for high-throughput, push-based, many-to-many messaging. Using Amazon SNS topics, your publisher systems can fan out messages to a large number of subscriber endpoints for parallel processing, including Amazon SQS queues, AWS Lambda functions, and HTTP/S webhooks. In addition, Amazon SNS can be used to fan out notifications to end users using mobile push, SMS, and email.

AWS Step Functions - As in the original Unix model above, there are many occasions in which microservices need to be stitched together following a particular workflow, which allows you to build and update apps quickly. Application development is simpler and more intuitive using step functions because it translates your workflow into a state machine diagram that is easy to understand, easy to explain to others, and easy to change. You can monitor each step of execution as it happens, which means you can identify and fix problems quickly. AWS Step Functions automatically triggers and tracks each step, and retries when there are errors, so your application executes in order and as expected. And, perhaps most important, AWS Step Functions is a great tool to help you refactor (or decompose) your monolithic applications. Yelp used AWS Step Functions to do exactly that in 2017/18.

A great example of an older, more established system is our monthly subscription billing cycle. The system is core to how Yelp collects revenue and has proven technically challenging and risky to transition. The Revenue engineering team knows these older systems should be moved into services, but the challenge of extracting tangled, business-critical code has proven expensive and dangerous. Luckily a new framework was announced by Amazon Web Services at the end of 2016, AWS Step Functions, that's allowed us to make this transition a reality.

AWS AppSync - AWS AppSync lets you create a flexible API to access, manipulate, and combine data from one or more data sources. AWS AppSync is a managed service that uses GraphQL to make it easy for applications to get exactly the data they need. GraphQL is an open-source data query and manipulation language for APIs, and a runtime for fulfilling queries with existing data.

With AWS AppSync, you can build scalable applications—including those requiring real-time updates—on a range of data sources such as NoSQL data stores, relational databases, HTTP APIs, and your custom data sources with AWS Lambda. For mobile and web apps, AWS AppSync also provides local data access when devices go offline, and data synchronization with customizable conflict resolution, when they are back online.

You can use AWS AppSync as a single interface to access and combine data from multiple microservices in your application, even if they're running in different environments such as containers in an Amazon VPC, behind a REST API on Amazon API Gateway, or behind a GraphQL API on another AWS AppSync endpoint.

Conclusion

Although distributed systems impose a number of unique architectural requirements, we would both be hard pressed to come up with a compelling reason to use monolithic architectures for any new development. The benefits of a loosely coupled, distributed, and highly scalable microservices architecture are simply too compelling to ignore. To help you along, AWS continues to offer innovative services that remove many of the complexities of distributed architectures.

We would like to give a very special thanks to Rachel Richardson for her help in writing this chapter. Her expertise definitely raised the bar.

5.3 RESILIENCE AND RELIABILITY

"Failures are a given, and everything will eventually fail over time."
– WERNER VOGELS, CTO AMAZON.COM, INC.

The 3:00 a.m. wake-up call that you receive as an IT leader when a critical technology system has failed is one of the perennial stresses of the job. The more senior you get, the more you are the final point of escalation for these incidents.

Dealing with these situations is not why we started a career in technology. The mean time to resolution (MTTR), wash-up, and explanations to customers internal and external saps time and energy and disrupts anything else you had planned. Worse, you can get caught in a continuous cycle where the more these events occur, the more they occur because you can't bring the necessary resources to bear to actually break the cycle and get to the root cause.

As we have touched on previously, 95 percent of what you deal with day in and day out as an executive are the decisions of yesterday. Actually, yesterday is the wrong word. *Yesteryear* would be a better word if it was real. IT systems have a habit of hanging around for decades, and we are stuck with the decisions that other leaders—who have long since moved on to other things—have "gifted" for us. We always smiled wryly when people would try and give us management advice on some shiny new widget that would supposedly solve all our ills. And few of these people had actually lived in the real world of looking after the professional well-being of large teams, running systems 24x7, and trying to move the organization forward efficiently. This while trying to keep everyone happy with the decisions we had to make all day, every day, as well as keeping up with the perpetual tsunami of new technology we needed to at least be aware of.

Attempts to break this cycle have been valiantly fought. The battle has raged between application versus infrastructure reliability elements, with seemingly ever-higher, yet meaningless availability figures being produced for components. These components still somehow always managed to fail at 3:00 a.m.—for one reason or another. What? You didn't know that the beta version of a patch that was installed a year ago would conflict with last night's emergency security patch and cause the system to fail? Sigh.

You may already be familiar with this table of the perennial availability battle we are fighting—the nines of availability.

Availability	Downtime per year	Categories
95% (1-nine)	18 days 6 hours	Batch processing, data extraction, load jobs
99% (2-nines)	3 days 15 hours	Internal tools, project tracking
99.9% (3-nines)	8 hours 45 minutes	Online commerce
99.99% (4-nines)	52 minutes	Video delivery, broadcast systems
99.999% (5-nines)	5 minutes	Telecom industry (ATM Transactions)

If you want to have 5-nines of availability, you can only afford 5 minutes of downtime a year. That is a high bar.

When we ran data centers, it was unfortunately wryly amusing to see availability figures like this bandied around regularly by different hardware providers. Because the availability you actually receive from an individual component is not related to the mathematical reality of running data centers full of these components with different availability figures.

For example, let's consider that you have two components, x and y respectively, with 99 percent and 99.99 percent availability. If you put those two components in series (one being dependent on the other), the overall availability of the system will get worse.

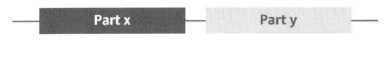

$$A = A_x A_y$$

Component	Availability	Downtime
x	99% (2-nines)	3 days 15 hours
y	99.99% (4-nines)	52 minutes
x and y combined	98.99%	3 days 16 hours 33 minutes

This explains how, when you have a single data center, but keep adding more and more components, you keep having failures. Because, ultimately, they are all in serial (even if some of the components have redundancy)—from the building to the electrical supply upward, through network, storage, compute, load balancer, application, and so forth.

Everything fails

One of the things—perhaps the most important thing—that attracted us to use AWS as customers, and eventually make the move professionally to work at AWS, were the very long-term decisions that

Amazon has made toward availability, reliability, and recoverability. We were also impressed by the lessons they had learned as they built and scaled to become one of the world's largest websites. Those hard-earned lessons were poured into AWS from the beginning back in 2006. And the lessons have continued to be learned. To quote Andy Jassy again, "There is no compression algorithm for experience."

As Werner Vogels says in the epigraph at the start of this chapter, "Failures are a given, and everything will eventually fail over time." This is the cold, stark reality of modern technology. You might install however many 99.9999999-available pieces of hardware into your data center, but the whole lot will fail if somebody hits the Emergency Power Off button or any of a multitude of other events happen. Which, if the experience of the authors is a benchmark, it absolutely does.

Murphy's law – "Whatever can go wrong, will go wrong."

During his keynote at the AWS re:Invent conference in 2018, Werner Vogels shared an interesting story of his worst day at Amazon.com. On December 12, 2004—the very last day that Amazon retail customers could place their orders and be assured delivery of their items before Christmas—Amazon.com experienced an outage. (Murphy's law picked a great moment.) At that time, Amazon was already running its system in a service-oriented architecture, with three very large datasets called Orders, Items, and Customers. The Customers database ran on an Oracle RAC cluster, and a bug that controlled the logging engine occurred, causing a 12-hour outage. This outage taught Amazon an awful lot of lessons. One key learning was that scaling up (bigger and more powerful individual compute instances) created a big blast surface when things go wrong. Another key learning was that Amazon had very little control or choices in the database space.

This is just one of many, many lessons that you can only learn as you go through various stages of significant growth and hit different elbows of the curve. Standing on the shoulders of giants and leveraging their economies of scale for lessons learned is how you can also get to a drastically more available place.

What is resiliency, and why you shouldn't be afraid of failing

Resilient systems embrace the idea that failures are normal, and that it's perfectly okay to run systems in what we call *partially failing mode*. When we are dealing with smaller systems of up to few tens of compute instances, 100 percent operational excellence is often the normal stage and failure is an exceptional condition. However, when dealing with large-scale systems, probabilities are such that 100 percent operational excellence is nearly impossible to achieve. Therefore, the normal state of operation is partial failure.

Running in partially failing mode is a viable option for nearly all web applications, from e-commerce services like Amazon.com to video-on-demand sites such as Netflix, to music services like Sound-Cloud, and yes, even financial services institutions. We are not saying it doesn't matter if your system fails, but we are saying you should design for failure up to and including entire data center failures.

The way out of the availability trap

One important thing to realize early on is that building resilient architecture isn't all about software. It starts at the infrastructure layer, progresses to the network and data, influences application design, and extends to people and culture. Let's take a deep dive into some of the core areas. This list is by no means exhaustive, but by incorporating and establishing deployment principles around these core areas, you can see a material shift.

- Redundancy
- Auto Scaling
- Infrastructure as code

- Immutable infrastructure and Blue Green Deployments
- Stateless applications

According to independent IDC research done in February 2018, titled "Fostering Business Organizational Transformation to Generate Business Value with Amazon Web Services," the customers they interviewed experienced 95 percent less unplanned downtime when running on AWS.

Redundancy

Now, instead of serial, let's consider the math when you are running things in parallel.

$$A = 1 - (1 - A_x)^2$$

Component	Availability	Downtime
x	99% (2-nines)	3 days 15 hours
Two x in parallel	99.99% (4-nines)	52 minutes
Three x in parallel	99.9999% (6-nines)	31 seconds

The math suddenly becomes very different. This is the deep thinking that went behind AWS Cloud's decision to use the Region *and* Availability Zone model. The takeaway here is that component redundancy increases availability significantly.

One of the first and most important things to do when you deploy an application in the cloud is to architect your application to be redundant. Simply put, redundancy is the duplication of components of a system in order to increase the overall availability of that system. In the AWS Cloud, that means deploying it across multiple Availability Zones (multi-AZ) or, in some cases, across multi-Regions.

While each AZ is fully independent from one another—with redundant power, networking, and connectivity, and housed in separate facilities—AZs are connected through links allowing for low single-digit millisecond latency between each AZ. Such a low latency allows for synchronous replications between the different AZs. This is a foundational principle for high availability and fault tolerance on AWS. Indeed, if one of the AZs in a particular Region experiences intermittent issues, the other AZs, independently, are able to continue operating.

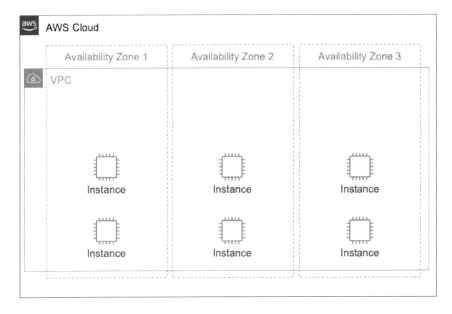

Just by deploying your applications and data in parallel now increases your overall system availability to 99.99 percent. And, if you put three component x in parallel, you get to the famous 6-nines. That is a high bar in terms of availability, and why AWS always advises customers to deploy their applications across multi-AZs, preferably three of them.

This is also why, what we call AWS regional services such as Amazon S3, Amazon Aurora, Amazon DynamoDB, Amazon SQS, Amazon Kinesis, AWS Lambda, or ELB, just to name a few, are built with this architecture in mind. There is some great further reading available here https://aws. amazon.com/builders-library/static-stability-using-availability-zones/

Auto Scaling

For many years in corporate IT, we would buy sufficient hardware and software for the most optimistic of peaks we could imagine and would still probably get it wrong. This purchase for peak was incredibly wasteful of time, effort, and money. The ability to programmatically scale your technology resources to meet demand and only pay for what you use is an absolute cornerstone of the AWS Cloud tenets. This is called Auto Scaling.

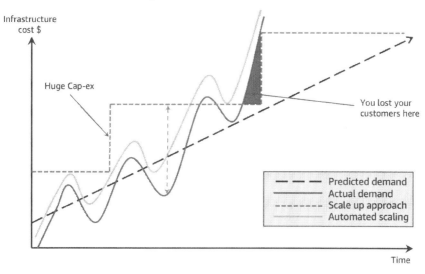

Typical traffic patterns for applications (above), lows and highs based on demand for traditional data centers.

Scaling your resources dynamically according to demand, as opposed to doing it manually, ensures your service can meet a variety of traffic patterns without anyone needing to plan for it. Instances, containers, and functions all provide mechanisms for Auto Scaling—either as a feature of the service itself, or as a support mechanism, Application Auto Scaling can be used to add Auto Scaling capabilities to services you build on AWS. This is a monumental change to how IT was traditionally delivered. Think of all the capacity projects you had to previously sponsor that took weeks, months, and sometimes years to mitigate risk and your best estimates were nearly always wrong. Think of the undifferentiated heavy lifting that is removed.

Infrastructure as code

An essential benefit of using infrastructure as code is repeatability. Let's examine the task of configuring a data center, from configuring the networking and security to the deployment of applications. Consider for a moment the amount of work that would be required if you had to do that manually, for multiple environments in each of these regions. First, it would be a tedious task, but it would most likely introduce configuration differences and drifts over time. Humans aren't great at undertaking repetitive, manual tasks with 100 percent accuracy, but machines are. Give the same template to a computer and it will execute that template 10,000 times exactly the same way.

Now, imagine your environment being compromised, suffering an outage, or even being deleted by mistake (yes, we've seen that happen). You have data backup. You have the infrastructure templates. All you have to do is re-run the template in a new AWS account, a new Amazon VPC, or even a new Region, restore the backups, and voilà, you're up and running in minutes. Doing that manually, and at scale, will result in a nightmare scenario, with a lot of sweat and tears, and worse, unhappy customers.

Another benefit of infrastructure as code is knowledge sharing. Indeed, if you version control your infrastructure (and you should), you can treat that code the same way you treat application code. You can have teams committing code to it and ask for improvements or changes in configuration. If that process goes through a pull-request, then the rest of the team can verify, challenge, and comment on that request, promoting better practices.

Immutable infrastructure and blue/green deployments

What is immutable infrastructure and why should you care about it as a leader?

The principle of immutable infrastructure is fairly simple: immutable components are replaced for every deployment, rather than being updated in place. Any of us who have needed to apply emergency patches to live systems in place know the rock and the hard place this puts us in between. Don't patch and risk a security event or patch and risk an outage. Untested patches can unfortunately often lead to outages. Yes, a horrible situation to be in. Did we mention that being an IT leader is a tough job?

With immutable infrastructure, as you need to deploy a patch or any type of new software code, your infrastructure as code, via API calls simply asks for a new Amazon EC2 node to be created in each AZ with your new AMI with the code incorporated onto it.

This ability when combined with blue/green deployments is particularly compelling.

When we used to deploy applications on-premises, we had to reuse existing infrastructure for new versions of applications. We often had to install updated applications on the same hardware and sometimes we were even compelled to doing risky in-place upgrades.

In the cloud, you can create new infrastructure, programmatically, for new versions of your applications. Then you can keep the previous version running in parallel for a while before tearing it down. This technique is called blue/green deployment. It allows you to progressively switch traffic between two versions of your apps to monitor business and operational metrics on the new version, and to switch traffic back to the previous version in case anything goes wrong.

This type of deployment is called "canary deployment" with "blue/green" testing. The origin of the name canary deployment comes from the old British mining tradition where miners used canaries to detect toxic gases such as carbon monoxide in coal mines. To make sure mines were safe to work in, miners would bring a canary along with them, and if the canary died or got ill, the mine was quickly evacuated.

When you have assured yourself that your performance and experience baselines are appropriate for your new application version, you simply turn the old ones off, and stop paying for them. This is immutable infrastructure, and it works at the compute, container, and serverless levels. Once you deploy this way, you will never, ever want to go back to any other way.

This deployment strategy supports the principle of the golden Amazon Machine Image. This golden AMI is the latest version of your preferred operating system with the minimum appropriately secured and hardened configuration and the application itself is often installed automatically on top of the golden AMI using perhaps Puppet or Chef for your automated software install. Suddenly the risk of updating underlying operating system or applications can be reduced if not eliminated when you use blue/green deployments with infrastructure as code.

No updates should ever be performed on live systems. When deploying a new patch, software update, or code of any kind, you always start from a new instance of the resource being provisioned: Amazon

EC2 instance, container, or an AWS Lambda function. The benefit of canary deployment is, of course, the near-immediate rollback it gives you. But more important, you get faster and safer deployments.

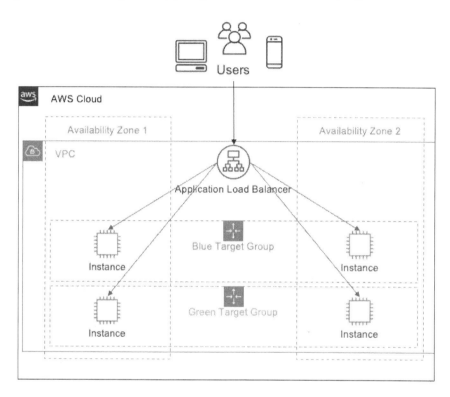

There are few considerations to keep in mind during canary deployment:

1. Being stateless: You should preferably not be dependent on any state between the different old and new versions deployed. If you need stickiness, keep it to the bare minimum.

2. Since fast rollback is a feature, your application should be able to handle it gracefully.

3. Managing canary deployment with database schema changes is hard—*really* hard. We often get asked how to do it. Unfortunately, there's no silver bullet. It depends on the

changes, the application, and the architecture around the database.

For your serverless applications, you also have the option of using Amazon API Gateway since it now supports canary release deployments. Or you can implement canary deployments of AWS Lambda functions with alias traffic shifting.

Stateless applications

Stateless applications are a prerequisite to Auto Scaling and immutable infrastructure since any request can be handled by available computing resources, regardless of whether it's Amazon EC2, a container platform, or a set of AWS Lambda functions.

Stateless service in a multi-AZ setup with Auto Scaling

In a stateless service, the application must treat all client requests independently of prior requests or sessions and should never store any information on local disks or memory.

Sharing state with any resources within the AWS Auto Scaling group should be conducted using in-memory object caching systems such as Memcached, Redis, EVCache, or distributed databases like Cassandra or Amazon DynamoDB, depending on the structure of your object and requirements in terms of performances.

Putting it all together

In order to have a resilient, reliable, auditable, repeatable, and well-tested deployment and scaling process with a fast spin-up time, you'll need to combine the idea of golden AMI, infrastructure as code, immutable infrastructure, and stateless application. And, to do that at scale, you'll have to use automation. In fact, it's your only option. So, "Automate all the things," is a critical foundational tenet for your teams.

Testing your availability

Netflix is an incredible customer for AWS. The company has been one of the pioneers of pushing the envelope and has not been shy about the level that they both automate and test their automation and reliability on AWS. We have personally benefited greatly from hearing our good friend and evangelist teammate, Adrian Cockcroft, talk many times about his journey as both Director of Web Engineering and Cloud Architect at Netflix, and about how they handled availability and reliability testing at scale.

Netflix has developed a suite of open-source tools—collectively called the Simian Army—that can generate latency, shut down compute nodes, and even shut down entire Availability Zones to test and ensure their software is as reliable as they can make it. This mechanism is now collectively known as *reliability engineering* or *chaos engineering* and more information can be found here.

What does this mean for disaster recovery?

For decades in corporate IT, the words "disaster recovery" have been laden with fear, loathing, angst, and seemingly endless money being spent on systems that are, more often than not, never ever used—let alone trusted to perform as needed—when they are needed.

With the new availability tools and methods described above, you can see that the idea of maintaining a cold/hot/primary/secondary/tertiary system that can keep step with the congruence of digital demands placed upon on them for very modern hyperscale systems is frankly like trying to put gasoline in an electric car.

The ability to real-time test failure scenarios, all the time, across your application and data landscape, is how you ensure you can stay online and in-service. Some customers have actually migrated their entire primary data centers into a single Availability Zone, and their secondary data centers in a second Availability Zone to get off the never-ending hardware upgrade train, remove costs, and get to a radically better infrastructure availability space.

Then they can adopt Cloud-First and Cloud-Native principles for all new development. When you do this, you can typically still maintain the existing mechanisms you had in place for replication and system fail over, while you establish the new.

Replication and recovery

The ability to securely replicate your data stores as you deem appropriate to other AWS Regions to hold copies of that data has fundamentally and forever changed how enterprises view disaster recovery. There is a comprehensive set of services to help with this including S3 Cross-Region Replication (CRR) to securely replicate your data objects to other AWS Regions as you deem appropriate, and Amazon DynamoDB global tables to give you a fully managed, multi-region and multi-master database. Amazon Aurora Global Databases allows you to have a secondary, read-only version to replicate objects into AWS Regions around the world. Along with Amazon S3 Glacier Deep Archive, Amazon DynamoDB global tables, and Amazon Aurora global tables, you can now achieve the level of backup and resiliency you have been looking for.

Final note on AWS Backup

While leveraging all of the innate capabilities of AWS Cloud is incredibly empowering with regards to resilience and reliability, you still need to ensure your data and application logic are backed up. To help with that, you have AWS Backup. This is a fully managed backup service that allows you to centralize and automate the backup of data across AWS services in the cloud as well as on-premises using the AWS Storage Gateway. You can centrally configure backup policies and monitor backup activity for AWS resources, such as Amazon EBS volumes, Amazon RDS databases, Amazon DynamoDB tables, Amazon EFS file systems, and AWS Storage Gateway volumes. It automates and consolidates backup tasks previously performed service-by-service, removing the need to create custom scripts and manual processes.

We want to give a heartfelt special thanks to our good friend Adrian Hornsby, Principal Technical Evangelist at AWS, for his help in writing this chapter. His graphics and narrative were invaluable and more and deeper information can be found at https://medium.com/@adhorn

5.4 MIGRATING YOUR APPLICATIONS

"How emigration is actually lived—well, this depends on many factors: education, economic station, language, where one lands, and what support network is in place at the site of arrival."

– DANIEL ALARCÓN

So, you have had some early wins with your first workloads, the engineers are learning frenetically and having fun, your business customers are excited about the potential here, and your CFO is now eyeing some serious savings.

It's at this point that the Cloud Business Office will likely turn its focus toward the migration of existing workloads. There have probably already been lots of statements thrown around—assumptions with regards to which workloads are going to move when and where. These are almost certainly bleeding into timeline commitments (even though they shouldn't exist for Agile) for the different new customer features that you want to build.

In our own experience, a couple of things will happen next.

Initially, the engineers and developers will be convinced that everything will have to be rewritten to take advantage of the cloud. They will be passionate about this. Unless they can turn everything into

CI/CD and run everything Cloud Native, it just won't be right. As engineers, we can relate to this point and have been culpable of pursuing such an imperative in this past. At the start of our own journeys, we too wanted to ensure a perfect tower of CI/CD infrastructure as code perfection. However, as many of us know, perfect is the perpetual enemy of good enough in business (to paraphrase Voltaire). The grizzled and battle-scarred leaders we have become now think a little differently.

The fiscal reality will soon hit home that rewriting a long time of intellectual property locked into your existing application suites and data stores will a) potentially take decades, and b) the CFO would quite like those cost savings in 24 months, please. That data center is darn expensive you know—how fast can we close it?

The importance of momentum

As you move forward with production workloads on AWS Cloud and running your existing Private Data Centers, you have now officially entered *hybrid* mode. This is a perfectly acceptable transitional state. It is not, however—as some have asserted—a valid long-term strategy unless you have workloads with specific latency or specific regulatory data residency requirements. In fact, running in hybrid for an extended period of time (many years) without a clear target, and removing as much undifferentiated heavy lifting as possible, can actually present a risk to your business across people, process, and technology. All three are left in a transitional state and you can't get closure in any of them.

Of the thousands of migrations that AWS has worked on, the most effective (delivery goals met) are the migrations that have a very clear leadership goal, engage clearly with accredited partners, focus very seriously on the reskilling, and stick to a migration target. Keeping momentum of migrations going is critical—some of the best migrations actually start with 50-in-50 goals: 50 apps moved in 50 days.

And, yes, this has been done many times. Either <u>AWS Partners</u> or the <u>AWS Managed Services</u> offering can help. Keep the focus on moving forward and removing any roadblocks with the CBO!

The Power of the 7 R's

As the leader, it's right about now that you are normally shown a tremendous amount of architectural and engineering decision points for each of your applications—as detailed and deep as the proverbial rabbit hole each would take you down. Some organizations we have worked with have had their cloud plans significantly derailed and distracted by overthinking this. However, there is a way that has become a critical core component of powerful conversations for hundreds of executive briefings we have had with customers, the wider Enterprise Strategy team, and countless Amazonians the world over. This way is the migration 7 R's.

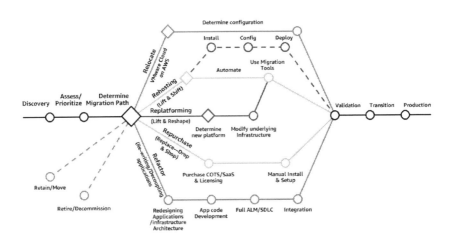

The above diagram of the 7 R's is one we often spend an entire Executive Briefing Session on with customers. Key customer stakeholders typically mentally sense check it against their own architecture portfolios. The conversation is always fascinating, and we love seeing the complexity ease in people eyes as they finally see a way through for them. Each R has a unique use—we have seen different models from other people and organizations. Frankly, however, none has been used as much in the field and been proven to work countless times over.

Let's take a closer look at each of the 7 R's.

Relocate - With VMware Cloud on AWS, you can use the same VMware Cloud Foundation technologies including vSphere, vSAN, NSX, and vCenter Server from your on-premises data centers and on the AWS Cloud without having to purchase any new or custom hardware, rewrite applications, or modify your existing operating models. The service automatically provisions infrastructure and provides full VM compatibility and workload portability between your on-premises environments and the AWS Cloud.

Rehosting - In its most succinct form, this means taking the existing operating system and any applications it hosts, and moving it from the existing hypervisor and/or bare metal server instance, copy seeding the data, and then finally moving the runtime components over to a similar-sized Amazon Elastic Compute (EC2) instance and size-matched Amazon Elastic Block Store (EBS) volume(s). This has been done hundreds of thousands of times for customers who are migrating to cloud. ENEL is one of the best examples in public reference. They clearly established their bold goal and migrated 5,500 instances in 9 months using rehosting. That's 25 a day, including weekends.

After the migration, not only can you bank a huge cost saving, you can optimize to reduce costs further. You'll then truly have your technical teams focused on maintaining and developing those software features on what matters most for your business. The significant majority of your moves should be made using rehosting.

There are some very powerful AWS tools available including the AWS Server Migration Service (SMS), which is an agentless service that makes it easier and faster for you to migrate thousands of on-prem-ises workloads to AWS. AWS SMS allows you to automate, schedule, and track incremental replications of live server volumes, making it easier for you to coordinate large-scale server migrations. And there are many other migration tools available from our partners in the AWS Marketplace, specifically built for migrations including CloudEn-dure (now an AWS company) and RiverMeadow.

Replatforming - Often called "lift, shift, and tinker," replatforming is when you take the existing application or database, transform it slightly, and then move it. This could, for example, mean you want to move an existing application, but upgrade the underlying operating system from Microsoft Windows 2008 to Microsoft Windows 2016. Or you want to move from Oracle WebLogic to an Apache Tomcat execution engine instead. Or you want to move from a bespoke, managed database to an Amazon RDS database instance that is maintained by AWS instead.

If you go this way for your workloads, follow the example of AWS Enterprise Strategy's Philip Potloff—previously CIO at Edmunds. com—and timebox your teams to two weeks to do this. As Parkinson's law suggests, "work expands so as to fill the time available for its completion," so give the engineer teams just two weeks or re-host. It's amazing the miracles, creativity, and passion engineers and develop-ers will put in if they want to avoid a re-host.

Replatforming can be a very powerful choice. When done correctly, you get a win-win-win outcome:

- Lower running costs by hosting an Amazon EC2 compute instance from AWS, saving money.
- Reduce and remediate technical operating system debt, reduc-ing risk.
- Remove the need to ever procure or upgrade the hardware for this application again, saving time.

A key part of replatforming is the ability to migrate your database. Replatforming is something you'll want a tool to automate for you. The AWS Database Migration Service is an extremely useful tool. As of December 2019, the AWS Database Migration Service has helped enterprises move more than 170,000 databases into AWS, and there are currently 184 migration tools available in the AWS Marketplace.

Repurchasing - Is also sometimes known as "shop and drop." Who, after all, wants to be looking after email services onsite anymore, and/or legacy telephone switches, payroll, human resources products, and so on? This adds zero differentiation to your business. There are many Software-as-a-Service offerings—from AWS WorkSpaces to Workday—and numerous partner and standalone solutions available in the AWS Marketplace. Executing the migrations to get these servers out of your data center will allow further focus of your technical teams onto the services that truly matter for your customers.

As you go through your portfolio, mark up these apps appropriately and assign resources to execute on their move. If the timelines look elongated for a repurchase, go with a rehost and move them later. Keeping momentum of apps moving is the goal.

Refactor - Cloud-Native and Cloud-First principles will lead you to the refactoring path. This path delivers the highest potential reliability and availability, and typically the lowest cost. When refactoring, you will be able to take the most appropriate services available in the AWS toolkit to build your apps from the ground up in a scalable and efficient way. If you so choose, you can leverage Auto Scaling Amazon EC2 instances and a multitude of database and file storage technologies and/or leverage serverless to create a powerful fulcrum effect that will dramatically lower your costs and remove the maximum amount of heavy lifting required. This path, however, can also take the longest amount of time. The path is best leveraged for new workloads and those non-x86 architectures that you may want to move to the cloud.

It is entirely appropriate to thoughtfully use refactoring to be Cloud First and Cloud Native as you migrate those services which truly differentiate your business from your competitors and where you want the benefits of doing so.

Retire/Decommission - Carefully choosing when it is not appropriate to take an application and/or virtual server with you to the cloud is crucial. It can be hard work unpicking systems, and it can be complex. That said, when you weigh the pros and cons of each type of move, choosing to retire assets and simplify your application portfolio can generate serious savings.

When emptying data centers, you will be utterly amazed at how much waste exists. It's not at all unusual, for example, to find hundreds of old and expensive servers reduced to doing small copy jobs. Over the years, workloads have moved off and these servers have been orphaned, but will continue to be religiously and expensively patched, secured, and upgraded. This compounded with the vast array of bespoke and often poorly implemented and used monitoring tools that are left running to look after vast amounts of hardware is normal. It's not unusual to find that double-digit percentages of workloads in a data center are simply switched off at the end of a migration, with the team realizing they are simply not used any more.

Retain/Not Moving - Some incumbent systems—be they AIX, Mainframe, HPUX, AS/400 (yes many still exist), or bespoke network connections—can be impractical to refactor in an appropriate time scale to actually meet your "close data center target" and release the monies being habitually spent there. In this case, there are realistically three possible scenarios: 1) Move the hardware/application to an appropriate specialist supporter of these technologies and access them remotely. 2) Move the hardware/applications to one of the AWS Direct Connect partners that exist around the globe (Equinix, for example). These have the benefit of being able to provide highly secure and resilient floor space with very low-latency access to the AWS Regions. 3) Retain a proportion of minimal on-premises data center space to keep the legacy systems running.

Case in point, one customer we know chose to take the four-year (never-ending) mainframe refresh cycle and purchase and install the next new mainframe into a co-lo of an AWS Partner to get really lower latency to the cloud, but also get it physically out their data center. As a result, they realized the tremendous fiscal benefit of closing the data center while giving themselves the time to properly deconstruct the mainframe in a timely way.

Creating your migration "strawman"

One of the techniques we use with customers—and that you can apply yourself—is to take the 7 R's and seven different colors of sticky notes, a spare meeting room with whiteboards, a drawn timeline (matched to your business goal), and a little uninterrupted time (one day is doable). Simply write the name of each application in your port-folio and match it to a sticky note that is most appropriate. As a rule of thumb, you should aim to Rehost the majority, Replatform where you have to, Repurchase when it makes sense, and Refactor the key business differentiating elements that you are going to change every day and that you want to get to the full potential of DevOps with CI/CD and you are prepared to invest to get them there.

When you complete this exercise, you will end up with a contiguous timeline showing when and how an application could move. Will it be 100 percent accurate? No. Does it *need* to be 100 percent accurate? No. And that is a clear assumption you should state to everyone at the outset. In our experience, this initial cut will very often be approx-imately 80 percent accurate, which is good enough. Remember: per-fect is the enemy of good enough.

This annotated timeline can then be used by any and all as a point of reference. As you get more information, the timeline will change. This is absolutely fine and indeed necessary, and it will feed directly into your detailed business case and migration acceleration program (MAP). Don't hide these whiteboards away—if you have a central floor or office area, place them where everyone can easily see them. There is nothing to hide here. They should be open to review and can be modified with new data points. These sticky note boards become a living Agile board in their own right.

Enriching your detailed business case

Now that you have categorized your entire existing application portfolio with a strawman analysis on a timeline, you can include a number of other elements to enrich and inform your detailed business case creation.

For example, you can now add in all of your known hardware CAPEX investments. There are always a multitude of multiyear investment upgrade and maintenance decisions when owning and operating your own data center. Everything from physical security to power, compute, network, storage arrays, and so on. The list is seemingly endless. And these renewal dates are typically always known for budgeting purposes.

One of the very big carrots/sticks that traditional on-premise hardware vendors use to encourage you to purchase new hardware is escalating maintenance costs. For example, following a new purchase of a storage array, in Year 1 the maintenance charge from the vendor will likely be zero. However, by Year 5, it will have grown so much that it will be cheaper to buy a new array than to pay the annual maintenance bill. This "upgrade train" is never ending within your own data centers, and it consumes exorbitant time, resources, and money to maintain. It provides us with probably the most compelling case for undifferentiated heavy lifting that exists.

Taking both the annotated application timeline and these renewal data points—and any other appropriate contract of business goal inflection points—enables you to then start working with either an in-house Financial Analyst or, if you prefer, with the AWS Economics teams who have direct experience with thousands of business cases to help you build the detailed business case you will need for your CFO and key stakeholders.

AWS Migration Acceleration Program (MAP)

The AWS Migration Acceleration Program (MAP) was born from the collective learnings of thousands of migrations and is designed to help enterprises committed to a migration journey achieve a range of business benefits by migrating existing workloads to Amazon Web Services. AWS MAP has been created to provide consulting support, training, and services credits to reduce the risk of migrating to the cloud, build a strong operational foundation, and help offset the initial cost of migrations. It includes a migration methodology and tooling to automate and accelerate common migration scenarios.

MAP comprises a three-step approach for migrating to AWS:

Step 1: Migration Readiness Assessment (MRA) phase

The MRA phase determines the current state of your readiness to migrate—identifying areas where you already have strong capabilities and where further development is needed to migrate at scale. The MRA is based on the AWS Cloud Adoption Framework (CAF) and it evaluates cloud readiness along eight dimensions (landing zone, operating model, security and compliance, migration process experience, skills and center of excellence, migration plan, and business plan). Priorities and gaps identified during the assessment help define the scope for the Migration Readiness & Planning (MRP) phase. The MRA typically involves a one-day workshop conducted by AWS and/or an AWS MAP Partner.

Step 2: Migration Readiness & Planning (MRP) phase

During the Migration Readiness & Planning (MRP) phase, you will team with AWS Professional Services and/or an AWS MAP Partner to build the foundation for a large-scale migration while gaining experience migrating and operating several workloads on AWS. AWS and its AWS MAP partners have developed a prescriptive methodology and approach based on best practices gleaned from hundreds of customer migration projects that significantly reduce time to migrate while lowering cost and risk. To prepare a cloud operational foundation, you will follow an Agile approach with workstreams for Cloud Enablement Engine, Landing Zone, Target Operating Model, and security and compliance. In addition, AWS will work with you to develop a strong migration plan and compelling business case that articulates the total cost of ownership (TCO) and return on investment (ROI) for a cloud migration. At the end of this phase, which is usually completed in two to four months, you will be ready to migrate at scale.

Step 3: Migration phase

In the Migration phase, you will execute the migration plan developed during the Migration Readiness & Planning phase, typically with the assistance of AWS Professional Services and/or an AWS MAP Partner. A key component is establishing a "migration factory" composed of teams, tools, and processes to streamline the movement of workloads from on-premises to AWS. The migration factory teams work through a prioritized backlog of workloads based on migration patterns identified in the portfolio discovery and planning process. Where possible, we apply known migration and operational patterns to accelerate the movement of workloads, reduce risk, and improve the final outcome. With this approach, you will quickly start to achieve the business benefits of lower operating costs with increased agility and scalability. Once in the cloud, you can focus on optimization of applications, processes, operations, and costs. This phase typically takes 12-24 months to execute.

Ensuring the right partner and tools for migration

In our time at AWS, we have had to retrospectively engage with a few customers who have been ill advised by their incumbent partners (not AWS Certified Partners) on cloud adoption. Often, the incumbents are attempting to protect and grow their on-premise revenue. In every case, the migrations have stalled or never even started as a result of bad recommendations and lack of experience from those "partners."

Both of us were fortunate to choose "born-in-the-cloud" partners who had both the accreditation and certified practitioners, and the real work experience (always ask for customer references of previous AWS Cloud migration work) for our own journeys. Finding the right partner is literally like putting rocket fuel in the migration engine for reskilling and the momentum of moving things we talked about in the beginning of this chapter.

Migration Delivery Partners

Migration Delivery Partners help enterprises through every stage of migration—accelerating the overall process by providing personnel, tools, and education of experience engineers, developers, and migration professionals. All are continually audited and evaluated against AWS current migration best practices.

Migration tooling

In our time, we often grew weary of unkept "tool promises"—especially those software products that needed to deploy "agents" on host compute. In networks with multiple demilitarized zones (DMZs) separated by firewalls, with different operating systems and applications, it can in reality take many months if not years to fully deploy these tools. It can take even longer to get the full value out of these tools and/or have a team with knowledge of how to support and use them properly.

While "agents" aren't a bad thing, *per se*, it's a note to be wary of the time implications that could be involved.

But the truth about cloud migrations is that you simply cannot move hundreds or thousands of compute nodes and terabytes of data without appropriate tooling to relieve massive amounts of manual work. While it is beyond the scope of this book to delve too deep, AWS Professional Services or an approved AWS Partner with the migration competency can provide sage advice on tooling.

Migration tracking

Understanding how you are maintaining momentum with your migrations as well as keeping real-time tracking of important key performance indicators (KPIs) is crucial for the credibility and actual delivery of your migration.

AWS Migration Hub provides a single location to track the progress of application migrations across multiple AWS and partner solutions. It provides critical visibility into the status of migrations across your portfolio of applications. AWS Migration Hub also provides key metrics and progress for individual applications, regardless of which tools are being used to migrate them. For example, you might use AWS Database Migration Service, AWS Server Migration Service, CloudEndure Migration, and partner migration tools such as ATADATA ATAmotion or RiverMeadow Server Migration SaaS to migrate an application comprised of a database, virtualized web servers, and a bare metal server. You can view the migration progress of all the resources in the application. This allows you to quickly get progress updates across all of your migrations, easily identify and troubleshoot any issues, and reduce the overall time and effort spent on your migration projects.

Having the hub displayed prominently so that everyone can see the momentum being made on the journey is a great mechanism to inspire all on the journey.

Migration tooling for discovery and planning

Nearly every enterprise aims to keep an updated Configuration Manager Database (CMDB) of their assets. Unfortunately, they are nearly always manually updated inventories of compute and their potential applications integrations, often linked back to a change management system. In our own experience, we have yet to meet one that is 100 percent up to date, unless it is programmatically driven. Having an understanding of what you need to move is, of course, a prerequisite of a migration. Discovery tools fundamentally are aiming to a) increase your CMDB to an accurate level, and b) understand the specific application—(often network-) level interdependencies between systems so that if you migrate system x and it talks to system y through a hard-coded IP address, you know about that challenge and can remediate as you migrate.

The AWS Application Discovery Service—as well as partner tooling from ATADATA, Cloudamize, CloudHealth, Risc Networks, Turbonomic, and TSOLogic (now an AWS company)—can all help with the challenge depending on what your specific requirements are. Some tools will attempt to match your current estate with AWS EC2 equivalents with a view to assisting your business case requirements.

Migration technology for application profiling

Make sure when you move apps that you have *all* the dependencies programmatically captured, and not what people *think* they are will be crucial. Also, having the right performance data, usage, and monitoring before and after can be unbelievably valuable. Understanding how your database performed at 3:00 a.m. before migration, compared with 3:00 a.m. after migration can be extremely helpful should a potential problem arise. Many customers, including us in our prior enterprise roles, took the opportunity to "right select" their monitoring tooling to go even faster when moving to cloud. There are a multitude of SaaS monitoring tools now available to give you powerful comprehensive telemetry views of your existing application interdependencies, many of them operating without agents needing to be installed. AppDynamics, Dynatrace, and New Relic are three examples of this cohort of SaaS tools now available.

The mainframe question

The term mainframe computer was created to distinguish the tra-ditional, large, institutional computer intended to service multiple users from the smaller, single user machines. These computers are capable of handling and processing very large amounts of data quickly. Mainframe computers are used in large institutions such as government, banks and large corporations. (Source: Wikipedia)

If you are blessed with not running mainframes, you can stop reading now and skip to the next section. If, however, you still have main-frames that are central to some if not all of your processes and appli-cations, then read on.

Customers have compelling business reasons to modernize and migrate mainframe workloads to AWS Cloud. However, mainframe modernization projects often require patience, strong leadership, and a robust approach to achieve the intended ROI. Fortunately, based on our experience from successful customer modernization projects to AWS Cloud, we have identified patterns, lessons learned, and best practices that facilitate new mainframe-to-AWS initiatives.

We have found that there are many reasons customers desire to mod-ernize their mainframe workloads with AWS. First, cost reduction is a strong benefit of moving workloads from mainframes to AWS by eliminating capital expenditure and millions of instructions per second (MIPS), shrinking independent software vendor (ISV) license costs, and leveraging elastic pricing models. Second, customers gain agility with reduced development cycles via continuous integration/continuous delivery (CI/CD), and virtually unlimited infrastructure resources consumed on demand. Third, customers gain the advantage of leveraging the mainframe data, which can contain decades of business transactions and can feed data analytics or machine-learning initiatives seeking competitive differentiators. Fourth and finally, modernizing with AWS often resolves the mainframe retirement skill gap and attracts new talent to modernize core business workloads.

There is no one-size-fits-all approach for mainframe modernization to AWS Cloud. Depending on the business and IT strategy, and depending on the mainframe-specific technical constraints, customers select the pattern most suitable for them. If the mainframe is large enough to process multiple workloads, each workload's characteristics can favor different patterns. Workloads are more easily identified when they are program or data independent. Within one mainframe, a stabilized application can follow one pattern, while an evolving application can pursue another pattern. This ability to choose multiple strategies specific to the workload is how customers are most successful with the four drivers discussed above—most specifically, the business agility and skills gap.

These are the most popular and successful patterns implemented by our customers:

Pattern 1: Short-term migration with automated refactoring
Automated refactoring automates both the reverse engineering and forward engineering for transforming a legacy stack (such as COBOL-based) to a newer stack (such as Java-based or .Net-based). For efficiency and quality, there is as much automation as possible in this

transformation, but no manual rewrite of code. Typically, the resulting application follows the twelve-factor app best practices similar to Cloud-Native applications, providing elasticity, horizontal scalability, and easier integration with a wide range of AWS services.

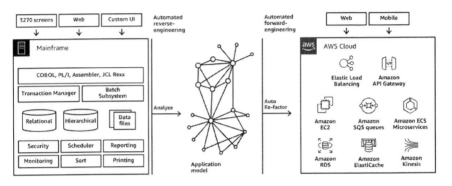

Figure 1: Short-term migration with automated refactoring

This pattern is not to be confused with language translation tools, which do basic line-by-line code conversion—for example, from procedural COBOL to procedural-like Java (sometimes called JOBOL)—which are difficult to maintain and integrate. Automated refactoring tools take a comprehensive approach by analyzing and transforming the complete legacy stack, including code, data access, data stores, frameworks, transaction subsystems, and dependency calls. It results in the automated creation of a coherent and functionally equivalent target stack, which is service oriented, service enabled, and has packaged optimizations for AWS services. It facilitates service decomposition toward the creation of microservices.

The value and differentiators of automated refactoring tools rely mainly on their automated forward-engineering capabilities. Many tools have reverse-engineering capabilities, but few have strong and extensive automation for forward engineering.

As an example, a U.S. Department of Defense customer automatically refactored a complete mainframe COBOL and C-logistics system (millions of lines of code) to Java on AWS, removing the legacy code technical debt. The APN Blog shows some automated refactoring tools with "How to Migrate Mainframe Batch to Cloud Microservices with Blu Age and AWS," and "High-Performance Mainframe Work-loads on AWS with Cloud-Native Heirloom."

Pattern 2: Short-term migration with middleware emulation

This pattern is a replatform to a middleware emulator that runs on AWS Cloud. With this approach, the legacy application code is ported to the emulator with as few code changes as possible, retaining and requiring the same application maintenance and development skills. This migration is seamless from an end-user perspective, keeping the same interfaces, look, and feel of the application.

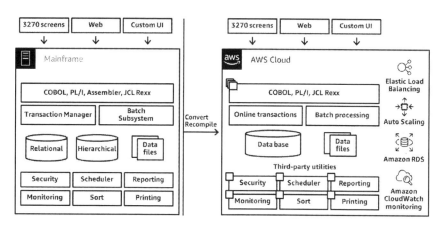

Figure 2: Short-term migration with middleware emulation

Typically, supported source code is recompiled, while unsupported language code is first converted to a supported language and then recompiled. Code changes or refactoring are necessary to integrate with differing third-party utility interfaces or when modernizing the data store and data access along the way. For this pattern, the tools include the middleware emulator, the compiler, as well as all the utilities required to automate the programs and data migration.

This pattern is often seen as an intermediate step within a larger modernization journey, or a target state for stabilized applications. As an example, a multinational beverage company used a middleware emulator on AWS to recreate and migrate the batch mode and online transaction processing capabilities while offering the same mainframe green-screen experience. The AWS website shows some middleware emulator tools with "Micro Focus Enterprise Server on AWS Quick Start," "Re-Hosting Mainframe Applications to AWS with NTT DATA Services," and "Migrating a Mainframe to AWS in 5 Steps with Astadia."

Pattern 3: Augmentation with data analytics

This pattern is not about migrating workloads but about augmenting mainframes with Agile data analytics services on AWS. Mainframe data, which can include decades of historical business transactions for massive amounts of users, is a strong business advantage. Therefore, customers use big-data analytics to unleash mainframe data's business value. Compared to mainframe alternatives, customers using AWS's big-data services gain faster analytics capabilities and can create a data lake to mix structured and unstructured data, giving them a much more comprehensive view of the company data assets.

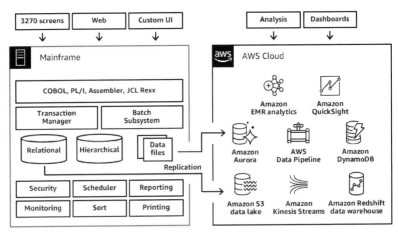

Figure 3: Augmentation with data analytics

AWS provides services for the full data lifecycle, from ingestion, to processing, storage, analysis, visualization, and automation. Replication tools copy mainframe data in real time, from the mainframe's relational, hierarchical, or legacy file-based data stores to Agile AWS data lakes, data warehouses, or data stores. This real-time data replication keeps the data fresh, allowing for up-to-date analytics and dashboards while keeping the mainframe as the source of record.

As an example, a United States passenger railroad corporation enabled mainframe data using real-time dashboards and reporting for sales, marketing, revenue, and fraud analytics, following the patterns described in this section. The AWS APN Blog shows a real-time data replication tool with "How to Unleash Mainframe Data with AWS and Attunity Replicate" and "Real-Time Mainframe Data Replication to AWS with tcVISION from Treehouse Software."

Pattern 4: Augmentation with new channels
Because mainframe development cycles with legacy languages are slow and rigid, customers use AWS to build new services quickly while accessing real-time mainframe data in local AWS data stores. This is a variation of Pattern 3, where the local mainframe data is not used for analytics but for new communication channels and new functionalities for end users. The new AWS Agile functions augment the legacy mainframe applications. Examples of new channels can be mobile or voice-based applications, and can be innovations based on microservices or machine learning.

This pattern avoids increasing the expensive mainframe MIPS by deploying new channels on AWS. Because data is duplicated, the data architect needs to be careful about potential data consistency or integrity concerns across the mainframe and AWS data stores.

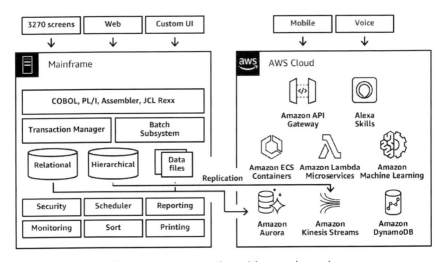

Figure 4: Augmentation with new channels

As an example, a large United States commercial bank developed new AWS Lambda-based serverless microservices on AWS, accessing replicated mainframe data in Amazon DynamoDB, and made these new services available to mobile users via Amazon API Gateway. Tools for this pattern are similar to Pattern 3 tools, which perform real-time data replication from legacy data stores or from mainframe messaging systems.

Best Practices

Learning from the experience of past projects, customers, and partners, AWS continuously develops and improves mainframe-to-AWS best practices. These include:

- **Complex proof of concept (POC)**—Projects can fail when selected tools are not able to address the most complex technical aspects of a mainframe workload. In order to reduce risks, customers have to request a complex POC, evaluating the tool capabilities with the most challenging customer-specific scenarios. It does not mean the POC scope needs to be large, but it means the few POC test cases need to be of highest complexity. Depending on the customer mainframe workload, complexity can reside in batch duration, numerous program and data dependencies, complicated logic, uncommon legacy technology or versions, latency requirements, high throughput or transactions per second, or large quantities of code or data. A complex POC validates the tool's abilities, shows the quality of the tool's outcome, and reassures both the tool vendor and the customer for a successful collaboration.

- **Maximum automation**—Mainframes typically host millions of lines of code and petabytes of data. Human intervention increases errors, risks, tests, duration, and cost. Consequently, short-term modernization projects use proven software stacks along with as much automation as possible without manual rewriting: automation for applying migration rules, automation for code refactoring, automation for data modernization, and automation for tests execution (CI/CD pipeline).

- **Decide pattern, then tool, then architecture, then activities**— The pattern frames the overall approach, with different sets of tools for each pattern. The tool is a critical success factor for mainframe modernization and must be technically tested with a complex POC as early as possible. Once the tool is validated, the overall architecture is created based on the tool and AWS best practices. The technical architecture then drives the modernization implementation activities.

- **Vendor-neutral pattern selection**—There is no one-size-fits-all and no one-tool-fits-all for mainframe modernization. Tool vendors tend to focus on only one pattern. There are also multiple vendors and multiple tools for each pattern. Consequently, pattern selection should be vendor agnostic, driven by the customer's business and IT strategy priorities, and by the customer's mainframe stack technical constraints.

- **System integrators selection**—Consulting and system integrator services firms can help to various degrees during all phases of the mainframe modernization project to AWS. Some system integrators specialize in only one pattern and one preferred tool, while others cover multiple patterns and multiple tools per pattern. Before selecting a modernization tool, consulting professional services should be pattern neutral and vendor neutral in order to advance the customer's best interest and not a system integrator's specialty with one specific tool. On the other hand, once a tool is selected by the customer system integrator, professional services should have expertise in the selected mainframe modernization tool and in AWS. Because of the different skillsets involved (consulting, mainframe, AWS, modernization, tools, integration, tests), it is common to see a combination of teams or professional services companies engaged.
- **Modernize legacy data stores**—Keeping legacy data stores, such as hierarchical databases or indexed data files, on AWS also keeps legacy technical debt and constraints, such as single points of failure, bottlenecks, or archaic data models and interfaces. For any pattern, modernizing the data store and the data access layer is typically a smaller investment, providing larger benefits for scalability, availability, agility, operations, skills, cost reduction, data integration, and new functions development.
- **Workload-based modernization**—For large mainframes hosting multiple independent workloads, each workload can follow a different modernization pattern.
- **Serialize technical then business-level modernizations**—Tools are typically optimized for quick technical modernizations. Doing business-level changes or refactoring requires manual interventions, involvement of business teams, and prevents the performance of some functional equivalence tests between the mainframe and AWS. As a result, mixing business and technical modernizations at the same time increases complexity, duration, risks, and costs.

- **Define tool evaluation factors**—For example: legacy technical stack support, complex POC success, IT strategy alignment,
project speed (such as the number of lines of code migrated per
month), target application stack agility, target data store agility,
target code maintainability, migration cost per line of code, target stack license costs, and return on investment (ROI) speed.
- **Estimate modernization and runtime costs**—Modernization
costs include both the licensing cost for the tools used during
modernization, along with professional services costs required
for delivering the modernization activities. Furthermore, target architecture recurring runtime costs are key, as they directly
impact the ROI speed. Runtime costs include both tool licensing
costs (if any) and the AWS service costs. For example, if a customer
makes an 80 percent reduction in annual recurring runtime costs,
the modernization cost could be recouped after three years, generating significant savings onward for new investments.

Next steps for mainframe migrations

Customers modernize mainframes leveraging AWS. AWS patterns,
best practices, and partners facilitate these initiatives. The AWS team
is glad to assist with many aspects of mainframe modernization initiatives. To get started, we suggest taking the following actions:

1. Collect the mainframe technical architecture along with the
   business and IT priorities.

2. Understand possible AWS modernization patterns and decide
   which is the preferred one.

3. Identify tools and vendors best supporting the selected pattern and the mainframe characteristics.

4. Evaluate the tool's value propositions and confirm the selection with a complex proof of concept.

To learn more about mainframe-to-AWS capabilities, feel free to reach out and review the AWS Partner value propositions on the <u>APN Blog mainframe section</u>. AWS also has similar patterns and best practices for non-x86 legacy systems including AS/400, OpenVMS, or UNIX proprietary systems.

A sincere thank you to our Amazonian colleague Phil de Valence for his mainframe expertise and experience, and for letting us borrow from his amazing blogs.

5.5 USING THE AWS WELL-ARCHITECTED FRAMEWORK

"Success is neither magical nor mysterious. Success is the natural conse-quence of consistently applying basic fundamentals."
– JIM ROHN

Ensuring you can use the 175+ AWS services in a consistent, repeat-able, and well-architected way will give you a sure and repeatable foundation to build upon. How do you do this? And more important, how do you ensure that your teams can do this?

There are millions of customers using AWS today. Their combined experience—and the experience of AWS's Solutions Architecture, Pro-Serve, and Product Owners and Partners—has been poured into the AWS Well-Architected Framework. This is a living, documented set of best practices that is continually and relentlessly tuned and refined to provide the very best pragmatic guidance to help you build.

Creating a software system is a lot like constructing a building. If the foundation is not solid, structural problems can undermine the integ-rity and function of the building. In the worst case, it can unexpect-edly collapse.

When architecting technology solutions on AWS, if you neglect the five pillars of operational excellence, security, reliability, performance efficiency, and cost optimization, it can become challenging to build a system that delivers on your expectations and requirements. Incorporating these five pillars into your architecture, however, helps produce stable and efficient systems. This allows you to focus on the other aspects of design, such as functional requirements.

The advantages of the AWS Well-Architected Framework are fourfold.

1. It allows your teams to build and deploy faster and avoid common mistakes

2. You are continually and actively lowering or mitigating risks

3. You are making informed decisions, knowing the tradeoffs if you use component x rather than y

4. Your teams will continually learn current best practices, so your design patterns will continually pivot to the best they can be

From our experience, it is very reassuring to effectively have the bases covered with a Well-Architected review as you move to cloud. You should find the right cadence that suits you as to when to do this. From experience, we can share that having a Well-Architected review that supports your standard design review cadence or before initiating a major change could become a very useful part of your risk management practice. The Well-Architected reviews can be conducted by AWS Solutions Architects or via AWS Well-Architected Accredited Partners.

The five pillars

As you can see from the previous page's illustration, the AWS Well-Architected Framework is comprised of five pillars:

- Operational excellence
- Security

AWS Well-Architected

Operational Excellence

Prepare

OPS 1—Operation priorities
OPS 2—Design for workload insights
OPS 3—Development and Integration
OPS 4—Mitigation of deployment risks
OPS 5—Operational readiness

Operate

OPS 6—Workload health
OPS 7—Operations health
OPS 8—Event response

Evolve

OPS 9—Operations evolution

Security

Identify Access Management

SEC 1—Credential management
SEC 2—Human access
SEC 3—Programmatic access

Detective Controls

SEC 4—Security events
SEC 5—Security awareness

Infrastructure Protection

SEC 6—Network protection
SEC 7—Compute protection

Data Protection

SEC 8—Data classification
SEC 9—Data protection at rest
SEC 10—Data protection in transit

Incident Response

SEC 11—Incident response

Reliability

Foundation

REL 1—Credential management
REL 2—Human access

Change Management

REL 3—Demand handling
REL 4—Resource monitoring
REL 5—Change management

Failure Management

SEC 6—Data backup
SEC 7—Resiliency implementation
SEC 8—Resiliency testing
SEC 9—Disaster recovery

Performance Efficiency

Selection

PERF 1—Architecture selection
PERF 2—Compute selection
PERF 3—Storage selection
PERF 4—Database selection
PERF 5—Networking selection

Review

PERF 6—Evolving architecture

Monitoring

PERF 7—Monitor performance

Tradeoffs

PERF 8—Performance tradeoffs

Cost Optimization

Expenditure Awareness

COST 1—Usage governance
COST 2—Usage and cost monitoring
COST 3—Resource decommissioning

Cost-Effective Resources

COST 4—Service selection
COST 5—Resource type and size selection
COST 6—Pricing model selection
COST 7—Data transfer planning

Matching Supply & Demand

COST 8—Matching supply with demand

Optimizing Over Time

COST 9—New service evaluation

- Reliability
- Performance efficiency
- Cost optimization

Let's take a look at each pillar in turn.

1. Operational excellence

The operational excellence pillar includes the ability to run and monitor systems to deliver business value and continually improve supporting processes and procedures. You can find prescriptive guidance on implementation in the Operational Excellence Pillar whitepaper.

Design principles
There are six design principles for operational excellence in the cloud:

- Perform operations as code
- Annotate documentation
- Make frequent, small, reversible changes
- Refine operations procedures frequently
- Anticipate failure
- Learn from all operational failures

Best practices
Operations teams need to understand their business and customer needs so they can support business outcomes. Ops creates and uses procedures to respond to operational events, and validates their effectiveness to support business needs. Ops also collects metrics that are used to measure the achievement of desired business outcomes.

Everything continues to change—your business context, business priorities, customer needs, and so on. It's important to design operations to support evolution over time in response to change and to incorporate lessons learned through their performance.

2. Security
The security pillar includes the ability to protect information, systems, and assets while delivering business value through risk assessments and mitigation strategies. You can find prescriptive guidance on implementation in the Security Pillar whitepaper. We cover security in great depth in Chapter 7.1 Security Is Always Job Zero.

Design principles

There are six design principles for security in the cloud:

- Implement a strong identity foundation
- Enable traceability
- Apply security at all layers
- Automate security best practices
- Protect data in transit and at rest
- Keep people away from data
- Prepare for security events

Best practices

Before you architect any system, you need to put in place security practices. You will, for example, want to control who can do what when and where. In addition, you want to be able to identify security incidents, protect your systems and services, and maintain the confidentiality and integrity of data through data protection.

You should have a well-defined and practiced process for responding to security incidents. These tools and techniques are important because they support objectives such as preventing financial loss or complying with regulatory obligations. The AWS Shared Responsibility Model enables organizations to achieve security and compliance goals. AWS is responsible for protecting the infrastructure that supports the company's cloud services, while customer responsibility will be determined by the AWS Cloud services that a customer selects. This determines the amount of configuration work the customer must perform as part of their security responsibilities.

3. Reliability

The reliability pillar includes the ability of a system to recover from infrastructure or service disruptions, dynamically acquire computing resources to meet demand, and mitigate disruptions such as misconfigurations or transient network issues. You can find prescriptive guidance on implementation in the Reliability Pillar whitepaper.

Design principles

There are five design principles for reliability in the cloud:

- Test recovery procedures
- Automatically recover from failure
- Scale horizontally to increase aggregate system availability
- Stop guessing capacity
- Manage change in automation

Best practices

To achieve reliability, a system must have a well-planned foundation and monitoring in place, with mechanisms for handling changes in demand or requirements. The system should be designed to detect failure and automatically heal itself.

Before architecting any system, foundational requirements that influence reliability should be in place. For example, you must have sufficient network bandwidth to your data center. These requirements are sometimes neglected, often because they are beyond a single project's scope. This neglect can have a significant impact on the ability to deliver a reliable system. In an on-premises environment, these requirements can cause long lead times due to dependencies and therefore must be incorporated during initial planning.

With AWS, most of these foundational requirements are already incorporated or may be addressed as needed. The cloud is designed to be essentially limitless, so it is the responsibility of AWS to satisfy the requirement for sufficient networking and compute capacity, while you are free to change resource size and allocation, such as the size of storage devices, on demand.

4. Performance Efficiency

The performance efficiency pillar includes the ability to use computing resources efficiently to meet system requirements and to maintain that efficiency as demand changes and technologies evolve. You can find prescriptive guidance on implementation in the Performance Efficiency Pillar whitepaper.

Design principles

There are five design principles for performance efficiency in the cloud:

- Democratize advanced technologies
- Go global in minutes
- Use serverless architectures
- Experiment more often
- Mechanical sympathy

Best practices

Take a data-driven approach to selecting a high-performance architecture. Gather data on all aspects of the architecture, from high-level design to the selection and configuration of resource types.

By reviewing your choices on a cyclical basis, you will ensure you are taking advantage of the continually evolving AWS Cloud. Monitoring will ensure you are aware of any deviance from expected performance and can take action on it.

Finally, your architecture can make tradeoffs to improve performance, such as using compression or caching, or relaxing consistency requirements.

The optimal solution for a particular system will vary based on the kind of workload you have, often with multiple approaches combined. Well-architected systems use multiple solutions and enable different features to improve performance.

5. Cost Optimization

The cost optimization pillar includes the ability to avoid or eliminate unneeded cost or suboptimal resources. You can find prescriptive guidance on implementation in the Cost Optimization Pillar whitepaper.

Design principles

There are five design principles for cost optimization in the cloud:

- Adopt a consumption model
- Measure overall efficiency
- Stop spending money on data center operations
- Analyze and attribute expenditure
- Use managed services to reduce cost of ownership

Best practices

As with the other pillars, there are tradeoffs to consider. For example, do you want to optimize for speed to market or for cost? In some cases, it's best to optimize for speed—going to market quickly, shipping new features, or simply meeting a deadline—rather than investing in upfront cost optimization.

Design decisions are sometimes guided by haste as opposed to empirical data, as the temptation always exists to overcompensate "just in case" rather than spend time benchmarking for the most cost-optimal deployment. This often leads to drastically over-provisioned and under-optimized deployments.

Using the appropriate instances and resources for your system is key to cost savings. For example, a reporting process might take five hours to run on a smaller server but one hour to run on a larger server that is twice as expensive. Both servers give you the same outcome, but the smaller one will incur more cost over time. A Well-Architected system will use the most cost-effective resources, which can have a significant and positive economic impact.

Final thought

The AWS Well-Architected Framework provides architectural best practices across the five pillars for designing and operating reliable, secure, efficient, and cost-effective systems in the cloud. The framework provides a set of questions that allows you to review an existing or proposed architecture. It also provides a set of AWS best practices for each pillar.

Ultimately, it's a fundamentally important framework to ensure that your teams and partners are building in the best way possible. We strongly advise you build it in as part of your run books.

With thanks to the Well-Architected team.

PART 6
DATA AND INTELLIGENCE

6.1 CLOUD DATABASES & ANALYTICS

"In God we trust. All others must bring data."

– W. EDWARDS DEMING

Data is the new oil, or so the cliché goes. However, data has always been valuable, and organizations have always found new ways to leverage data to create value.

Most large enterprises have preserved a quasi-archeological record of data-management technology dating back to the 1960s. Thomas cut his teeth in IT on a mainframe managing and analyzing data stored in flat files. We routinely meet with executives who want to know how to migrate their vintage AS/400s into the cloud. These were first introduced in 1988, while many of the subroutines still running on these venerable workhorses were written in COBOL, which was introduced in 1959.

The first workable version of a relational database (Oracle 2.3) was released in 1979, beating IBM to the punch, which released its first RDBMS called SQL/DS in 1981. DB2 soon followed in 1983, and SQL Server was introduced five years later.

The 1990s ushered in the age of the data warehouse under the intellectual leadership of Bill Inmon. In 1998, Thomas worked on one of his first transformation team projects: to implement a standard US Congressional report on the statistics of military personnel from a flat file system into an OLAP system. Around the same time, Ralph Kimball popularized the architectural patterns of star schemas and data marts, which are still prevalent in many enterprise data architectures today.

The term "big data" first appeared in a 1999 paper published by the Association for Computing Machinery (ACM) titled, "Visually Exploring Gigabyte Datasets in Real Time," which lamented the lack of adequate compute power to analyze the amount of data that could be stored. The Defense Manpower Data Center (DMDC), where Thomas worked at the time, celebrated reaching 1TB of data stored that same year!

In software engineering, multitier architecture (often referred to as n-tier architecture) or multilayered architecture is a client–server architecture in which presentation, application processing, and data management functions are physically separated. The most widespread use of multitier architecture is the three-tier architecture. (Source: Wikipedia)

N-tier architectures made use of the ability to store and retrieve data from a centralized data store. This has been the predominant architectural pattern for more than 30 years, and for good reason. The success of this pattern is at the root of the challenge that was supposed to be addressed by business intelligence (BI). The proliferation of systems and applications with disparate data stores resulted in enterprises wanting to correlate data across these disparate systems. Since data was stored in many different formats, and database schemas were based on divergent business rules and assumptions, trying to correlate data became a core task for entire departments. Companies invested in big iron data warehouse and BI appliances such as IBM Netezza, Oracle Exadata, or Teradata to name a few. These required significant expertise and planning in order to manage the high cost, complexity, and overhead of the extract, transform, and load (ETL) processes.

With the rampant growth of new data sources, and the explosion of data volumes, the appliances were soon found to be too expensive to scale, and teams were forced to make tough choices on which data to load and process.

Loading and transporting data emerged as an additional challenge, with institutions moving large amounts of "batched" data across networks into systems to be processed during off hours. The continued growth of data volumes has presented these batch processes with a natural limit, where more data has to be moved and processed than can reasonably be accomplished in the available time, usually at night, when transactional volumes decline to a fraction of daytime activity.

Since 2005, new technologies have emerged to address what came to be known as the "big data challenge." Approaches included MapReduce and Hadoop, data streaming, and NoSQL databases.

Data governance has also become more complex over time. Who has access to what data under which circumstance has always been a challenge. Compliance regulations (and good practice) require the understanding of data provenance. Where did the data come from, who has had access, and how has it been transformed?

Enterprises have accreted this hodgepodge of data management solutions and are still trying to find a way forward, where they can unlock the value of the new "oil" and provide better solutions to their customers.

Since 2006, AWS has been working on solving the pain points related to this data conundrum.

> *Polyglot programming [is] the idea that applications should be written in a mix of languages to take advantage of the fact that different languages are suitable for tackling different problems.*

In 2006, Neal Ford of ThoughtWorks coined the term "polyglot programming," and soon thereafter, thought leaders started to think about polyglot database models and polyglot persistence. In essence, this simply means using the best tool for the job. So, a web cache layer would be better served by, let's say, Redis than an RDBMS, while a social network data store might be best implemented as a graph in Neo4J or Amazon Neptune. Of course, the side effect of this newer architectural pattern is a further proliferation of siloed data.

Although social media had existed in nascent form with bulletin board services and AOL in the '90s, social media really came to the fore in 2006 when Twitter and Facebook emerged in the public sphere. Data streams have been growing at astronomical rates ever since, and not only social media streams, but also streams generated by the explosion of connected devices and sensors in every domain, in the most inaccessible regions of the earth, and increasingly, in space.

Let's regroup for a minute. We had been presented with some of these challenges in our previous roles within enterprises. Of particular importance were the many customer-facing applications that, following the venerable n-tier design, had an underlying database that stored customer and transaction data. Of course, every application had its own schema, and business rules defined customers and their identities in subtly different ways. When the CFO wanted to know details about transaction volumes by unique customers, we were hard pressed to furnish an answer. Worse, depending on who analyzed the cleansed and collated data, the CFO might get different answers. And even when pressed, teams could not declare absolute truth with any certainty. Why? Because merging data catalogued under different underlying business rules is incredibly hard. How do you guarantee that two accounts in two different applications belong to the same person? Is it as simple as matching first and last name? What if they used two different email addresses? What if they connected from two different IP addresses? This becomes a very difficult problem very quickly.

The inverse challenge presented by many discreet databases comes in the form of large centralized databases. Monolithic applications come with large and complex databases, often with business logic buried deep within the RDMBS—typically in the form of stored procedures. A common pattern had been to create new applications and new functionality by expanding the existing monolithic database. This continuous accretion of tables, materialized views, stored procedures, and connection pools serving a variety of endpoints has led to database implementations that are as convoluted and complicated as monolithic applications. Database experts are often afraid to make changes, much less refactor or migrate these database Borg cubes.

Part of the universe of Star Trek, the Borg cube is one of the most formidable alien technologies known to the Federation. Its lack of identifiable function spaces — such as a bridge, engineering, or personnel quarters — reveals the hive-like Borg collective consciousness and its drones.

And these kinds of challenges exist across many business domains. Whether in marketing, supply chain management, oil and gas exploration, education, or government systems, we often hear that a re-architecture of these systems would cost tens of millions of dollars and take five years to complete. And this is only if no new requirements are added. Good luck with that!

Yet, there is a way forward. Increasingly, organizations are collecting all their data—structured and unstructured, which commonly represents 80 percent of the data of an organization—in a data lake. The data lake then serves as a staging environment to load data into right-sized data stores, or it can be queried directly by increasingly powerful and simple-to-use tools. Efficiencies in terms of cost, performance, and resilience can be achieved simply by migrating into the cloud. Before we embark on a further examination of what this looks like, lets declare a few tenets of managing and analyzing data in the cloud.

Principles

Operational excellence through data—We must ensure databases are operational to support business needs. We ensure security, availability, and usability in that order.

Never constrain the business—Database services are focused on enabling the organization to meet business objectives. We will never constrain the business as a result of changes in our database technologies or services.

Be a force multiplier—Enable self-service functionality whenever possible. Empower teams to leverage data without the help of the database team.

Be transparent—We will share everyone's mutual success, failures, and lessons learned across the wider community.

Never change existing critical data—Only change derived information.

Protect the source—Maintain source data in its original form and quality, and maintain data provenance.

Fix data problems at the source—We reveal data problems so they can be addressed at the source.

Use the right tool for the job—And keep it as simple as possible

Expose data through APIs—All teams will henceforth expose their data and functionality through service interfaces.

Data access only via API—Teams must communicate with each other through these interfaces.

Get the code out of the Database—Do not use and remove stored procedures whenever possible.

ACTION STEPS

There are a variety of actions you can take to democratize data. Here are the steps that we have seen to have efficacy.

Step 1: Build a data lake

A data lake is a single platform combining storage, data governance, and analytics. So, what should it do?

1. Ingest and store data from a wide variety of sources into a centralized platform.

2. Build a comprehensive data catalog to find and use data assets stored in the data lake.

3. Secure, protect, and manage all of the data stored in the data lake.

4. Use tools and policies to monitor, analyze, and optimize infrastructure and data.

5. Transform raw data assets in place into optimized usable formats.

6. Query data assets in place.

7. Use a broad and deep portfolio of data analytics, data science, machine learning, and visualization tools.

8. Quickly integrate current and future third-party data-processing tools.

9. Easily and securely share processed datasets and results.

We have had customers tell us that creating a data lake is too hard, and that getting the data out of the many data silos is nearly impossible. Until recently, a data lake had been more concept than reality. Setting up and managing data lakes involves manual, complicated, and time-consuming tasks. This work includes loading data from diverse sources, monitoring those data flows, setting up partitions, turning on encryption and managing keys, defining transformation jobs and monitoring their operation, reorganizing data into a columnar format, configuring access control settings, deduplicating redundant data, matching linked records, granting access to data sets, and auditing access over time.

Thankfully, this task is no longer as difficult as it once was. Creating a data lake with AWS Lake Formation is as simple as defining where your data resides and what data access and security policies you want to apply. AWS Lake Formation then collects and catalogs data from databases and object storage, moves the data into your new Amazon Simple Storage Service (S3) data lake, cleans and classifies data using machine-learning algorithms, and secures access to your sensitive data. The beauty of Amazon S3 is that you can store any kind of data from virtually any source. Amazon S3 can easily support the largest petabyte-scale collection of data.

Says Joshua Couch, VP Engineering at Fender Digital,

We are generating tons of user and usage data from our digital applications and devices. We are planning to build a data lake on AWS to operate alongside our Amazon Redshift-based data warehouse. I can't wait for my team to get our hands on AWS Lake Formation. Lake Formation will make it easy for us to load, transform, and catalog our data and make it securely available within our organization, across a wide portfolio of AWS services. With an enterprise-ready option like Lake Formation, we will be able to spend more time deriving value from our data rather than doing the heavy lifting involved in manually setting up and managing our data lake.

There are several additional options to moving large amounts of data into your data lake, including connecting to AWS Kinesis Data Firehose, physically shipping 80-100TB of data at a time using an AWS Snowball, or by employing an AWS Storage Gateway, which offers on-premises devices, applications, and network file share via an NFS connection. Files written to this mount point are converted to objects stored in Amazon S3 in their original format without any proprietary modification.

Transactional data stored in an RDBMs is typically the smallest source of data. Which system administrator has never experienced crashing a system because they ran out of disk space overflowing with log files? Both of us have had to explain this "event" to irate business stakeholders while in our previous careers. Modern application architectures make use of this constant stream of logs to perform performance and security analysis.

Organizations collect vast amounts of what is known as **dark data** just in case it may be useful someday. Sometimes the business need is to maintain data for reasons of regulatory oversight, other times, IT stores data to be used in root cause analysis after a failure occurs. This collection of data is unstructured, unorganized, and typically represents a cost without yielding any obvious value.

Take, for example, all the data that is collected in issue tracking systems, or the data that is collected by call centers, or the customer comments that can be left on the websites of many companies. The data is collected and may be analyzed in discreet instances, for example, during a call center interaction with a representative. Once the immediate problem has been dealt with, the collected data typically ceases to have value.

However, dark data such as these can still have tremendous value. Using machine-learning tools such as Amazon Comprehend, this dark data can now be rendered useful. You could, for example, dive deep into what topics most commonly come up in customer complaints, or the sentiment of people leaving comments. The possibilities are nearly unlimited.

Streaming data is now the single largest source of data ingest. In addition to streaming log files, most organizations stream social media data, IoT device data, sensor data, clickstream, and other user-behavior data, to name a few sources. Then, there are industry-specific data sources such as weather, genomic, pharmaceutical, energy production and distribution, and many more. While much of this data can be analyzed in near-real time and discarded, enormous amounts of data are stored to yield further insights using machine learning and other advanced data analytics.

A data lake based on Amazon S3 and leveraging AWS and marketplace services offers some pretty amazing capabilities. There are use cases where it makes sense to store source data in its original raw form as an immutable object, either because there is an evidentiary requirement, or because there is valuable information hidden in the raw data that can only be unlocked over time. Whether you need to keep the raw data or not, a best practice is to preprocess data for further analysis. This preprocessing step is referred to as "extract-transform-load" (ETL), and it does just that. You extract the valuable bits, which are "cleansed" and transformed into a format that is more easily used or analyzed, and then this transformed data is loaded into another object store in Amazon S3 or directly into a database construct. At this stage, data may also be "enriched" by blending in additional data sources, or by extrapolating missing data.

AWS Glue was developed as an ETL service that automates data discovery, conversion, and job scheduling tasks. AWS Glue crawls your Amazon S3 data, identifies data formats, and then suggests schemas for use with other AWS analytic services. One common format used to facilitate further analysis is Apache Parquet, which organizes data in columnar format to reduce file size and improve query performance, both of which reduce the operating costs of your solution.

One of the many reasons we became AWS converts is the continuous innovation based on customer feedback and requests. One such request was to make data analytics easier and cheaper. Structured Query Language (SQL) is one of the fundamental IT skillsets large organizations have cultivated in their employees. AWS offers new ways to make use of data, but rather than supplanting the existing skills of an organization, AWS also offers ways to benefit from the existing skillsets in the organization. You can query and analyze data stored in your data lake in raw or columnar formats using standard SQL. This is possible due to the introduction of Amazon Athena, an on-demand query service that requires no infrastructure management.

At some point you may need to archive data, which we used to manage by physically shipping tape to secure archival facilities. Amazon S3 Glacier allows you to archive large amounts of data at a very low cost. This makes it feasible to retain all the data you want for use cases like data lakes, analytics, IoT, machine learning, compliance, and media asset archiving. To simplify retrieval, Amazon S3 Glacier allows you to query data in place and retrieve only the subset of data you need from within an archive.

Step 2: Create mechanisms for data governance
Data governance is frequently one of those implied disciplines. Many organizations do not have an explicit data governance process. Database administrators and/or business intelligence analysts might strive to create a data governance model because it is practical. Other organizations—financial institutions come to mind—must have a data governance policy, and they spend a great deal of money and effort to create and enforce policies that clearly define who can use what data for what purpose.

So, what is needed to effectively govern the creation and use of data? For one thing, you need to know what data you have. Where and how is it stored? Who can access data, and under what circumstances? How is data protected, and how and when is data destroyed? Can you prove that data has in fact been destroyed?

In the past, whoever was charged with answering these questions would start with the native capabilities of the individual databases that contained data. That approach didn't solve how to manage across multiple different data stores, so organizations invested in add-on tools that were superimposed or bolted onto the existing systems. But that was insufficient, since you still had to manage the movement of data between systems and between producers and consumers of data. So, we bolted on even more solutions, to encrypt and decrypt, to secure the network, to protect endpoints (remember the workaround using USB sticks as an "air gap?"), to understand usage patterns, and ultimately, to find signals in the vast noise of data streaming through all systems all the time in an effort to find patterns of unauthorized access or usage.

Sound complicated? It is—and expensive. Thankfully, by leveraging a fully integrated ecosystem of tools and technologies that surround the AWS data lake, this complexity becomes much easier to manage.

We've already spoken about Amazon Glue, which you can use to discover and catalog what data you have. Glue creates a data catalog and automatically creates schema for that data in the form of an Apache Hive Metastore. Using ODBC and JDBC connections, you can then connect to visualization tools such as PowerBi or Tableau.

Managing access within AWS is also extremely powerful. Using AWS Identity and Access Management (IAM), data access can be managed at a granular level. You can define security policy-based rules for your users and applications by role. Once the rules are defined, AWS Lake Formation enforces your access controls at table- and column-level granularity for users of Amazon Redshift Spectrum, Amazon Athena, and Amazon EMR (for Apache Spark.) AWS Glue access is enforced at the table level and is typically for administrators only. Amazon EMR users of Apache Spark can also be authenticated through Active Directory (AD) integration.

You also have the ability to designate data owners, such as data stewards and business units, by adding a field in table properties as custom attributes. Your owners can augment the technical metadata with business metadata that further defines appropriate uses for the data. You can specify appropriate use cases and label the sensitivity of your data for enforcement by using AWS Lake Formation security and access controls. Your data governance mechanism can make use of audit logs managed with AWS CloudTrail to monitor access and show compliance with centrally defined policies. You can audit data access history across analytics and machine learning services that read the data in your data lake. This lets you see which users, roles, or groups have attempted to access what data, with which services, and when.

Step 3: Utilize AWS Batch

Most enterprises will continue to leverage existing legacy systems until the time is right to modernize the last vestiges of these aging systems. Based on the historical limitations, legacy systems required the collection of data over some time interval, often a single day, and sometimes weeks or months. Another reason for batch processing was the cyclical nature of reporting requirements, such as a quarterly business review. AWS offers choices on how to manage batch processing, including open source and commercial solutions. And, of course, AWS offers a cloud-scale solution called AWS Batch, which manages all the infrastructure for you, avoiding the complexities of provisioning, managing, monitoring, and scaling your batch computing jobs.

One of the features we find particularly compelling is the ability to automatically bid on spot instances to drive down the cost of batch processing. If there is no business requirement for near-real time data processing, this capability provides the best of both worlds—asynchronous data processing *and* the compute spot market.

Step 4: Use microservices when possible
"Smart end points and dumb pipes." – Martin Fowler

One of the cringeworthy comments we still hear way too often is that companies are building multiple microservices that point to a shared data store. Of course, this is an architectural foul since a microservice by definition is supposed to be loosely coupled and independent— enabling a single Two-Pizza Team to manage everything needed for that service.

A shared data store is an anti-pattern for several reasons. First, the microservices are no longer loosely coupled, and second, the data model has to support multiple services. Or, as Werner Vogels, CTO of Amazon, has stated in the past, "Shared resources became shared obstacles, compromising speed." Instead, microservices should be built using their own data store, even if this sounds like heresy to a data architect schooled in the finer details of normalizing (and then de-normalizing it for performance) an underlying database.

> *Architectural note: This means in effect that the data store should be designed as simply as possible for each microservice. Microservices represent a different kind of complexity than traditional system architecture describes. While some microservices require create, read, update, and delete (CRUD) operations, the more common use case will benefit from Command Query Responsibility Segregation (CQRS).*

Step 5: Use the right database for the job
By picking the best database to solve a specific problem or a group of problems, you can break away from restrictive one-size-fits-all monolithic databases and focus on building applications to meet the needs of your business. AWS provides a large palette of purpose-built database options while enabling you to select third-party and/or open source database options as well. The selection of the database is based entirely on the specific use case.

If your business use case requires atomicity, consistency, isolation, and durability (ACID) transactions to maintain referential integrity and data consistency, then Amazon RDS or Amazon Aurora are great options. If you need data warehousing capability, then Amazon Redshift offers what is required.

If, on the other hand, you need to store and retrieve key-value pairs in large volumes and in milliseconds, or you need to store semi-structured data as documents, then Amazon DynamoDB is a great choice.

Some applications require real-time access to data. Amazon ElastiCache stores data directly in memory and provides microsecond latency.

Some data use cases are best served by representing data as a graph, such as applications that need to enable millions of users to query and navigate relationships between highly connected datasets with millisecond latency. Amazon Neptune provides this capability.

Telemetry applications, as well as DevOps and IoT-related applications, need to analyze data across time, and for these cases AWS has developed Amazon Timestream.

Systems of record, supply chain, registrations, and banking transactions are all use cases in which organizations are exploring distributed ledger technology (DLT) as a possible solution. DLT, however, has inherent scalability and performance limitations that make this an impractical approach. For this reason, AWS has developed Amazon Quantum Ledger Database (QLDB), which provides a scalable and performant solution for use cases that require a centralized, trusted authority to maintain complete and cryptographically verifiable record of transactions.

We fully expect AWS to continue to develop additional purpose-built database solutions in the future, as more enterprise customers identify additional use cases that are poorly served by the predominant paradigm of the past 30 years—the relational database. There remains a need for a traditional RDBMS, but modern architectures benefit from the more nuanced data management approach AWS has developed.

Step 6: Use the right analytics tool for the job

The same principle applies to analytics. In our past positions, we were faced with hefty price tags for big iron analytics systems—often after lengthy lobbying efforts and justifications presented by our BI teams. Without these large systems, it was said, they would not be able to analyze the massive amounts of data required, and the business would lose out on competitive insights, pricing information, customer analytics, and future product opportunities. So, reluctantly, we acquiesced and spent a small fortune, a lot of engineering time, and then massaged and moved data into position for analysis. Of course, the systems quickly ran out of storage, and we either had to buy additional (exorbitantly expensive) storage or we had to purge data from the BI system to make room for the most current data.

Happily, there is a better way now. While the need for a formal BI capability remains, enterprises increasingly democratize access to data and analytics. With flexible IAM roles, a variety of users can analyze data. Rather than routing all analytics requests through a central bottlenecked team, why not allow the accounting team to analyze financial data directly? Why not enable the consumer protection function to run their own queries? Why not empower the product team to visualize consumer behavior in the wild in near-real time? AWS offers a variety of tools that enable your team to do just that.

Amazon Athena for interactive analysis allowing users to analyze data directly in your data lake.

Amazon EMR provides a managed service for big-data processing using Spark and Hadoop framework. Importantly here, Amazon EMR supports 19 different open-source projects including Hadoop, Spark, HBase, and Presto and AWS updates each open-source project within 30 days of a version release, ensuring you have the latest and greatest from the community.

Amazon Redshift provides the ability to run complex, analytic queries against petabytes of structured data, and includes Amazon Redshift Spectrum that runs SQL queries directly against exabytes of structured or unstructured data in S3.

Amazon Kinesis for real-time analytics, to collect, process, and analyze streaming data such as IoT telemetry data, application logs, and website clickstreams. This enables you to process and analyze data as it arrives in your data lake, and respond in real-time instead of having to wait until all your data is collected before the processing can begin.

Amazon Elasticsearch Services for operational analytics such as application monitoring, log analytics, and clickstream analytics.

Step 7: Ensure security at rest and in motion

"Dance like nobody's watching, encrypt like everyone is." – Werner Vogels, 2017

In addition to fine-grained, role-based access control, best practice suggests that you encrypt most if not all of your data all the time. The most important service in this regard is AWS Key Management Service (KMS). (For a detailed technical description of how KMS functions, refer to AWS Key Management Service Cryptographic Details https://d1.awsstatic.com/whitepapers/KMS-Cryptographic-Details.pdf) KMS provides cryptographic keys and operations secured by FIPS 140-2 certified hardware security modules (HSMs) scaled for the cloud, and therefore offers a highly secure way to generate and manage encryption keys.

When you encrypt your data, your data is protected, but then you must protect your encryption key. One strategy is to encrypt it as well. *Envelope encryption* is the practice of encrypting plaintext data with a data key, and then encrypting the data key under another key.

Master key   Encrypts   **Data key**   Encrypts   **Data**

Your organization might require the encryption of all data that meets a specific classification. Depending on the specific service, you can enforce data encryption policies through preventative or detective controls. For some services, such as Amazon S3, a policy can prevent storing unencrypted data. For other services, the most efficient mechanism is to monitor the creation of storage resources and check whether encryption is enabled appropriately.

Amazon Relational Database Service (RDS) builds on Amazon EBS encryption to provide full-disk encryption for database volumes. When you create an encrypted database instance with Amazon RDS, it creates an encrypted Amazon EBS volume on your behalf to store the database. Data stored at rest on the volume, database snapshots, automated backups, and read replicas are all encrypted under the AWS KMS CMK that you specified when you created the database instance.

If your organization is subject to corporate or regulatory policies that require encryption of data in transit, we recommend using encryption of data in transit on every client accessing the file system. Having said that, we actually recommend that you implement encryption of sensitive information in motion wherever possible, whether it is required by policy or not.

6.2 MACHINE LEARNING WITH CLOUD

"Don't replace people: Augment them."

– TIM O'REILLY

Machine learning (ML) and artificial intelligence (AI) have been increasingly hot topics in our conversations with customers. Part of the reason for this is that ML has in the past been somewhat of an arcane art. ML required very specialized knowledge, massive compute power, and extremely large data sets, not to mention the need for labeled "training data."

Before we dive deeper. Let's define a few terms:

- **Artificial intelligence**: Software applications which exhibit human-like behavior, such as speech, natural-language processing, reasoning, or intuition
- **Machine learning**: Teaching machines to learn without being explicitly programmed
- **Deep learning**: Using neural networks, teaching machines to learn from complex data where features cannot be explicitly expressed

AWS's mission is to put machine learning into the hands of every developer and data scientist. AWS has put a great deal of effort into "democratizing AI"—the objective was and continues to be to provide all the services and tools an enterprise needs to generate value through ML and AI.

Take C-SPAN for instance. C-SPAN is a nonprofit public service funded by the U.S. cable television industry. Its mission is to open Washington, D.C. to the public and make government more transparent by broadcasting and archiving government proceedings, including live coverage of the United States Senate and House of Representatives.

In early 2016, C-SPAN Archives developed an internal tool that could tag speakers and topics of Congressional proceedings with a time hack. Unfortunately, it was relatively slow. Two human indexers used this tool, plus closed-captioning data, to index faces in about 50 percent of C-SPAN's footage, at a rate of about one hour of work per hour of video.

Alan Cloutier—then a technical manager at C-SPAN—heard about Amazon Rekognition, a highly scalable image-analysis service, at the AWS re:Invent 2016 keynote address. Within an hour, he had used Amazon Rekognition to search for "John McCain" and discovered that Amazon Rekognition could pick the correct face from a collection of more than 100,000 images with a high degree of certainty.

Within three weeks of the announcement, the C-SPAN Archives team had a working solution using Amazon Rekognition. Only one line of code is required to add an image or do a comparison, so very little development was required. The initial image collection—consisting of 97,000 known individuals—was indexed by Amazon Rekognition in less than two hours.

Why AI/ML matters

Generally speaking, ML can help you use historical data to make better business decisions. ML algorithms discover patterns in data and construct mathematical models using these discoveries. Then you can use the models to make predictions on future data. For example, one possible application of a machine-learning model would be to predict how likely a customer is to purchase a particular product based on their past behavior.

ML is not really a new invention. The mathematical principles under-lying machine learning have existed for decades. In 1950, Alan Turing proposed a "learning machine" that could learn and become artifi-cially intelligent, and a year later, Marvin Minsky (who much later founded the famed MIT Media Lab) and Dean Edmonds built the SNARC—the first neural network machine able to learn.

Over the following decades, these early leaders in AI and others researchers enthusiastically pronounced the imminent age of artifi-cial intelligence.

- 1958, Herbert Simon and Allen Newell (awarded the Turing award in 1975): "Within 10 years a digital computer will be the world's chess champion."
- 1965, Herbert Simon: "Machines will be capable, within 20 years, of doing any work a man can do."
- 1967 Marvin Minsky: "Within a generation, the problem of cre-ating 'artificial intelligence' will substantially be solved."
- 1970 Marvin Minsky: "In from 3 to 8 years, we will have a machine with the general intelligence of an average human being."

Shortly thereafter came the first "AI Winter," when research fund-ing all but disappeared in the 1970s, followed by a second AI Win-ter beginning in 1984. This culminated in a 2001 talk, given by none other than Marvin Minsky, titled "It's 2001: Where is HAL?" referring of course to the HAL computer in Stanley Kubrick's film *2001: A Space Odyssey*. Significantly, in 1968 Marvin Minsky had advised Stanley Kubrick during the making of the film. In this talk, Minsky stated: "No program today can distinguish a dog from a cat, or recognize objects in typical rooms, or answer questions that 4-year-olds can!"

Yet, a mere five years later, it finally happened. Artificial intelligence—and more important, machine learning—became generally available *and* affordable. The age of artificial intelligence was upon us, although in a different form than the early pioneers had predicted. Why then has AI taken so long to become useful?

While scientists were capable of running artificial-intelligence applications in the lab, the cost and complexity of running these algorithms made them scientific curiosities, rather than something with economic utility. The amount of compute power and data storage required was simply beyond the available capacity of all but the largest research institutions, and even then, only for short periods of compute time.

An important milestone was reached in December 2004, when Google released the famous MapReduce paper, which described "a programming model and an associated implementation for processing and generating large data sets." Not to be outdone, Yahoo implemented the ideas described in this paper and released a first version of their project—Hadoop—in April 2006.

In early 2006, AWS came into being, and with it the compute and storage capacity required to enable machine learning at scale for the very first time.

Internally, Amazon has been using machine learning for more than 20 years. With thousands of engineers focused on machine learning across the company, there are very few Amazon retail pages, products, fulfilment technologies, and stores which haven't been improved in one way or another through the use of machine learning. AWS's mission has been to take machine learning from something which had previously been available only to the largest, most well-funded technology companies, and put it in the hands of *every* developer. Amazon has also made use of ML with advances in robotics, drones, supply chain management, the family of Amazon Echo devices, and the Amazon Go store—which has abstracted and simplified the checkout process to the simple act of walking out the store with the goods you want to purchase.

"It is a renaissance, it is a golden age. We are solving problems with machine learning and artificial intelligence that were in the realm of science fiction for the last several decades. Natural language understanding, machine vision problems, it really is an amazing renaissance." – Jeff P. Bezos, Founder and CEO, Amazon.com, Inc.

Things really got going in late 2017, when AWS made the next generation of GPU-powered EC2 instances available for the first time. Powered by up to eight NVIDIA Tesla V100 GPUs, the P3 instances were designed to handle compute-intensive machine learning, deep learning, computational fluid dynamics, computational finance, seismic analysis, molecular modeling, and genomics workloads.

Jeff Barr, Chief Evangelist of AWS, described the impact of the P3 instances with the following anecdote:

Let's go back to the dawn of the microprocessor era, and consider the Intel 8080A chip that powered the MITS Altair that I bought in the summer of 1977. With a 2 MHz clock, it was able to do about 832 multiplications per second (I used this data and corrected it for the faster clock speed). The p3.16xlarge is roughly 150 billion times faster. However, just 1.2 billion seconds have gone by since that summer. In other words, I can do 100x more calculations today in one second than my Altair could have done in the last 40 years!

The AWS suite of ML services now offers support across the full spectrum of applications—from supporting the dyed-in-the-wool data scientist, to enabling programmers and business analysts who have no background in data science, all the way to facilitating the rapid implementation of high-level applications that can be leveraged with amazing ease.

AWS ML services can be grouped by the people they serve:

- Data scientists
- Developers who need a simple integration

- Developers who have no background in ML who need to create models

How to know when to use ML

Humans are not good at parsing through enormous piles of data quickly to extract gems of insight. We are slow, prone to error, and we get bored—further exacerbating the previous two problems. In 1996, for instance, Thomas was deployed to Bosnia as part of a NATO peacekeeping mission (IFOR). He routinely read hundreds of pages of reports per day in order to extract information that might be relevant and useful to the group's peacekeeping mission. Thomas could only dream of the power and ease with which he would do this task today.

The sheer volume of available data that is constantly generated makes it entirely impossible for humans to parse and extract data. Worse, trying to find connections or correlations in large, unstructured, often spurious datasets is impossible for most people unless they happen to be data scientists and/or mathematicians.

We recommend you use machine learning for the following situations:

- **You cannot code the rules.** Many human tasks (such as recognizing whether an email is spam or not spam) cannot be adequately solved using a simple (deterministic), rule-based solution. A large number of factors could influence the answer. When rules depend on too many factors and many of these rules overlap or need to be tuned very finely, it soon becomes difficult for a human to accurately code the rules. You can use ML to effectively solve this problem.
- **You cannot scale.** You might be able to manually recognize a few hundred emails and decide whether they are spam or not. However, this task becomes tedious for millions of emails. ML solutions are effective at handling large-scale problems.

Getting started (training your own models)

You can use Amazon Machine Learning to apply machine learning to problems for which you have existing examples of actual answers. For example, if you want to use Amazon Machine Learning to predict if an email is spam, you will need to collect email examples that are correctly labeled as spam or not spam. You then can use machine learning to generalize from these email examples to predict how likely new email is spam or not. This approach—of learning from data that has been labeled with the actual answer—is known as *supervised machine learning*.

You can use supervised ML approaches for these specific machine learning tasks: binary classification (predicting one of two possible outcomes), multiclass classification (predicting one of more than two outcomes), and regression (predicting a numeric value).

Examples of binary classification problems:

- Will the customer buy this product or not buy this product?
- Is this email spam or not spam?
- Is this product a book or a farm animal?
- Is this review written by a customer or a robot?

Examples of multiclass classification problems:

- Is this product a book, movie, or clothing?
- Is this movie a romantic comedy, documentary, or thriller?
- Which category of products is most interesting to this customer?

Examples of regression classification problems:

- What will the temperature be in Seattle tomorrow?
- For this product, how many units will sell?
- How many days before this customer stops using the application?
- What price will this house sell for?

ACTION STEPS

Building Amazon ML applications is an iterative process that involves the following sequence of five steps:

Step 1: Formulate the problem

The first step in machine learning is to decide what you want to predict, which is known as the *label* or *target answer*. Imagine a scenario in which you want to manufacture products, but your decision to manufacture each product depends on its number of potential sales. In this scenario, you want to predict how many times each product will be purchased (predict number of sales). There are multiple ways to define this problem by using machine learning. Choosing how to define the problem depends on your use case or business need.

Step 2: Collect labeled data

Do you want to predict the number of purchases your customers will make for each product (in which case the target is numeric and you're solving a regression problem)? Or do you want to predict which products will get more than 10 purchases (in which case the target is binary and you're solving a binary classification problem)? ML problems start with data—preferably, *lots* of data (examples or observations) for which you already know the target answer. Data for which you already know the target answer is called *labeled data*. In supervised ML, the algorithm teaches itself to learn from the labeled examples that we provide.

Each example/observation in your data must contain two elements:

- **The target**—The answer you want to predict. You provide data that is labeled with the target (correct answer) to the ML algorithm to learn from. Then, you will use the trained ML model to predict this answer on data for which you do not know the target answer.
- **Variables/features**—These are attributes of the example that can be used to identify patterns to predict the target answer.

For example, for the email classification problem mentioned earlier, the target is a label that indicates whether an email is spam or not spam. Examples of variables are the sender of the email, the text in the body of the email, the text in the subject line, the time the email was sent, and the existence of previous correspondence between the sender and receiver.

Often, data is not readily available in a labeled form. Collecting and preparing the variables and the target are often the most important steps in solving an ML problem. The example data should be representative of the data that you will have when you are using the model to make a prediction. For example, if you want to predict whether an email is spam or not, you must collect both positive (spam emails) and negative (non-spam emails) for the machine learning algorithm to be able to find patterns that will distinguish between the two types of email.

Once you have the labelled data, you might need to convert it to a format that is acceptable to your algorithm or software. For example, to use Amazon ML, you need to convert the data to comma-separated (CSV) format with each example making up one row of the CSV file, each column containing one input variable, and one column containing the target answer.

Step 3: Analyze your data

It is important to avoid overcomplicating the problem and to frame the simplest solution that meets your needs. However, it is also important to avoid losing information—especially information in the historical answers. Here, converting an actual past sales number into a binary variable "over 10" versus "fewer" would lose valuable information. Investing time in deciding which target makes the most sense for you to predict will save you from building models that don't answer your question.

Before feeding your labeled data to an ML algorithm, it is a good practice to inspect your data to identify issues and gain insights about the data you are using. The predictive power of your model will only be as good as the data you feed it.

When analyzing your data, you should keep the following considerations in mind:

- **Variable and target data summaries**—It is useful to understand the values that your variables take and which values are dominant in your data. You could run these summaries by a subject matter expert for the problem you want to solve. Ask yourself or the subject matter expert: Does the data match your expectations? Does it look like you have a data collection problem? Is one class in your target more frequent than the other classes? Are there more missing values or invalid data than you expected?
- **Variable-target correlations**—Knowing the correlation between each variable and the target class is helpful because a high correlation implies that there is a relationship between the variable and the target class. In general, you want to include variables with high correlation because they are the ones with higher predictive power (signal), and leave out variables with low correlation because they are likely irrelevant.

In Amazon ML, you can analyze your data by creating a data source and by reviewing the resulting data report.

Step 4: Build the model

The fundamental goal of ML is to *generalize* beyond the data instances used to train models. We want to evaluate the model to estimate the quality of its pattern generalization for data the model has not been trained on.

You are now ready to provide the ML algorithm (that is, the *learning algorithm*) with the training data. The algorithm will learn from the training data patterns that map the variables to the target, and it will output a model that captures these relationships. The ML model can then be used to get predictions on new data for which you do not know the target answer.

The goal of the ML model is to learn patterns that generalize well for unseen data instead of just memorizing the data that it was shown during training. Once you have a model, it is important to check if your model is performing well on unseen examples that you have not used for training the model. To do this, you use the model to predict the answer on the evaluation dataset (held out data) and then compare the predicted target to the actual answer (ground truth).

Step 5: Generate predictions and inferences
Batch prediction is useful when you want to generate predictions for a set of observations all at once, and then take action on a certain percentage or number of the observations. Typically, you do not have a low latency requirement for such an application. For example, when you want to decide which customers to target as part of an advertisement campaign for a product, you will get prediction scores for all customers, sort your model's predictions to identify which customers are most likely to purchase, and then target maybe the top 5 percent of customers that are most likely to purchase.

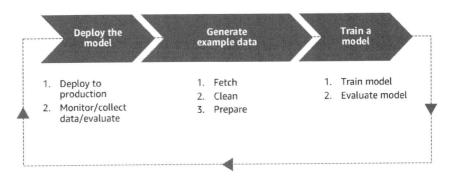

Online prediction scenarios are for cases when you want to generate predictions on a one-by-one basis for each example independent of the other examples, in a low-latency environment. For example, you could use predictions to make immediate decisions about whether a particular transaction is likely to be a fraudulent transaction.

Getting started (without the heavy lifting)

If you don't have the appetite (yet) to build your solutions from scratch with the help of your data scientists (you do have data scientists on your team, right?), then there is a much easier way to get you started *without* needing data scientists on your team. You can simply use Amazon SageMaker, which is a service designed to accelerate this process significantly. Amazon SageMaker is a fully managed service that allows you to label and prepare your data, choose the appropriate algorithm, train the algorithm, and then tune and optimize it for deployment. Deployment into Auto-Scaling production clusters can be done with a single click in the console. Once deployed, you can use the service to reliably make predictions that inform decisions and actions.

AWS also provides a new way to label data in Amazon SageMaker, with the release of Amazon SageMaker Ground Truth in late 2018. This reduces the time and effort required to create datasets for training by using machine learning to automatically label data in a training set, based on labels applied by humans. Over time, the labeling algorithm progressively improves by continuously learning from human labelers. This, in turn, allows you to apply labels to larger datasets faster and cheaper.

There is a straightforward, four-step process to develop and deploy a model that can fuel your applications and products. Although development work is involved, the team does not have to understand machine learning in order to implement an Amazon SageMaker solution.

Step 1: Create an Amazon SageMaker notebook instance

Step 2: Train a model with a built-in algorithm and deploy it

Step 3: Clean up

Step 4: Integrate Amazon SageMaker endpoints into internet-facing applications

A couple examples to get you thinking

Application developers without formal data-science training have developed remarkable solutions in days or weeks, rather than months or years of development time. Here are some examples:

Formula 1 Racing

In 2018, Formula 1 announced plans to move the vast majority of its infrastructure from on-premises data centers to AWS, and to standardize on AWS's machine learning and data analytics services to accelerate its cloud transformation.

Using Amazon SageMaker, Formula 1's data scientists are training deep-learning models with more than 65 years of historical race data, stored in both Amazon DynamoDB and Amazon S3 Glacier. With this information, Formula 1 can extract critical race performance statistics to make race predictions and give fans insight into the split-second decisions and strategies adopted by teams and drivers. Says Pete Samara, Director of Innovation and Digital Technology at Formula 1:

> *For our needs, AWS outperforms all other cloud providers in speed, scalability, reliability, global reach, partner community, and breadth and depth of cloud services available. By leveraging Amazon SageMaker and AWS's machine learning services, we are now able to deliver these powerful insights and predictions to fans in real time. We are also excited that the Formula 1 Motorsports division will run High Performance Compute workloads in a scalable environment on AWS. This will significantly increase the number and quality of the*

simulations our aerodynamics team can run as we work to develop the new car design rules for Formula 1.

Fender Guitars

Fender went all in on AWS to better engage with customers and gain supply-chain efficiencies. Fender, made famous by the likes of Jimi Hendrix, runs its Fender Play, Fender Tune, and Fender Tone apps on AWS, which help customers learn to play guitar, tune their instruments, and control digital amplifiers. Ethan Kaplan, chief product officer at Fender, spoke at re:Invent 2018. He described how they are using Amazon SageMaker to scan images of pieces of wood in order to find the perfect match between two pieces needed to make a guitar body. The images are fed into SageMaker and compared to thousands of others to determine the optimal wood grain.

Final thought

You don't need a specialist ML team to get started. Throughout this book, we have talked about the ability of small outcome/product-centric heterogeneously skilled teams to execute and deliver value quickly when the heavy lifting is removed for them. This, of course, is true in the context of ML as well. With these higher-level services, some of which can be used with just single API call (Amazon Rekognition for example) it is possible for your existing teams to go really fast.

We want to give a special shout out to our good friend Julien Simon, Principal Technical Evangelist at AWS, for his help in writing this chapter. His insight and narrative (and wit) were and continue to be invaluable. To learn more—and go much, much, much deeper into the world of artificial intelligence and machine learning—visit him at https://medium.com/@julsimon

PART 7

SECURITY AND GOVERNANCE

7.1 SECURITY IS ALWAYS JOB ZERO

"There's so much security built into cloud computing platforms today, for us, it's our No. 1 priority—it's not even close, relative to anything else."
– ANDY JASSY, CEO, AWS

In the piece that follows, Thomas tells the story of Experian's migration to cloud when he served as Vice President, Emerging Technologies, with this large financial enterprise:

> When we first explored the idea of migrating to the cloud in 2014, I thought that the biggest hurdle to overcome would be the executive team's natural concerns around security and compliance. At the time, there was a widespread belief among executives that Experian could never go to the cloud because of security concerns. Nevertheless, we decided to push on, because we knew that going to cloud would enable our business to become nimble and fast.

> Before submitting our proposal to the executive leaders and then to the funding committee, we wanted to first get buy-in from our global CISO. When we met, he shared his concerns about cloud security and expressed doubt whether this was the right thing to do. I wasn't surprised by this response, in fact, I would have been surprised if he had not shared these concerns. But I was prepared to address them.

I asked him if better security might look like having more standard-ized hardened components and systems. I wanted to know if being able to lock down access to systems by role with a detailed audit trail might be of interest. I asked him if he thought if it would be beneficial to have the ability to conduct a system audit more than once per year, and without incurring the ire of IT operations. I asked him how much time it took to examine and approve requests for innovation and new product ideas, and whether he would like to have a way to preapprove reusable core infrastructure and software components that would allow his team to focus only on the truly novel elements of any new system. I told him that we had an oppor-tunity to bring security thinking as a practice directly into the devel-opment teams—to create a stronger culture of security within IT.

Needless to say, those were the kinds of things security profession-als have wanted for a long time. They don't really relish the idea of starting with "no," of being a wet blanket on innovation, or of being perceived as the brakes on the business. And they also don't want to heedlessly give approvals knowing that the security of their business, their customer and corporate data, and their personal rep-utation could be compromised by one careless oversight.

So, I told him we could create such a future together. I asked for and received his support to start with a smallish project with his team deeply involved from the beginning. I promised we would bring world-class experts in to validate our architecture, and we would increase the number of scheduled penetration tests with an out-side firm. He asked that we help in creating a cross-reference docu-ment to map and compare traditional security controls against new cloud-based security controls and mitigation measures.

And so, our journey began. Along the way, we learned that secu-rity is a shared responsibility between the customer and AWS. We learned that leveraging security capabilities offered by AWS required thoughtful architectures, and we learned that our security posture could be improved when compared to some of our established systems. Above all, we learned that security doesn't have to be difficult to implement. In fact, by using the tooling AWS provides, we were able to enhance security and simplify our operations. Ultimately, we were much better able to ensure the information security triad of confidentiality, integrity, and availability (CIA).

Confidentiality

In information security, confidentiality "is the property that information is not made available or disclosed to unauthorized individuals, entities, or processes."[11] This is not the same thing as privacy, although confidentiality is a prerequisite for privacy since privacy expectations by definition cannot be met by a system that fails to meet confidentiality requirements.

Integrity

In information security, data integrity means maintaining and assuring the accuracy and completeness of data over its entire lifecycle.[12] This means that data cannot be corrupted or accidentally deleted and cannot be modified in an unauthorized or undetected manner.

Availability

For any information system to serve its purpose, the information must be available when it is needed. Ensuring availability involves using systems that are resilient to unforeseen events, whether they are natural disasters, scaling to meet the demands of an unexpectedly successful marketing campaign, or surviving denial-of-service attacks, to name just a few examples from our own experience. We've already discussed availability in Chapter 5.3 Resilience and Reliability.

AWS considers information security—not just confidentiality, but integrity and availability as well—as its "Job Zero," referring of course to the penchant of developers to start any count from "zero," not "one." In other words, security is AWS's absolute top priority. In our experience, security testing and validation at most organizations is done at the end of the implementation, or very late in the lifecycle of any new initiative. Almost as if security were this annoying and unwanted thing that one has to grudgingly deal with. Almost as if security was something you could bolt on at the end, some kind of hardened wrapper around soft-and-smushy application code.

Many organizations conduct security reviews and security testing toward the end of the software development lifecycle. Many of you who read this will recognize the uncomfortable moment when security audits reveal a flaw, and you have to decide whether to postpone the release, or whether to formally accept the risk in your risk register in order to launch on time. If you chose the latter, your very next release will likely need to contain the fix for the discovered flaw. Either way, you are forced to slow down the business. Security is often seen as a necessary evil, to be endured and resolved with the least amount of effort and cost at the last (responsible) moment.

Contrast this with Ralf Kleinfeld's (CISO at Otto Versand in Germany) comment to Thomas in a conversation that security is a business driver for Otto! Or the idea that security is a measure of quality! Everything should start with security, just as much as cost, performance, features, and other core design elements. New services must pass through well-defined quality gates—including security elements—not just once, but from inception and forever more, using automated security tests whenever *any* change is made.

While constantly passing through the right security gates, development can and should go very, very fast through the use of guardrails. Guardrails, as previously discussed, greatly simplify software development *and* provide automated tools to enable security by design and from the ground up.

So how is it that AWS helps customers meet the requirements of confidentiality, integrity, and availability? We'll answer that question in the next section.

Understanding the AWS secure global infrastructure

The AWS secure global infrastructure and services are managed by AWS and provide a trustworthy foundation for enterprise systems and individual applications. AWS establishes high standards for information security within the cloud and has a comprehensive and holistic set of control objectives, ranging from physical security through software acquisition and development to employee lifecycle management and security organization. The AWS secure global infrastructure and services are subject to regular third-party compliance audits. (See the "Amazon Web Services Risk and Compliance" whitepaper for more information.)

Security and compliance are shared responsibilities between AWS and the customer. This shared model can help relieve the customer's operational burden as AWS operates, manages, and controls the components intrinsic to the service. At a minimum, which is the EC2 virtualization service, AWS takes care of everything from the virtualization layer down to the physical security of the facilities in which the service operates. At a maximum, AWS manages everything beyond proper configuration of a service via its APIs. In the virtual-machine service, the customer assumes responsibility and management of the guest operating system (including updates and security patches), other associated application software, as well as configuration of the AWS-provided security group firewall. Even for the virtual-machine service, however, AWS makes it extremely easy to manage operating system patching, configuration, and updates with another service called AWS Systems Manager. For many other higher-level services,

customer responsibility is minimal—just configure a good authentication and authorization model, and away you go with storage, databases, and other things. You have no operational responsibility, only
configuration responsibility.

Customers should carefully consider which services they choose since
responsibilities vary depending on the services used, the integration of
those services into their IT environment, and applicable laws and regulations. The nature of this shared responsibility also provides the flexibility and customer control that permits the deployment. As shown
in the chart below, this differentiation of responsibility is commonly
referred to as "security *of* the cloud" versus "security *in* the cloud."

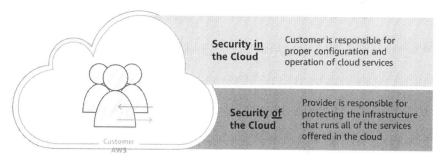

One of the things about this model that we loved when *we* were customers is that AWS continuously innovates to improve their security
offering for customers. As a matter of fact, AWS constantly makes
changes that decrease the level of responsibility *in favor* of customers! For example, Amazon Elastic Block Store (EBS), which is used for
throughput and transaction intensive workloads, used to require that
customers explicitly encrypt volumes. Since May 2019, however, customers can specify with a global account-level flag that they want
all newly created EBS volumes to be created in encrypted form. And
after that, even if the user specifies no encryption at the API level,
volumes are encrypted anyway. AWS constantly raises the bar in ease
of use and security-service capabilities. Other recent examples include

Amazon S3 Block Public Access to give an "easy button" to override possible configuration errors for Amazon S3 storage; Amazon Guard-Duty and AWS Security Hub with one-click enablement of deep visibility into workload configuration and behavior; and AWS Control Tower, which enables you to deploy new AWS environments with best practices not only preconfigured, but enforced via policy.

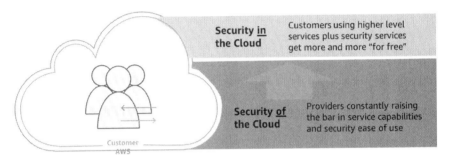

Source: https://aws.amazon.com/compliance/shared-responsibility-model/

It is actually worth diving a bit deeper, since the model changes depending on the level of abstraction you are using. Largely, you can think of three levels of abstraction:

1. Infrastructure services

2. Managed services that "contain" existing non-cloud software (the name isn't great but some AWS documents call these "container" services)

3. Abstracted services

Let's take a look at each

1. Shared responsibility model for infrastructure services

Infrastructure services, such as Amazon EC2, Amazon EBS, and Amazon VPC, run on top of the AWS global infrastructure, but give you relatively low-level access to the kind of IT primitives that you're used to using outside the cloud: virtual machines, block-storage volumes, subnets and network gateways, firewall rules, etc. While in many respects they are very similar to and compatible with on-premises technologies, one fundamental difference is that *everything* is created, managed, and deleted via API calls. These lower-level services vary in terms of availability and durability objectives, but always operate within the specific Region where they have been launched. You can build systems that meet availability objectives exceeding those of individual services from AWS by employing resilient components in multiple Availability Zones.

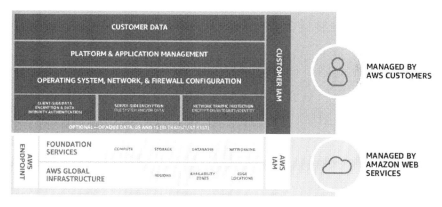

Figure 1: Shared Responsibility Model for Infrastructure Services

Building on the AWS secure global infrastructure, you install and configure your operating systems and platforms in the AWS Cloud just as you would do on-premises in your own data centers. Then you install your applications on your platform. Ultimately, your data resides in and is managed by your own applications. You need to evaluate whether additional layers of protection beyond what is provided by the AWS secure global infrastructure are necessary.

For certain compliance requirements, you might require an additional layer of protection between the services from AWS and your operating systems and platforms, where your applications and data reside. You can impose additional controls—such as protection of data at rest, and protection of data in transit—or introduce a layer of opacity between services from AWS and your platform. The opacity layer can include data encryption, data-integrity authentication, software- and data-signing, secure timestamping, and more.

2. Shared responsibility model for managed "contained" services

The AWS shared responsibility model also applies to managed, "contained" services (the AWS best practices paper dated August 2016 describes this model as "container services"), such as Amazon Relational Database Service (RDS), Amazon Elastic MapReduce service (EMR), and Amazon Elasticsearch. For these services, AWS manages the underlying infrastructure and foundation services, the operating system, and the application platform, but also orchestrates the deployment, update, and eventual deletion of software—whether proprietary or, in most cases, open source—that also can be used outside the cloud. For example, Amazon RDS for Oracle is a managed database service in which AWS manages all the layers of the container, up to and including the Oracle database platform. For services such as Amazon RDS, the AWS platform greatly eases the creation and management of the database engine and provides highly automated, high-availability, and horizontal-scaling capabilities through master/slave copies, as well as easy-to-use data backup and recovery tools. But it is your responsibility to configure and use all these tools in relation to your business continuity and disaster recovery (BC/DR) policy. Similarly, the Amazon EMR and Amazon Elasticsearch services take care of a lot of complex work around the creation and maintenance of Hadoop and Spark and Elasticsearch clusters in highly automated fashion, but in the end you still control the environments and run your own data analytics jobs using the same kinds of tools you would use outside the cloud.

For AWS-managed "contained" services, you need to determine what data goes where (and whether or not it should it be encrypted), who or what systems need access, and from which networks this data can be accessed.

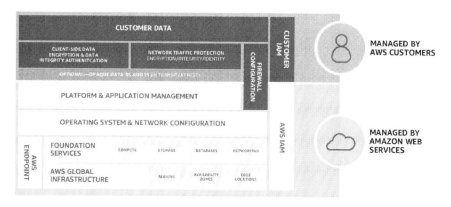

Figure 2: Shared Responsibility Model for Managed Self-Contained Services

3. Shared responsibility model for abstracted services

For abstracted services, such as Amazon S3 and Amazon DynamoDB, the service presents itself as nothing other than a set of APIs. The service itself is a black box, completely "abstracted away" behind those APIs. AWS operates the infrastructure layer, the operating systems, the distributed transactions and failover layers, and all the service code needed to perform the features presented to you via the API endpoints that you use to configure the system, then to store and retrieve your data—all maintained with zero scheduled downtime through highly automated, modern DevOps pipelines. All these services also tightly integrate with the IAM service—unlike infrastructure and "contained" services, which still often utilize traditional access layers once APIs are used to deploy the systems—all access to every feature is managed via IAM. You are responsible for managing your data (including classifying your assets), and for using IAM tools to apply ACL-type permissions to individual resources at the platform level, or permissions based on user identity or user responsibility at the IAM user/group level. For most abstracted services, you can also use platform-provided encryption of data at rest, while maintaining rich control over encryption keys stored in the AWS Key Management Service (KMS). And you should use HTTPS encapsulation for your payloads for protecting your data in transit to and from the service.

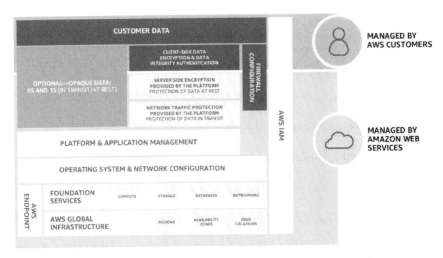

Figure 3: Shared Responsibility Model for Abstracted Services

Whenever possible, it is worth exploring and using abstracted services, since AWS does a lot of the heavy lifting of managing security to enhance confidentiality, integrity, and availability of your data and applications. For all use cases across the three abstraction levels, AWS offers a growing number of services and capabilities to simplify security management.

AWS Security Services to help manage security in the cloud

Identity	Detective control	Infrastructure protection	Data protection	Incident response
AWS Identity & Access Management (IAM)	AWS Security Hub	AWS Systems Manager	AWS Key Management Service (KMS)	AWS Config Rules
AWS Single Sign-On	Amazon GuardDuty	AWS Shield	AWS CloudHSM	AWS Lambda
AWS Directory Service	AWS Config	AWS WAF—Web application firewall	AWS Certificate Manager	Amazon CloudWatch Events
Amazon Cognito	AWS CloudTrail	AWS Firewall Manager	Amazon Macie	AWS CloudFormation
AWS Organizations	Amazon CloudWatch	Amazon Inspector	Server-Side Encryption	
AWS Secrets Manager	VPC Flow Logs	Amazon Virtual Private Cloud (VPC)		
AWS Resource Access Manager	AWS Security Hub	AWS Control Tower		

Best-practice areas

In the cloud, there are a number of principles that can help you strengthen your system security. These principles have been well understood in theory for many decades, but were difficult to consistently implement without severely curtailing business agility in practice. AWS rigorously implements these and other security principles, and thus ensures "security of the cloud," removing a very large burden from organizations that can instead focus their security resources on "security in the cloud." In this shared-security model, organizations can finally focus on data and application security in the knowledge that AWS will secure the components "of the cloud."

AWS is improving security of the cloud and is advancing the field of cybersecurity by developing *automated reasoning* to create and check mathematical proofs of the correctness of systems. What is automated reasoning, you ask? It's a method of formal verification that automatically generates and checks mathematical proofs which help to prove the correctness of systems—that is, fancy math that proves things are working as expected. If you want a deeper understanding of automated reasoning, check out the re:Invent session at https://www.youtube.com/watch?v=U40bWY6oVtU

AWS defines five best-practice areas:

1. Identity and access management
2. Detective controls
3. Infrastructure protection
4. Data protection
5. Incident response

1. Identity and access management

AWS Identity and Access Management (IAM) enables you to manage access to AWS services and resources securely. Using AWS IAM, you can create and manage AWS users and groups, and use permissions to allow and deny their access to AWS resources.

Identity and access management are key parts of an information security program, ensuring that only authorized and authenticated users are able to access your resources, and only in a manner that you intend. For example, you should define users, groups, services, and roles that take action in your account, build out policies aligned with these principles, and implement strong credential management. These privilege-management elements form the core of authentication principles and authorization.

In AWS, privilege management is primarily supported by the AWS Identity and Access Management (IAM) service, which allows you to control user and programmatic access to AWS services and resources. You should apply granular policies, which assign permissions to a user, group, role, or resource. You also have the ability to require strong password practices, such as complexity level, avoiding re-use, and enforcing multi-factor authentication (MFA). You can use federation with your existing directory service. For workloads that require systems to have access to AWS, AWS IAM enables secure access through roles, instance profiles, identity federation, and temporary credentials.

AWS IAM allows you to:

- Manage IAM users and their access—You can create users in AWS IAM, assign them individual security credentials (in other words, access keys, passwords, and multi-factor authentication) or request temporary security credentials to provide users access to AWS services and resources. You can manage permissions in order to control which operations a user can perform.
- Manage IAM roles and their permissions—You can create roles in AWS IAM and manage permissions to control which operations can be performed by the entity or AWS service that assumes the role. You can also define which entity is allowed to assume

the role. In addition, you can use service-linked roles to delegate permissions to AWS services that create and manage AWS resources on your behalf.

- Manage federated users and their permissions—You can enable identity federation to allow existing identities (users, groups, and roles) in your enterprise to access the AWS Management Console, call AWS APIs, and access resources without the need to create an IAM user for each identity. Use any identity-management solution that supports SAML 2.0, or use one of our federation samples (AWS Console SSO or API federation).

2. Detective controls

You can use detective controls to identify a potential security threat or incident. They are an essential part of governance frameworks and can be used to support a quality process, a legal or compliance obligation, and for threat identification and response efforts. There are different types of detective controls. For example, conducting an inventory of assets and their detailed attributes promotes more effective decision making (and lifecycle controls) to help establish operational baselines. You can also use internal auditing, an examination of controls related to information systems, to ensure that practices meet policies and requirements and that you have set the correct automated alerting notifications based on defined conditions. These controls are important reactive factors that can help your organization identify and understand the scope of anomalous activity.

In AWS, you can implement detective controls by processing logs, events, and monitoring that allows for auditing, automated analysis, and alarming. AWS CloudTrail logs, AWS API calls, and Amazon Cloud-Watch provide monitoring of metrics with alarming, and AWS Config provides configuration history. Amazon GuardDuty is a managed threat-detection service that continuously monitors for malicious or unauthorized behavior to help you protect your AWS accounts and workloads. Service-level logs are also available. For example, you can use Amazon Simple Storage Service (Amazon S3) to log access requests.

3. Infrastructure protection

Infrastructure protection encompasses control methodologies, such as defense in depth, necessary to meet best practices and organizational or regulatory obligations. Use of these methodologies is critical for successful, ongoing operations in either the cloud or on-premises.

In AWS, you can implement stateful and stateless packet inspection, either by using AWS-native technologies or by using partner products and services available through the AWS Marketplace. You should use Amazon Virtual Private Cloud (Amazon VPC) to create a private, secured, and scalable environment in which you can define your topology—including gateways, routing tables, and public and private subnets.

Multiple layers of defense are advisable in any type of environment. In the case of infrastructure protection, many of the concepts and methods are valid across cloud and on-premises models. Enforcing boundary protection, monitoring points of ingress and egress, and comprehensive logging, monitoring, and alerting are all essential to an effective information security plan.

AWS customers are able to tailor, or harden, the configuration of an Amazon Elastic Compute Cloud (Amazon EC2), Amazon EC2 Container Service (Amazon ECS) container, or AWS Elastic Beanstalk instance, and persist this configuration to an immutable Amazon Machine Image (AMI). Then, whether triggered by AWS Auto Scaling or launched manually, all new virtual servers (instances) launched with this AMI receive the hardened configuration.

Other services you can leverage here are Amazon CloudFront, which is a global content delivery network that securely delivers data, videos, applications, and APIs to your viewers, which integrates with AWS

Shield for DDoS mitigation. AWS WAF is a web application firewall that is deployed on either Amazon CloudFront or AWS Application Load Balancer to help protect your web applications from common web exploits.

4. Data protection

Before architecting any system, foundational practices that influence security should be in place. For example, data classification provides a way to categorize organizational data based on levels of sensitivity, and encryption protects data by way of rendering it unintelligible to unauthorized access. These tools and techniques are important because they support objectives such as preventing financial loss or complying with regulatory obligations.

In AWS, the following practices facilitate protection of data:

- As an AWS customer, you maintain full control over your data.
- AWS makes it easier for you to encrypt your data and manage keys, including regular key rotation, which can be easily automated by AWS or maintained by you.
- Detailed logging that contains important content, such as file access and changes, is available.
- AWS has designed storage systems for exceptional resiliency. For example, Amazon S3 Standard, Amazon S3 Standard–IA, Amazon S3 One Zone-IA, and Amazon Glacier are all designed to provide 99.999999999 percent durability of objects over a given year. This durability level corresponds to an average annual expected loss of 0.000000001 percent of objects.
- Versioning, which can be part of a larger data lifecycle-management process, can protect against accidental overwrites, deletes, and similar harm.
- AWS never initiates the movement of data between Regions. Content placed in a Region will remain in that Region unless you

explicitly enable a feature or leverage a service that provides that functionality.

- AWS provides multiple means for encrypting data at rest and in transit. We build features into our services that make it easier to encrypt your data. For example, we have implemented server-side encryption (SSE) for Amazon S3 to make it easier for you to store your data in an encrypted form. You can also arrange for the entire HTTPS encryption and decryption process (generally known as SSL termination) to be handled by Elastic Load Balancing (ELB).

5. Incident response

Even with extremely mature preventive and detective controls, your organization should still put processes in place to respond to and mitigate the potential impact of security incidents. The architecture of your workload strongly affects the ability of your teams to operate effectively during an incident, to isolate or contain systems, and to restore operations to a known good state. Putting in place the tools and access ahead of a security incident, then routinely practicing incident response through game days, will help you ensure that your architecture can accommodate timely investigation and recovery.

In AWS, the following practices facilitate effective incident response.

- Detailed logging is available that contains important content, such as file access and changes.
- Events can be automatically processed and trigger tools that automate responses through the use of AWS APIs.
- You can pre-provision tooling and a "clean room" using AWS CloudFormation. This allows you to carry out forensics in a safe, isolated environment.

One word of caution: You will inevitably have exceptions to your security controls. It's tempting to hardcode these exceptions or write configuration files that allow for exclusions to rules. However, this approach can create hidden complexity in your control. If a resource is identified as being noncompliant, it may be better to allow it to remain as such and to document it as an exception to be periodically reviewed. Remember to keep a clean separation between your risk-evidence and risk-management processes here. Exception lists in code are difficult to maintain and ultimately mean that your AWS Config dashboard can show a distorted evaluation of your resources' compliance. We advise against codified exceptions in most cases. In fact, if you find yourself preparing to write out exceptions in code, consider that maybe your user story needs rewriting. And the cycle begins again!

How do you manage security governance using DevOps methodologies?

There are a variety of ways to manage security governance using DevOps methodologies—specifically, removing gates and adding guardrails. Here are some key approaches to consider:

Fewer gates

Given that application security is critical to modern software development, then why do so many developers have disdain for something that is so fundamental? Developers and engineers are builders, and builders want to build. They do not want to spend their time butting up against artificial gates because a legacy AppSec tool has implemented a barrier within a waterfall workflow.

This model—when developers are required to get in line, submit to a security scan, and wait to see the results—can be terribly demoralizing. When the results are produced, developers inevitably spend significant time and energy investigating red flags raised by security. In far too many cases, these red flags turn out to be false positives generated by legacy tools that are incapable of accurately identifying real security concerns. Thus, developers find themselves jumping through hoops, chasing down suspects, and wasting time. It's no wonder developers "hate the gates" and view traditional security programs as inhibitors to innovation.

More guardrails

As Marc Andreessen famously said, "software is eating the world. Contrary to what some people might think, these practices are not an excuse to cut security corners. Rather, they represent the perfect opportunity to do security better than ever. But how?

Modern application-security tools need to be automated, largely invisible to developers, and minimize friction within the DevOps CI/CD pipeline. To do this, these security tools must work the way developers want to work. Security controls must integrate into the development lifecycle early and everywhere. These controls should live within the developer's tool stack and create rapid feedback loops so mistakes can be instantly remediated at the time they're made.

Such controls cannot take the form of "tollgates." Instead, they must take the form of high-performance guardrails and create a governance environment in which developers can go fast, and security professionals can focus on the *verify* part of the principle of trust, but verify.

Preventive and detective guardrails

Guardrails are prepackaged governance rules for security, operations, and compliance that customers can select and apply enterprise-wide or to specific groups of accounts. A guardrail is expressed in plain English and it enforces a specific governance policy for your AWS environment that can be enabled within an AWS organization's organizational unit (OU). Each guardrail contains two dimensions—it can be either preventive or detective, and it can be either mandatory or optional. Preventive guardrails establish intent and prevent deployment of resources that don't conform to your policies (for example enable AWS CloudTrail in all accounts, and prevent the disabling of this critical service). Detective guardrails (disallow public read access for S3 buckets) continuously monitor deployed resources for nonconformance. For reference, AWS Control Tower automatically translates guardrails into granular AWS policies by:

- Establishing a configuration baseline using AWS CloudFormation
- Preventing configuration changes of the underlying implementation using service control policies (for preventive guardrails)
- Continuously detecting configuration changes through AWS Config rules (for detective guardrails)
- Updating guardrail status on the AWS Control Tower dashboard

Mandatory and optional guardrails

AWS Control Tower offers a curated set of guardrails based on AWS best practices and common customer policies for governance. You can automatically leverage mandatory guardrails as part of your landing zone setup. Some examples of mandatory guardrails include:

- Disallow changes to IAM roles set up for AWS Control Tower
- Disallow public read access to log archive
- Disallow policy changes to log archive

You can also choose to enable strongly recommended guardrails at any time on OUs. All accounts provisioned under enabled OUs will automatically inherit those guardrails. Some examples of strongly recommended guardrails include:

- Disallow public read or write access to Amazon Simple Storage Service (Amazon S3) buckets
- Disallow access as a root user without multi-factor authentication

- Enable encryption for Amazon Elastic Block Store (Amazon EBS) volumes attached to Amazon Elastic Compute Cloud (Amazon EC2) instances

Getting these guardrails established and agreed by the Cloud Leadership Team (CLT) is crucial. Let's go a little deeper into why that is the case.

Guardrail: Only approved AMIs are allowed to be used

On the surface, this looks like an easy preventative control to implement, but it immediately raises multiple questions, including:

- Who approves AMIs, and how are they approved?
- How can users get AMIs to use?
- What constitutes "use?" "Starting?" "Connecting to?"

This is where DevOps comes in. Many DevOps practices use the notion of a user story to help define the requirements for solutions. A *user story* is simply a syntax for defining a requirement. In other words: As a <user>, I want to <requirement>, so that <outcome>. If you use the same approach to define your security controls, you'll notice that a lot, if not all, of the ambiguity fades:

> *As a Security Operations Manager, I want only images tagged as being hardened by the Security Operations Team to be permitted to start in a VPC so that I can be assured that the solution is not vulnerable to common attack vectors.*

Great! Now the engineer trying to implement the security control has a better understanding of the intention behind the control, and thus a better idea of how to implement and test it.

Documenting these guardrails for your CLT security stakeholders (legal, audit, risk, CISO, and so on) in an accessible, Agile project-management tool rather than in a spreadsheet is also a good idea. While spreadsheets are a very common method of documentation, a project-management tool makes it easier for you to update your controls, ensuring that they keep pace with your company's innovations. There are many Agile project-management suites that can assist you here. We have used Jira by Atlassian with most of our customers, but there are a few other tools that achieve similar outcomes: Agilean, Wrike, Trello, and Asana, to name a few.

Continuous integration and evaluation of security controls

Once you've written your security control as a user story, you can borrow from DevOps again and write some acceptance criteria. This is done through a process that's very similar to creating a threat model in the first place. You'll create a scenario and then define actions for actors plus expected outcomes. The syntax used is that we start by defining the scenario we're testing, and then use: "Given that <conditions of the test> when <test action> then <expected outcome>." For example:

> Scenario: User is starting an instance in a VPC
> "Given that I am logged in to the AWS Console
> and I have permissions to start an instance in a VPC
> When I try to start an instance
> and the AMI is not tagged as hardened
> Then it is denied" [Preventative]

> "Given that I am logged into the AWS console
> and I have permission to start an instance in the VPC
> When I try to start an instance
> and the AMI is not tagged as hardened
> Then an email is sent to the Security Operations Team."
> [Responsive]

> "Given that I am logged into the AWS Console

And I have permission to start an instance in the VPC
When I try to start and instance that is tagged as hardened
Then the instance starts." [Allowed]

After you write multiple action statements and scenarios supporting the user story (both positive and negative), you can write them up as a runbook, an AWS Config rule, or a combination of both as required.

There are numerous benefits to this approach:

- You get immediate feedback on compliance to your security controls and thus your business's security posture
- Unlike traditional annual security compliance audits, you have a record that, not only are you compliant now, but you've been compliant all year. And publication of this evidence to provide support to audit processes requires almost negligible effort on your part
- You may not have to take weeks out of your schedule to audit your security controls. Instead, you can check your AWS Config dashboard and run some simple procedural runbooks
- Your developers are now empowered to get early feedback on any solutions they're designing
- Changes to your threat model can quickly radiate down to applicable security controls and acceptance tests, again making security teams enablers of innovation rather than blockers

A word on encryption and security

"Encryption is the tool we have to make sure that nobody else has access to your data," Vogels said. Amazon Web Services (AWS) built encryption into nearly all of its 165+ cloud services, he added. "Make use of it. Dance like nobody is watching. Encrypt like everyone is." – Werner Vogels, CTO, Amazon

In 1949, on the heels of World War II, Claude Shannon published *Communication Theory of Secrecy Systems* where he described the properties of "secret systems." In this text, he famously stated that "the enemy knows the system." He went on to say that "one ought to design systems under the assumption that the enemy will immediately gain full familiarity with them." This concept is widely embraced by cryptographers, in contrast to "security through obscurity," which is not.

So, in addition to good system design and architecture, cryptography is an essential tool in the practice of protecting information. In our view, encrypting data should be the default state whenever possible. Data in cleartext should be a documented exception. Werner Vogels, the CTO of Amazon, is often seen wearing a black t-shirt emblazoned with the words "Encrypt Everything." We agree wholeheartedly!

Cryptography can be difficult to manage, and to this end AWS has created a set of tools that help meet cryptographic requirements. AWS has created the AWS Key Management Service (KMS) to manage encryption using a key hierarchy and a technology known as envelope encryption. AWS KMS is a Cloud-Native, horizontally scalable key management and manipulation service built on top of a fully FIPS 140-2 Level 3 certified set of Hardware Security Modules (HSMs). These HSMs have been custom designed by AWS to meet the unique requirements of the cloud.

KMS stores the keys at the root of the key hierarchy—those keys are used to "wrap" (encrypt) other keys, which can "wrap" other keys, and so forth. By using a hierarchy, finer-grained controls can be used and the impact of a compromised encryption key or "blast radius" is dramatically reduced.

For example, customer master keys (there can be many of these) in AWS KMS never leave the boundaries of the service. Those keys are used to encrypt data keys, which do leave the service (but only over encrypted network transports). An AWS service that needs to store data relatively permanently first asks AWS KMS for a data key and an encrypted copy of that data key. The service then uses the data key to encrypt the data, stores the encrypted data—and alongside it the encrypted data key—and throws away the unencrypted key. When called upon to read the data, the service is not able to do so on its own! The only thing it stores is cyphertext: an encrypted copy of the data, and an encrypted copy of the key used to encrypt the data. So, in order to proceed, the service retrieves the encrypted data key, calls the AWS KMS service, and sends in the encrypted key using an authenticated, authorized, and audited API. AWS KMS decrypts the data key using the customer master key, and sends back an unencrypted copy of the data key. The service can now decrypt the customer data and send it to an authenticated and authorized caller, after which it once again deletes the unencrypted data key.

This hierarchical model provides many benefits. For one thing, master keys can be rotated without unencrypting all the original data. Only the data keys need to be unencrypted and then re-encrypted with the new master key. Also, this model provides an easy way to "crypto-delete" data: the customer simply deletes the master key that governs that storage volume (or volumes), "bucket" (as in Amazon S3 object storage), database, or whatever. At that point, there is no way to decrypt the stored data key, and thus no way to decrypt the original data.

We would be remiss if we did not also acknowledge the progress that is being made in quantum computing. There is a great deal of speculation about the impact of quantum computing on cryptography—speculation and hype! Quantum computing and quantum cryptography are a complex set of topics that are, unfortunately, often munged together.

First, how real is the possibility of a fully functional quantum computer? Several large companies including Google and IBM are working on experimental quantum computers, and although there have been impressive demonstrations of capabilities, these were impressive in the same way AI lab experiments were impressive in the 1950s. It took 60 more years to advance technological underpinnings before AI could become both practical and commercially viable. [13] [14]

Quantum computers essentially have the capability to calculate multiple possible solutions to a problem at the same time. Asymmetric/public-key encryption protocols are based on multiplying large prime numbers with each other. With current technology, it is computationally impractical, for example, to factor all possible large primes that might make up a public/private key pair of an RSA2048 key. (The odds of accidentally finding such a prime-number pair have been described as the odds of winning the lottery dozens of time in a row after purchasing a single ticket each time.) A quantum computer, however, could theoretically solve such problems in seconds, minutes, or perhaps days, at which time public key encryption would become vulnerable. Importantly, quantum computing would only have a very small impact on the security of symmetric key cryptography. So, what does all this really mean then?

What it means in practice is that quantum computers would have little impact on data stored and encrypted in storage systems like Amazon S3 or Amazon EBS. According to some academic researchers, it would be like downgrading systems from AES-256 to AES-128, which is still practically unbreakable. Quantum computers, however, could compromise captured or stored network traffic, because TLS implementations use an asymmetric key to encrypt the first symmetric session key of a session (as a bootstrap). Subsequent session keys are encrypted using the previous session key. If you can capture the first session, a quantum computer could break the initial session key, and thus you could decrypt all subsequent session keys. Using the session keys, you could decrypt the content of the transmission.

If you are really concerned about this eventual threat, then use symmetric encryption of the content prior to transmission, and securely send the key over a different channel. Of course, it will be better to fix the underlying network encryption protocols to protect them from the future (and distant) threat of quantum computers. To this end, AWS is actively participating in proposals to develop post-quantum key exchange algorithms,[15] and is integrating two algorithms[16] into S2N for testing by interested users. A more esoteric approach to secure key exchange is quantum entanglement, and although there have been fascinating theoretical experiments in 2019, this possible future is even more distant than quantum computing.

Culture

Throughout this book, we have talked about the importance of culture and organization. Security culture is not an exception. In 2019, Thomas sat in a meeting next to Stephen Schmidt, the AWS CISO, as he explained one of the many ways AWS maintains security as the top priority of the business. He explained that, in most organizations, the CISO reports to the CIO, sometimes they report to the head of risk or the COO, but rarely do they report directly to the CEO, as Stephen does. Andy Jassy convenes a regular security review with the AWS CISO and all senior VPs in the company. Leaders are accountable for resolving any open issues and must adhere to strict timelines for resolution.

Stephen holds routine cloud service security review meetings with all of the service team owners—these are, as we have seen, akin to product owners with P&L responsibility. New services will not launch if there are any known security issues. Stephen has the authority to bring all resources to bear to harden AWS against new threats immediately, as was done when we were both thinking about becoming customers in 2014. That year, *heartbleed* was discovered. This was a vulnerability of OpenSSL that could compromise TLS/SSL, and thus one of the very pillars of security on the Internet. AWS security engineers patched all systems that were vulnerable within hours of the announcement of *heartbleed* without disrupting customers!

That wasn't all they did, however. Soon thereafter, they began to develop a new SSL implementation to address other inherent problems of OpenSSL, and in 2015, publicly released s2n (https://github.com/awslabs/s2n). This was a complete rewrite of the library that implements the TLS protocol with approximately 6,000 lines of code compared to OpenSSL's approximately 500,000 lines. Interestingly, the lines of *test* code for s2n exceed the implementation code by about 10:1! And formal verification tests for the correctness of key algorithms provided by AWS's Automated Reasoning Group are built into the automated build and integration process for s2n. Any code changes that cause the formal proofs to break are automatically rejected.

AWS also contributed back to the open-source implementations of TLS (BoringSSL and LibreSSL, both forks of OpenSSL) to assist in improving the underlying security of the internet.

In addition to making security a leadership priority, adopting cloud is an opportunity to create a security-conscious culture throughout your organization. Developers can use automated testing—often provided by the security team—to continuously look for security defects and vulnerabilities. If such a defect is discovered, we recommend you give the developer the authority to "pull the Andon cord" and prevent this defect from finding its way into production. The cost of repair is lowest at this early stage, and thus a wise upfront investment.

Training at least one engineer in every team to be a security expert (and with a direct line of communication to the security team) is another good investment, as they can proactively improve code, architecture, and the security skills of the team. Software security will also benefit from peer review, as we discussed elsewhere in the context of software quality and resiliency. In our view, and that of AWS, security is really *everyone's* responsibility. At AWS, *everyone* is expected to report a security issue, and they are empowered to escalate security issues to the highest levels if necessary.

For decades, leaders have striven to enable a culture of security—we are, of course, only as strong as our weakest link in this regard. Security will always be Job Zero at AWS. It will always be the area of highest investment for us. We will not hesitate to move engineers from new-feature development to security development if we aren't satisfied with where it needs to be. As Isaac Newton said in 1675, "If I have seen further, it is by standing upon the shoulders of giants."

A very special thanks goes to Mark Ryland, Director in the Office of the CISO, and to Clarke Rodgers, Enterprise Security Strategist, for their help in editing and for pushing us to raise the bar on this chapter.

7.2 GOVERNANCE, RISK MANAGEMENT, AND COMPLIANCE

"We have to conduct ourselves so when we are scrutinized, we pass with flying colors."

– JEFF P. BEZOS, FOUNDER AND CEO, AMAZON.COM, INC.

Internal controls have existed from ancient times. In Hellenistic Egypt, from 323 BC to 31 BC, there was a dual administration, with one set of bureaucrats charged with collecting taxes and another with supervising them. Internal controls are not new—they have had different names and different drivers over the millennia.

Fast forward a few millennia.

The term "corporate governance" originated in 1960 with Richard Eells, an authority on corporate philanthropy, to denote "the structure and functioning of the corporate polity." The concept of "corporate government" has been around even longer—appearing in finance textbooks since the beginning of the 1900s.

Due to questionable corporate campaign practices, in the mid-1970s the U.S. Securities and Exchange Commission (SEC) and the U.S. Congress enacted campaign-finance law reforms. And, in response to foreign corrupt practices, they enacted the 1977 Foreign Corrupt Practices

Act (FCPA), which criminalized transnational bribery and required companies to implement internal control programs. In response, the Treadway Commission—a private-sector initiative—was formed in 1985 to inspect, analyze, and make recommendations on fraudulent corporate financial reporting. As a result of their initial report, the Committee of Sponsoring Organizations (COSO) was formed.

In September 1992, the four-volume report entitled "Internal Control—Integrated Framework" was released by COSO and later re-published with minor amendments in 1994. This report presented a common definition of internal control and provided a framework against which internal-control systems may be assessed and improved. This report is one standard that U.S. companies use to evaluate their compliance with FCPA.

During this same period, there was concern raised about the money spent on information technology and the lack of perceived value actually received. (Erik Brynjolfsson's 1993 article "The Productivity Paradox of Information Technology: Review and Assessment" offers an interesting glimpse into the past.) Subsequently, in an effort to bridge this gap, in 1993 IT governance was born from the concept of corporate governance—focusing on the intersection of the business goals, strategic objectives, and IT management of an organization.

Regulated oversight got far more intensive during the early 2000s following a period of corporate failures at two large conglomerates. This led to passage of the Sarbanes-Oxley Act. In February 2002, the term "governance, risk management, and compliance" (GRC) was popularized by Michael Rasmussen while at Forrester Research. According to Rasmussen, GRC is

A capability to reliably achieve objectives while addressing uncertainty and acting with integrity...The reliable achievement of objectives is the governance piece, addressing uncertainty is about risk management, and acting with integrity is the compliance angle. All

three of these provide a natural flow. Governance provides direction and objectives giving the context for risk management. Risk management in turn aims to comprehend uncertainty and set boundaries which then relies on compliance to ensure that we stay within those boundaries.

According to a poll by *CFO* magazine released in 2006, 82 percent of respondents claimed they used COSO's framework for internal controls. Other frameworks used by respondents included COBIT, AS2 (Auditing Standard No. 2, PCAOB), and SAS 55/78 (AICPA).[17]

We see both COSO and COBIT being used by customers, and indeed we used them both as customers ourselves. This article from Reciprocity ("What Are The Differences Between COBIT & COSO") covers it well.

COSO only responds to those controls related to fiduciary duty. Primarily designed to enable Sarbanes-Oxley (SOX) 404 requirements, COSO limits itself to a certain area of an organization's IT environment. Meanwhile, COBIT 5 extends beyond financial reporting to the whole environment. Therefore, the two complement each other as well as the overarching risk, compliance, and governance program.

Okay let's reset for a moment.

While we hope that everyone appreciates a brief historical overview of primarily U.S. corporate governance and the seriousness with which we all take it, diving deep into modern business governance is beyond the scope of this book. GRC frameworks can provoke as much debate as the three-letter term itself.

In the modern era of cloud adoption, there are primarily three main frameworks that regulated and well-managed companies utilize as the broad structure they utilize to govern their operations: COSO, COBIT, and the relatively newer NIST Cybersecurity Framework. The first two being more derived from accounting and audit standards and adopting technology controls as it developed, and the last being focused on the fact that every IT control is related to the secure operations of an organization (both for public institutions and commercial enterprises alike). An overarching governance program should be seen through this lens: All three frameworks can provide value for helping any organization systematize their structured approach to GRC in the cloud, and each should be evaluated to determine which best fits the organization's objectives as it begins to utilize the cloud as part of its journey.

IT governance, risk management, and compliance

PwC breaks down IT governance, risk, and compliance objectives as follows:

> *Combining disciplines for better enterprise security. Adopting a unified IT governance, risk management, and compliance (IT GRC) approach, and managing the associated activities coherently will create efficiencies, provide a holistic view of the IT environment, and ensure accountability.*

Through evolution, we now find GRC programs are well established within modern enterprises.

The decision-making, resource-and-portfolio-management, risk-management, and regulatory-compliance functions included in a GRC framework will not be effective unless the organization's executive leadership is both involved and supportive. It is for this reason we went into such detail back in Chapter 3.4 Creating the Cloud Leadership Team. Engagement and approval of any amendments of the standards and policies of an organization that will ensure effective and secure use of AWS Cloud by the leadership team from the start are crucial. Subsequent effective engagement with the Cloud Center of Excellence—and eventually the Cloud Business Office when it is formed—can provide part of an inclusive oversight and engagement mechanism should holistic amendments be required.

Governance, risk management, and compliance programs are sometimes looked upon as the bureaucracy getting in the way of exciting work. But a good GRC program establishes the foundation of the business's objectives. It is the proactive approach to cloud adoption that, if done well, minimizes a failure of operational controls. We always want to be working to mitigate that unwanted 3:00 a.m. call.

Although governance, risk management, and compliance are often viewed as separate functions, there is a symbiotic relationship between them. Governance establishes the strategy and guardrails for meeting specific requirements that align and support the business. Risk management connects specific controls to governance and assessed risks, and provides business leaders with the information they need to prioritize resources and make risk-informed decisions. Compliance is the adherence and monitoring of controls to specific governance requirements. It is also the "ante" required to play the game in certain industries, and with continuous monitoring it closes the feedback loop regarding effective governance. Security architecture, engineering, and operations are built upon the GRC foundation.

For example, when forced to make investment tradeoffs and progress, does a Chief Information Security Officer invest in a large, access-management practice or do they invest in improving application security across their enterprise? GRC would guide this in terms of relative priority and level of investment.

Consistently agreed and well-constructed principles, as we have discussed throughout the book, are a great mechanism to hold employees accountable for the bar they hold. Establishing a consistent set of rules and processes that all teams have to follow creates "sameness" across the control framework, allowing for the automation of compliance evidence in a consistent way.

GRC requirements are key to the evaluation process of what applications can be moved to the cloud in a way that does not create exceptions to standards, and those that must be redesigned to meet the control consistency that the cloud can bring.

As was the case on our own journey, and from the many customers we have worked with, when moving to cloud, leaders ask for a breakdown of each element of GRC and what they should review. While the list that follows is not exhaustive, nor will all of it apply to everyone, it can provide you with a solid foundation to start. The key takeaways are: base governance on objectives and capabilities, include risk context in decision making, and automate monitoring and response.

Governance

Identify compliance requirements
- Identify and be aware of required compliance frameworks (such as HIPAA or PCI) and any contract and agreement obligations, and ensure an approach to compliance is established.
- Identify any restrictions or limitations to cloud adoption or emerging technologies. For example, is there a local regulatory or legal consideration to be taken in account?
- Identify required or chosen audit standards to implement (for example COSO or COBIT)

Conduct program assessment
- Conduct a program assessment based on industry processes such as the NIST Cyber Security Framework (CSF) or ISO/IEC TR 27103:2018 to understand the capability and maturity of your current profile.
- Determine desired end-state capability and maturity—also known as *target profile*—and ensure overall portfolio management provides a mechanism to manage overall desired business outcomes and ensure that success is tracked and reported.

- Document and prioritize gaps (people, process, and technologies) for resource allocation.
- Establish a CCoE, as covered in Chapter 3.5 Creating the Cloud Center of Excellence.
- Draft and publish a cloud strategy alongside your communication plan.
- Define and assign functions, roles, and responsibilities across the entire organization. It is critical that everyone from the development teams to internal auditors be included in the development of responsibilities required for the cloud journey
- Ensure effective program and project management that helps you manage technology projects using methodologies that take advantage of the agility and cost-management benefits inherent to cloud services.

Update and publish policies, processes, and procedures
- Develop the overall strategy for the documentation that you will use to manage your migration to the cloud. We discussed this in detail in Chapter 5.4 Migrating Your Applications.
- Determine if you going to add cloud to your current documentation profiles or develop new documents that better meet the faster pace of change in the cloud. For example, a policy is usually approved at the C-suite or board level, so it cannot evolve as quickly as lower-level documents. As a result, it needs to contain control elements that won't change frequently.
- The common flow of corporate governance for the cloud usually looks like: 1) Risk Profile; 2) Policy; 3) Standard; 4) Procedure; 5) Runbooks.
- Develop a Cloud Control Framework with clear differentiation between control objectives, control implementations, and control testing. This becomes the baseline for automation—both implementation and monitoring—and helps each line of defense

in a regulated institution (1st, 2nd, 3rd) understand where their needs are being met.

Typically, in regulated entities there are "lines of defense" overseeing risk management. "In the Three Lines of Defense model, management control is the first line of defense in risk management, the various risk control and compliance oversight functions established by management are the second line of defense, and independent assurance is the third."[18]

- Update procedures to integrate cloud services and other emerging technologies. This is commonly referred to a Service Adoption Framework and it creates a well-understood process to approve new service usage while defining all the controls required to be implemented for the service across the company. This is done with a cross-functional team representing all relevant departments with control requirements that need to be meet. At scale, this is a dedicated process that enables innovation rather than slows it down.
- Establish technical-governance principles that map to your overall GRC objectives.

Risk management

Conduct a risk assessment*

In our experience as leaders, the ability to make balanced, risk-based decisions thoughtfully—considering the impact, probability, and judgement to then reject, accept, or mitigate a perceived risk—is fundamental to the success of any transformation. Leaders who are connected in a visceral way to the daily stand-up and/or progress meetings will (or need to) establish a cadence risk decisioning to maintain progress. Areas for the leaders to consider in this regard are:

- Conducting or updating an organizational risk assessment (e.g., market, financial, reputation, legal, etc.).

- Conducting or updating a risk assessment for each business line (such as mission, market, products/services, financial, etc.).
- Conducting or updating a risk assessment for each asset type. This can be both for the data and application types that you plan to move to the cloud. This should also be done in a repetitive manner as your application portfolio in the cloud grows.
- Conducting a risk assessment for the overall utilization of cloud-based technologies to fulfil previous on-premise requirements. Cloud service providers have unique ways of delivering services, and that model must be evaluated as it changes the norms of current procurement, operational, and security models.

The use of preestablished threat models can simplify the risk-assessment process, both initial and updates. However, the risk plan must incorporate feedback from all across the company, no one should be left out of the process. Everyone's voice must be heard for it to be a complete process.

Draft risk plans
- Conduct cross-functional reviews of all risks, and develop the appropriate stance to accept, mitigate, or transfer. Some initial risks can be retired after consideration by the team that they are not relevant, but all documentation should be kept to demonstrate that there were no biases to leave anything out of the process.
- Implement plans to mitigate, avoid, transfer, or accept risk at each tier, business line, and asset (for example, a business-continuity plan, a continuity-of-operations plan, a systems-security plan).
- Implement plans to mitigate any specific risk areas (such as supply-chain risk, insider threat). For example, are you going to implement a "2-person" rule for all production changes? Or are you going to utilize a "Security Red Team" to assess organizational security, often unbeknownst to client staff?

- Develop a risk-review process that is more frequent and iterative than traditional annual reviews. Technology will change on a regular basis, so new risks will need to be developed. Mitigation plans can change with the advent of new services or features that implement compensating controls.

Authorize systems
- Evaluate using the NIST Risk Management Framework (RMF) or other process to authorize and track systems.
- Evaluate using NIST Special Publication 800-53, ISO ISO/IEC 27002:2013, or other control set to select, implement, and assess controls based on risk.
- Implement continuous monitoring of controls and risk, employing automation to the greatest extent possible.

Incorporate risk information into decisions
- Link system risk to business and organizational risk.
- Automate translation of continuous system risk monitoring and status to business and organizational risk.
- Incorporate "What's the risk?" (financial, cyber, legal, reputation) into leadership decision making.
- Be sure to carefully evaluate the "risk of doing nothing" into your overall decisions. The benefits of cloud in many cases effectively mitigate or remove existing risks related to incumbent on-premises technology.

Compliance

Monitor compliance with policy, standards, and security controls
- Automate technical-control monitoring and reporting.
- Automate the workflow and validation of manual-control monitoring so it can be measured with the same tooling that is used

for automated controls. This creates a single view of your Cloud Control Framework that is much easier to track.

- Implement manual monitoring of non-technical controls that can't be tracked in automation (for example, periodic review of visitor logs) and reserve special attention for any non-automated technical controls you may have put in place.
- Evaluate the utilization of new cloud-based continuous compliance tooling that provides all lines of defense real-time views into the status of the cloud environment to provide transparency.
- Link compliance monitoring with security information and event management (SIEM) and other tools utilized by control owners so there are no gaps in knowledge about the status of the environment.

Continually self-assess

- Automate application security testing and vulnerability scans
- Continuously review testing and models to keep up to date with changes to the threat landscape.
- Conduct periodic self-assessments from sampling of controls, entire functional area, and pen-tests.
- Develop testing plans for the automation you are relying on to protect your cloud environment.
- Be willing to be self-critical of assumptions, perspectives, and artifacts.
- Develop a process to conduct more-frequent reviews of cloud service changes and improvements to incorporate new functionality into current controls implementations.

Respond to events and changes to risk

- Integrate security operations with the compliance team for response management to ensure that security events do not impact control effectiveness.
- Establish standard operating procedures to respond to unintentional changes in controls.

- Mitigate impact and reset affected control(s); automate as much as possible.

Communicate events and changes to risk
- Establish a reporting structure and thresholds for each type of incident or control deviation.
- Include general counsel in reporting.
- Ensure applicable regulatory authorities and identified stakeholders are notified when required.
- Automate where appropriate.
- Conduct regular incident-management drills across the non-technical aspects of the company so teams can rely on experience when managing an event.

Going global

One of the frequent questions we receive in our travels is, "What should the governance organizational model look like in truly large or global enterprises?" In PART 3, we discussed the Cloud Leadership Team (CLT), Cloud Center of Excellence (CCoE), and Cloud Business Office (CBO). In an enterprise, having these clearly defined functions will aid the establishment of your security and governance objectives. But what about in a global or group companies-type situation? Well, it's actually very straightforward—you establish a central CLT, CCoE, and CBO.

The Single-Threaded Leaders of each subdivision or group should have appropriate mirrored versions of this three-part structure—ideally, with the Single-Threaded Leaders (often CTO or CIO) of each reporting back to the central CLT as required for holistic governance. You can then choose to centralize or federate different elements of your governance framework. For example, you may choose to negotiate for pricing with AWS at the central CLT level, along with negotiating any contractual agreements you may enter with AWS. But how each division uses the cloud could be different based on their own individual needs.

Going a little deeper

In June 2012, COSO published their "Enterprise Risk Management for Cloud Computing Guide." For those institutions using the COSO framework, this will probably be a go-to starting place for your Risk and Audit functions to review when you go to the cloud. The framework is a thoughtful, albeit 2012 dive into cloud computing.

Penultimate thought

When moving to cloud, GRC can appear a little daunting for leaders who know they can get great benefits from AWS Cloud, but are also aware they might need to be thoughtful of any governance adjustments they want to make.

While many organizations tend to focus on the economics or security of cloud adoption, it's critical to understand the entire governance, risk, and compliance framework for a more holistic approach to well-managed migrations.

Failure to include the critical areas of a broader GRC framework as part of your initial plans will create a much slower migration path, and you'll regret the missed opportunities to build GRC capabilities directly into your technical designs from the beginning of your program.

The most significant challenge for most customers is to admit that they need to do things differently. No matter how well managed you are outside of a cloud environment, the people, process, and technology affected by your migration require an objective review of your current controls.

Ultimately, enterprises need to be able to properly consider their journey to cloud within the concept of the GRC. And it is necessary to bring first-line leaders, risk leaders, and audit together on the journey—each needs to be aware of the needs of the others with regards to GRC.

Going deeper on risk and compliance

Many customers find themselves wanting to go deeper into this topic than what space allows in this chapter. We suggest having a look at the following documents, as well as those in the bibliography, for a deeper review.

It doesn't have to be hard work though. Going beyond the scope of this chapter, AWS Solutions Architects can offer practical advice with regards to this topic. In addition, working in conjunction with AWS Professional Services or an AWS Approved Partner, you can go deeper and conduct a Cloud Adoption Framework Governance Session. This will provide you with a deeper review to ensure your cloud governance aligns with your overall corporate and technology governance targets.

For a more detailed description of risk and compliance in AWS please see the whitepaper here.

For a more detailed description of AWS Compliance programs, please see AWS Compliance page: https://aws.amazon.com/compliance/

Thanks to Jonathan Jenkyn, Michael South, Mark Ryland, Bill Shinn, and John McDonald for some of their material and the overall guidance on this chapter.

AFTERTHOUGHT

"If you want to build a ship, don't drum up people together to collect wood and don't assign them tasks and work, but rather teach them to long for the endless immensity of the sea."
– ANTOINE DE SAINT-EXUPÉRY

This book was obviously written with no specific context of how your business operates today. That said, the common question we have found that resonates with leaders around the world is this: How can we survive the wave of disruption that is cascading over and around us?

As we know, technology has become an entwined part of virtually every business. In this age of cloud, knowing which part of technology to focus on, and when to leverage other parts is fundamental knowledge that is required to survive and thrive.

The very best of luck with your cloud transformation.

ACKNOWLEDGEMENTS

The difference between saying "you want to write a book" and the reality of publishing one, are so utterly separate that the metaphor of "chalk and cheese" does not do it justice. In practice, writing this book was a two-year journey of compressing experiential lessons, and ensuring what we were writing was appropriate and accurate (in spite of AWS's relentless innovation).

Fellow authors that we spoke to prior and during writing all acknowledged it was many times harder than they had initially presumed. We too are humbled by the sheer amount we have had to learn, not just in the processing of writing a book itself and publishing, but of the amount of resources, support, and goodwill from others you need to bring a book to reality.

It is faced with that reality that we have many people to thank.

First, we need to thank our leaders Philip Potloff, Candace Worley, Leah Bibbo, Rachel Thornton and Stephen Orban for their support in the creation of this book (and in Stephen's case, for hiring us in the first place). And thanks to all our colleagues in the AWS Enterprise Strategy team for their thought leadership—we learn from them every day.

Second, we want to thank our Amazon mentor Miguel Alva, for his unwavering advice, support, and curiosity to what we were doing and to Darren Mowry for his ever-infectious support. To Werner Vogels— not only for kindly writing the foreword for this book but also for sharing stories of the Amazon early days with us. To Adrian Cockcroft for his foreword and helping us look around corners we didn't know existed. Mark Schwartz for his foreword and for answering the unending stream of questions about being an author and how things work and providing extremely valuable (at times difficult) feedback that we needed to hear.

Third, we want to pay special thanks to those Amazonians who unselfishly gave us their time to help, edit, or write, and to those from whom we borrowed of their intellectual archives: Jeff Barr, Joe Chung, Clarke Rodgers, Adrian Hornsby, Danilo Poccia, Julian Simon, John Enoch, Zehra Syeda-Sarwat, Mark Ryland, Bill Shinn, Matt Walburn, Jonathan Jenkyn, Michael South, John McDonald, Phil DeValance, Doug Vanderpool, Stephanie Lavocat, Christie Gifrin, Shiri Blatt, Rachel Richardson, Monica Benjamin, Matt Lambert, Emily Neumann, and Anand Pillai.

Finally, we would like to thank those folks outside of AWS who also helped including everyone who helped at Silverfox, Simon Wardley from Leading Edge Forum, Peter Hinssen from Nexxworks, Drew Firment from A Cloud Guru, and a special thanks to our copy editor Pete Economy.

Jonathan would like to thank his wife Mandy for her patience, support, love and understanding, as his role takes him away from home often. A special shout out to his children Jessica, Matthew, and Emilia who keep him young at heart. Thanks to his coach James Caplin (*lux ex tenebris*).

Thomas would like to thank Mike Kilander for his friendship, loyalty, support, and inspiration for more than two decades. Thomas has learned from many over the years, but wants to especially thank Frank

Hespe for his friendship and the importance of asking the right question; James Isom for his friendship and for talking him into getting into IT in the first place; Ed Gerck for his wisdom in system design, cryptography, and for introducing him to the theories of Claude Shannon; Joe LoPiccolo on how to think about customers, procurement, and operations; and Eric Tao for teaching him about teaching, software, and architecture. Most of all, Thomas is grateful to his family, and to Barbara for putting up with his crazy travel schedule.

AUTHOR BIOGRAPHY

Jonathan Allen

Jonathan joined AWS in early 2017. As a Director in the Enterprise Strategy team, he works with enterprise executives around the globe to share lessons learned and strategies on how cloud adoption can help them increase speed and agility while devoting more of their resources to their customers.

He has worked with hundreds of enterprises helping them successfully complete migrations and transition their organizations to help them realize the benefits of AWS Cloud. Including working with many of the world's leading brands. Jonathan is a frequent public speaker and writes frequently on the AWS Enterprise and Amazon Day One Blog.

Prior to joining AWS, Jonathan spent 17 years working as a leader in Capital One Financial Corporation, where his final role was Senior Director and UK divisional CTO. He was part of the technology leadership team that selected AWS as their predominant cloud partner in 2014, and was accountable for architecting, engineering, and an agile DevOps execution of the technical build out and system migrations of the UK divisions AWS Cloud strategy in partnership with the US divisions until 2017.

Prior to Capital One, Jonathan was a software and systems engineer working for multiple independent systems houses.

In 2012, he was awarded IT Manager of the Year by The Chartered Institute for IT. He holds a Diploma in Computer Studies from Loughborough College, a CIO MBA from Boston University, and is a certified AWS Solutions Architect. He has previously held Cisco and Microsoft advanced accreditations and can still program in Cobol(!), although Python is his language of choice today.

twitter.com/jonatallen

linkedin.com/in/jonatallen

Thomas Blood

Thomas joined AWS in October of 2016 as an Enterprise Evangelist and Strategist, and now leads AWS Digital Innovation for Europe, the Middle East, and Africa (EMEA).

Diffusion of innovation research shows individuals evaluate an innovation based on a subjective assessment conveyed from other individuals like themselves who have already adopted the innovation. Thomas has worked with more than 400 enterprise technology customers to share experiences and strategies for how AWS can help them increase speed and agility in order to innovate on behalf of their customers. Thomas is a frequent speaker, having covered over 100 events in his tenure at AWS.

Prior to joining AWS, Thomas was VP of Emerging Technologies at Experian Consumer Services, where he led an effort to re-architect the technology platform using a Cloud-Native approach in AWS. This transformation has changed how the business develops software, systems, and business solutions and has caused a ripple effect throughout the global enterprise with multiple business units pursuing their own journey to the cloud.

Over the previous 20 years, Thomas has worked in diverse technical leadership roles at Edmunds, the Department of Defense, the Naval

Postgraduate School as well as two technology startups. He spent a number of years in the U.S. Army where he served as an intelligence analyst in Europe and the Middle East.

Thomas earned his master's degree in interdisciplinary studies from California State University at Monterey Bay. He also holds a BA in Economic Development and Environmental Studies. He has studied intermediate Arabic at the American University in Cairo and has completed postgraduate courses in biometrics and identity management at the Naval Postgraduate School in Monterey. He speaks German, English, Spanish, and some Arabic and French.

twitter.com/groberstiefel

linkedin.com/in/thomasblood

BIBLIOGRAPHY

Chapter 2.4 Measuring Business Agility

(2018). *Accelerate—DORA State of DevOps—Strategies for New Economy*. DORA.

Economist Intelligence Unit, E. (n.d.). *Organizational Agility*. Retrieved from www.emc.com: https://www.emc.com/collateral/leadership/organisational-agility-230309.pdf

Gene Kim, K. B. (2013). *The Phoenix Project*. Portland: IT Revolution.

Group, I. T. (n.d.). https://www.infotech.com/browse/management-and-governance. Retrieved from https://www.infotech.com/browse/management-and-governance: https://www.infotech.com/browse/management-and-governance

Sullivan, F. a. (2017). *Why Business Agility Matters*. Retrieved from www.pega.com: https://www1.pega.com/system/files/resources/2018-08/1791-FS-Business-Agility.pdf

Weill, P. (n.d.). *The Agility Paradox*. Retrieved from http://ebusiness.mit.edu/: http://ebusiness.mit.edu/ciosummit/weillslides.pdf

John Doerr, *Measure What Matters: How Google, Bono, and the Gates Foundation Rock the World with OKRs*, Portfolio (2018) p.16

Chapter 5.2 APIs and Microservices

https://martinfowler.com/articles/microservices.html

https://www.amazon.com/Building-Micro-services-Designing-Fine-Grained-Systems/dp/1491950358

https://d1.awsstatic.com/whitepapers/microservices-on-aws.pdf

https://aws.amazon.com/modern-apps/

To read the full story about Yelp's use of AWS Step Functions, go to https://engineeringblog.yelp.com/2017/11/breaking-down-the-monolith-with-aws-step-functions.html

Chapter 7.2 Governance, Risk Management, and Compliance

How to manage security governance using DevOps methodologies

Migrating to the cloud requires a change of mindset for compliance and audit

GRC and the cloud—Embracing new technologies requires changes in behaviour

AWS re:Invent 2018: Architecting Security & Governance across your AWS Landing Zone (video)

Architecting Security & Governance across Your AWS Environment

Governance as Code Using Security by Design

AWS Governance at Scale

Scaling a governance, risk, and compliance program for the cloud, emerging technologies, and innovation

AWS Governance at Scale (whitepaper)

NOTES

1   References to accelerate and DORA SODR TBD

2   https://aws.amazon.com/blogs/enterprise-strategy/
    todays-it-executive-is-a-chief-change-management-officer/

3   L.D. Holder, "Concept of the Operations: See Ops Overlay," Military Review
    (August 1990): 28)

4   https://www.amazon.de/Turn-Ship-Around-Building-Breaking/
    dp/1591846404

5   https://en.wikipedia.org/wiki/Metcalfe%27s_law

6   https://www.amazon.com/Extreme-Ownership-U-S-Navy-SEALs-ebook/
    dp/B00VE4Y0Z2

7   J. Xie, S. Sreenivasan, G. Korniss, W. Zhang, C. Lim, and B. K. Szymanski,
    "Social consensus through the influence of committed minorities," Phys.
    Rev. E 84, 011130 – Published July 22, 2011

8   https://www.nasdaq.com/symbol/vz/financials?query=income-statement

9   https://www.atlassian.com/devops

10 (April 1987). "No Silver Bullet — Essence and Accidents of Software
    Engineering". *IEEE Computer*. **20** (4): 10–19. CiteSeerX 10.1.1.117.315.
    doi:10.1109/MC.1987.1663532) and Mills, H. D., "Top-down programming
    in large systems," Debugging Techniques in Large Systems, R. Rustin, ed.,
    Englewood Cliffs, N.J., Prentice-Hall, 1971.

11 Kristian Beckers, *Pattern and Security Requirements: Engineering-Based
    Establishment of Security Standards, Springer (2015) p. 100. ISBN
    9783319166643.*

12   *J. Efrim Boritz, "IS Practitioners' Views on Core Concepts of Information Integrity," International Journal of Accounting Information Systems, Elsevier (2005)* **6** *(4): 260–279.* doi:10.1016/j.accinf.2005.07.001.

13   https://www.wired.com/story/googles-quantum-supremacy-isnt-end-encryption/

14   https://www.schneier.com/blog/archives/2018/09/quantum_computi_2.html

15   https://nvlpubs.nist.gov/nistpubs/ir/2019/NIST.IR.8240.pdf

16   https://github.com/awslabs/s2n/issues/904

17   https://en.wikipedia.org/wiki/Committee_of_Sponsoring_Organizations_of_the_Treadway_Commission#cite_note-3

18   https://www.theiia.org/3-lines-defense

Printed in Great Britain
by Amazon